They Teach That in Community College!?

College & Career Press
Chicago, Illinois

Project Staff

Managing Editor: Andrew Morkes

Additional Editorial Assistance: Amy McKenna, Jennifer Frisbie, Felicitas Cortez

Interior Design: The Glasoe Group

Cover Design: Meyers Design, Inc.

Proofreader: Jonathan Bieniek

Photo Credits

Front/Back Cover: courtesy of IndexOpen

Interior: courtesy of IndexOpen

Published and distributed by

College & Career Press, LLC
PO Box 300484
Chicago, IL 60630
773/248-6590
amorkes@chicagopa.com
www.collegeandcareerpress.com

Printed in the United States of America
06-04

Acknowledgments

The editors of *They Teach That in Community College!?* would like to extend their sincerest appreciation to the educators who provided their time and expertise to assist us in the creation of this book.

Other Titles in the *They Teach That in College!?* series:

They Teach That in College!?
They Teach That in Graduate School!?

Other Products Available From College & Career Press:

College Exploration on the Internet
College Spotlight newsletter

Table of Contents

Introduction

They Teach That in Community College!? provides information about interesting, lucrative, and cutting-edge college majors unknown to many counselors, educators, and parents. It includes profiles of 70 college majors and schools, course listings, potential employers, contact information for colleges and universities that offer these programs, professional associations that offer career information about these fields, and interviews with educators in the field. We hope that *They Teach That in Community College!?* becomes a valued and trusted resource as you navigate the challenges of college!

How This Book is Organized

The book has 70 main chapters—66 of which focus on unique and interesting majors and four of which focus on schools that are especially unique for reasons as varied as offering special instruction for students with learning disabilities (Beacon College and Landmark College), to offering assistance to deaf and hard-of-hearing students (National Technical Institute for the Deaf), to offering free college tuition (Deep Springs College).

Now that we've explained what a unique college is, you might be asking yourself, 'What is a unique major?' We used two official criterion to select majors to include in this book: 1) the major had to be fast-growing and offer good employment and salary prospects for students, and 2) the major had to be offered at less than 30 percent of community colleges in the United States. A third unofficial criterion was that the major had to capture our imagination—in short it had to be fun and, hopefully, interesting to our readers.

The following paragraphs provide an overview of the specific subsections that are contained in the unique major and school chapters:

The unique major chapters have the following subsections: 1) an opening paragraph that details the major in question; 2) a list of typical courses that students will take if they study the major; 3) a list of potential employers of students who study the major; 4) a list of schools that offer the major [(each entry includes contact information and the degree levels—such as certificate, diploma, and associate—that are available for the major) (note: some colleges may also offer bachelor's and master's degrees; in these cases, they are also listed)]; and, 5) a list of professional organizations that you can contact for more information on the field.

The unique schools chapters have the following subsections: 1) an opening paragraph that details the school in question; 2) a list of majors that are offered; and, 3) contact information for the school in question.

Additionally, both types of articles occasionally feature interviews with college educators. These educators offer an overview of their programs, suggest high school classes that will help you prepare for college, present information on the future of their fields, and provide other useful advice.

In addition to the aforementioned sections, *They Teach That in Community College!?* also features three appendices (Community Colleges in the United States by State, Top Community Colleges, Community College Associations) and three indexes (School, Schools by State, Association/Organization).

Finally . . . Important Things to Keep in Mind

Remember that the world of education is constantly changing: majors may be renamed, available degree levels may change, programs may be dropped due to lack of funding, etc. Be sure to contact the school in which you are interested in attending for the latest program information.

Additionally, the Internet is also always changing. Websites are redesigned, new information is added . . . you get the idea. If you have trouble locating any of the websites listed in this book, try shortening the web address to its basic address. For example, if you are having trouble reaching Kirkwood Community College's agriculture website (http://www.kirkwood.edu/agrisciences), shortening the address to the University's most basic address (http://www.kirkwood.edu) will usually allow you to access the site and locate the information at the site's home page or by using its search feature.

Accreditation is the process of determining whether an educational institution or academic program meets standards set by regional or national organizations of professionals. We have made every attempt to list accredited programs in this book (but have also listed programs that are not yet accredited—or approved by professional associations—if the number of schools that are accredited within a specific field is small). Since a good education is key to success in the workplace, be sure to investigate the accreditation status of the program in which you are interested. Attending an unaccredited program MAY limit your ability to transfer credits (if you plan to transfer to a four-year program to continue your education) and perhaps reduce employment opportunities.

Agricultural Education

Ask almost anyone to name typical agricultural careers, and you might hear "farmer" and "farm manager." While these careers remain very important to our food industry, today's agriculture and agricultural education involves much more than farming and managing farms. Agriculture students can now pursue dozens of majors that are far removed from planting crops and managing farms—majors as diverse as agricultural communications, finance, marketing, and sales; biochemistry; biological and food process engineering; food industry marketing and management; food manufacturing; international agronomy; landscape architecture; public horticulture; quantitative agricultural economics; turf science; and wood products manufacturing technology.

Typical Courses:

> Varies by major

Potential Employers:

> Agricultural industry
> Food industry
> Broadcasting industry
> Financial industry
> Government agencies (e.g., U.S. Department of Agriculture)
> Virtually any other industry that specializes in agricultural-related products and services

Available At:

The following programs are just a sampling of the unique opportunities that are available to students interested in agricultural careers. Agricultural education programs are available at community colleges throughout the United States. Visit the websites of schools in your area to learn more about unique majors that are offered.

Casper College
125 College Drive, Casper, WY 82601
800/442-2963
http://www.caspercollege.edu/lifescience/agriculture
Degrees available: Associate degree (four fields of study)

Dawson Community College
300 College Drive, PO Box 421, Glendive, MT 59330
800/821-8320
http://www.dawson.edu
Degrees available: Certificates (three fields of study), associate degrees (three fields of study)

A farmer harvests grain.

Kirkwood Community College
6301 Kirkwood Boulevard, SW, Cedar Rapids, IA 52404
800/332-2055
agsci@kirkwood.edu
http://www.kirkwood.edu/agrisciences
Degrees available: Certificate, diplomas, associate degrees (15 fields of study)

Northeast Community College
801 East Benjamin Avenue, PO Box 469, Norfolk, NE 68702-0469
402/371-2020
http://www.northeastcollege.com/PS/programs_of_study.php
Degrees available: Certificate, associate degrees (six fields of study)

4

Ohio State University Agricultural Technical Institute
1328 Dover Road, Wooster, OH 44691-4000
330/264-3911
ati@osu.edu
http://www.ati.osu.edu
Degrees available: Certificates, associate degrees (more than 25 fields of study)

Purdue University
School of Agriculture/Academic Programs in Agriculture
615 West State Street, West Lafayette, IN 47907-2053
765/494-8470
GOinAG@purdue.edu
http://www.agriculture.purdue.edu or
http://www.agriculture.purdue.edu/goinag/
programs.html#associate
Degrees available: Associate degrees (six fields of study), bachelor's degrees (nearly 50 fields of study)

Southwestern Community College
1501 West Townline Street, Creston, IA 50801
800/247-4023, ext. 352
http://www.swcciowa.edu/AgBusiness/Agbusiness.html
Degrees available: Associate degree

Williston State College
1410 University Avenue, PO Box 1326, Williston, ND 58802
888/863-9455
http://www.wsc.nodak.edu/academics/programs.htm
Degrees available: Associate degrees (three fields of study)

For More Information:

American Farm Bureau Federation
600 Maryland Avenue, SW, Suite 800, Washington, DC 20024
202/406-3600
http://www.fb.org

American Society of Agronomy
677 South Segoe Road, Madison, WI 53711
608/273-8080
http://www.agronomy.org

National FFA Organization
National FFA Center
PO Box 68960, Indianapolis, IN 46268-0960
317/802-6060
http://www.ffa.org

U.S. Department of Agriculture
1400 Independence Avenue, SW, Washington, DC 20250
202/720-2791
http://www.usda.gov

Interview: Jerry Bolton

Jerry Bolton is the Dean of the Agricultural Sciences Department at Kirkwood Community College in Cedar Rapids, Iowa. The College has the second largest two-year agriculture department in the nation. Mr. Bolton discussed his program and the education of agricultural students with the editors of *They Teach That in Community College!?*

Q. Please provide an overview of educational opportunities that are available in your program.

A. Kirkwood's Agricultural Sciences Department has 15 career programs. I will list each and the awards available: Agribusiness (AAS, diploma), Agriculture GPS/GIS technician (AAS, diploma, certificate), Agriculture Production (AAS, diploma), Agriculture Transfer (AA degree), Diesel Agriculture Technology (AAS), Diesel Truck Technology (AAS), Floral Careers (diploma), Golf Course and Turf Management (AAS, diploma), Horse Science (AAS, diploma), Landscape, Garden Center, and Nursery Management (AAS, Diploma), Landscape Maintenance (AAS), Parks and Natural Resources (AAS, diploma), Pet Grooming/Pet Shop Management (diploma), Veterinary Assistant (diploma), Veterinary Technician (AAS).

Q. What career opportunities are available in agriculture that might surprise high school students unsure of what to study in college?

A. High school students have little concept of the technology jobs available in agriculture. The image is one of cows, sows, and plows! In reality, the infusion of technologies such as genetic markers, geospatial equipment, ultrasound equipment, management information systems, biotechnology, and nanotechnology into agriculture has/is changing the entire career field of agriculture.

6

Q. What are the most important personal and professional qualities for agricultural students?

A. The successful agriculture student is punctual, ambitious,
inquisitive, and passionate about his or her career. Today, skills
in entrepreneurship and risk taking are also becoming needed.
From a professional perspective, students need to develop their
math and science abilities, because the new world of agriculture is being driven by technology—not only for production of
goods, but also for profitable decision making.

Q. What advice would you offer agricultural majors as
they graduate and look for jobs?

A. My advice for graduating agriculture majors is: be prepared to
work hard and long to succeed, stay abreast of technology
changes, and continually educate yourself in math and science.

American Sign Language/ Interpreter Training

Approximately 32.5 million people in the United States are deaf or hard of hearing, according to the U.S. Census Bureau. As government, and society as a whole, has become more aware of the rights and needs of people who are deaf, exciting career opportunities have emerged for persons interested in professional work in deaf-related fields. To meet this demand, community colleges are adding or improving their deaf studies programs, which teach students about American Sign Language, interpreting, deaf history, and deaf culture. This is a growing field, as increased understanding of the deaf community—within the broader national and international community—is necessary.

Typical Courses:

> Basic Sign Language
> Introduction to American Sign Language
> Sign Mime and Creative Movement
> Introduction to Deaf Studies
> Structure of American Sign Language
> Deaf Art/Deaf Artists
> Deaf Theater History
> Organizational Communication and the Deaf Employee
> Deaf Culture and Community
> Introduction to American Sign Language Teaching
> Civil Rights and Deaf People

Potential Employers:

> Human services organizations
> Government agencies
> Schools
> Deaf-related associations and organizations
> Employment agencies that serve the deaf or hard of hearing

Available At:

The following programs are just a sampling of the opportunities that are available to students interested in American Sign

Language/Interpreter Training. Educational programs in this subject are available at community colleges throughout the United States. Visit the websites of schools in your area to see if they offer study options in the field.

Bristol Community College
135 County Street, Attleboro, MA 02703
508/678-2811
http://www.bristolcommunitycollege.edu/catalog/ca7/degree/ca7_dst.html
Degrees available: Certificate, associate degree

College of Southern Idaho
315 Falls Avenue PO Box 1238, Aspen Building, Room 156
Twin Falls, ID 83303-1238
800/680-0274, ext. 6881
info@csi.edu
http://www.csi.edu/l4.asp?sign
Degrees available: Associate degree

Columbus State Community College
Interpreting/American Sign Language Education Program
550 East Spring Street, Columbus, OH 43215
800/621-6407
http://www.cscc.edu/DOCS/interp.htm
Degrees available: Certificate, associate degree

Community College of Philadelphia
American Sign Language/English Interpreting Program
1700 Spring Garden Street, Philadelphia, PA 19130
215/751-8010
http://www.ccp.edu/site/academic/degrees/sign_language.php
Degrees available: Associate degree

Cuyahoga Community College
Deaf Interpretive Services Program
11000 Pleasant Valley Road, Parma, OH 44130
216/987-5219
http://www.tri-c.edu/home/default.htm
Degrees available: Associate degree

Delaware Technical and Community College-Stanton/Wilmington Campus
333 Shipley Street, Wilmington, DE 19801
302/571-5336
http://www.dtcc.edu/stanton-wilmington/programs
Degrees available: Certificate, diploma

Delgado Community College-City Park Campus
615 City Park Avenue, New Orleans, LA 70119
800/377-7285
enroll@dcc.edu
http://www.dcc.edu/programs/programlist.htm
Degrees available: Certificate, associate degree

Florida Community College-Jacksonville
Sign Language Interpretation Program
501 West State Street, Jacksonville, FL 32202
http://www.fccj.org/prospective/programs/creativart_com/index.html
Degrees available: Associate degree

Georgia Perimeter College-Decatur Campus
3251 Panthersville Road, Decatur, GA 30034-3897
678/891-3600
http://www.gpc.edu/~acadaff/cat/programs/ITP.html
and
http://www.gpc.edu/~acadaff/cat/programs/ITPCert.html
and
http://www.gpc.edu/~gpcslip
Degrees available: Certificate, associate degree

Did You Know?

According to the Registry of Interpreters for the Deaf, interpreters who work as staff at agencies, businesses, government organizations, or school systems earn between $15,000 and $30,000+ per year. Highly skilled and credentialed interpreters can make $40,000 to $50,000 a year.

Hillsborough Community College-Dales Mabry Campus
Department of Health Sciences
PO Box 30030, Tampa, FL 33630-3030
813/253-7202; TDD 813/253-7552
http://www.hccfl.edu/depts/healthsci/interpreter/index.html
Degrees available: Associate degree

J. Sargeant Reynolds Community College
PO Box 85622, Richmond, VA 23285-5622
804/371-3000
http://www.jsr.vccs.edu/curriculum/programs/
American%20Sign%20LanguageCSC.htm
and
http://www.jsr.vccs.edu/curriculum/programs/
Interpreter%20EducationCSC.htm
Degrees available: Certificates

Kapiolani Community College-University of Hawaii
Department of Arts and Sciences
4303 Diamond Head Road, Honolulu, HI 96816
808/734-9000
kapinfo@hawaii.edu
http://programs.kcc.hawaii.edu/%7Eeia
Degrees available: Associate degrees

LaGuardia Community College
Natural and Applied Sciences Department
31-10 Thomson Avenue, Long Island City, NY 11101
718/482-7200
http://www.lagcc.cuny.edu/hsp/hsp2/deaf.htm
Degrees available: Associate degree

Lansing Community College
Sign Language/Interpreter Program
5200 Communication Department
PO Box 40010, Lansing, MI 48901-7210
517/483-1040
http://www.lcc.edu/communication/sign_lang
Degrees available: Certificate, associate degree

11

Montgomery College-Rockville Campus
Department of Speech, Dance, Theatre, and American Sign Language
51 Mannakee Street, Rockville, MD 20850
301/251-7556
http://www.montgomerycollege.edu/curricula/descriptions/cdasl.htm
Degrees available: Certificate, associate degree

Nassau Community College
Communications Department
One Education Drive, Garden City, NY 11530
516/572-7170
http://www.ncc.edu/dptpages/communications/ASL.html
Degrees available: Associate degree

Pikes Peak Community College
5675 South Academy Boulevard, Colorado Springs, CO 80906
800/456-6847
http://www.ppcc.cccoes.edu/CatalogSchedule/Programs/
Programs.cfm?Program=InPp
Degrees available: Associate degree

Pima County Community College
American Sign Language Program
4905 East Broadway Boulevard, Tucson, AZ 85709-1010
520/206-6857
infocenter@pima.edu
http://www.pima.edu/program/interpreter/index.shtml
Degrees available: Associate degree

Rochester Institute of Technology
National Technical Institute for the Deaf
52 Lomb Memorial Drive, Rochester, NY 14623
585/475-6809 (Voice/TTY), 585/475-6851 (TTY)
http://www.rit.edu/~932www/ugrad_bulletin/colleges/ntid/
specert.html#deafstudies
Degrees available: Certificate

Salt Lake Community College
Interpreter Training Program
4600 South Redwood Road, Salt Lake City, UT 84123
801/957-4111
http://www.slcc.edu/pages/1051.asp
Degrees available: Associate degree

Santa Ana College
Communication Department
1530 West 17th Street, Santa Ana, CA 92706
714/564-6005
http://www.sac.edu/degrees/sac/Communications.htm
Degrees available: Certificate

Santa Fe Community College
6401 Richards Avenue, Santa Fe, NM 87508-4887
505/428-1370
info@sfccnm.edu
http://www.sfccnm.edu/sfcc/pages/1043.html
and
http://www.sfccnm.edu/sfcc/pages/1007.html
Degrees available: Certificate, associate degree

Seattle Central Community College
Allied Health, Business, Languages, and Cultures Division
1701 Broadway, Room 2BE3210, Seattle, WA 98122
206/344-4347, 206/344-4347 (TTY)
http://seattlecentral.edu/proftech/PROdeafstudies.php
Degrees available: Associate degree

Sierra College
5000 Rocklin Road, Rocklin, CA 95677
916/789-2649, ext. 3705
http://www.sierracollege.edu/ed_programs/liberal_arts/disci-
plines.htm#deaf
Degrees available: Associate degree

Spokane Falls Community College
Human Services Department
3410 West Fort George Wright Drive, Spokane, WA 99204-5288
http://tech.spokanefalls.edu/HumanServices/
default.asp?menu=4&page=Interpreter
Degrees available: Certificate, associate degree

Tidewater Community College
American Sign Language and Interpreter Education Department
1428 Cedar Road, Chesapeake, VA 23322-7199
757/822-5015, 757/822-5018 (TTY)
http://www.tcc.edu/academics/divisions/academicC/asl/index.htm
Degrees available: Associate degree

Tulsa Community College
Interpreter Education Program
3727 East Apache, Tulsa, OK 74115
918/595-7494
http://www.tulsacc.edu/page.asp?durki=3728&site=85&return=3543
Degrees available: Associate degree

For More Information:

Alexander Graham Bell Association
for the Deaf and Hard of Hearing
3417 Volta Place, NW, Washington, DC 20007-2778
202/337-5220, 202/337-5221 (TTY)
info@agbell.org
http://www.agbell.org

American Speech-Language-Hearing Association
10801 Rockville Pike, Rockville, MD 20852
800/498-2071, 301/897-5700 (TTY)
actioncenter@asha.org
http://www.asha.org

Registry of Interpreters for the Deaf, Inc.
333 Commerce Street, Alexandria, VA 22314
703/838-0030
http://www.rid.org

Animation

When many people think of animation, they instantly think of the Saturday morning cartoons they watched as children. But animation has come a long way in the last couple of decades, with significant computerized software advances that have created a much broader range of opportunities in today's animation field. Television and film animation is still a viable career option, but animation is also used in many other applications—computer game development, medical simulations, advertising, industrial and architectural design, and more. Housed in most art departments, this major requires artistic vision and creativity along with an aptitude for computers and technology. Business savvy and communication skills are also important. Since this field offers diverse opportunities for graduates, it is fitting for the individual who wants a well-rounded education that is marketable across a variety of industries and applications, but which is also specialized enough to provide significant direction in post-graduation job seeking.

Typical Courses:

> Fundamentals of Design
> Rendering and Modeling Techniques
> Cartooning
> Storyboarding
> Digital Design with Photoshop
> Design for Advertising
> Multimedia Flash
> Digital Layout, Imaging, and Editing
> The Film as Art
> Television Video/Studio Production
> 3D Animation and Commercial Applications

Potential Employers:

> Television and film production companies
> Corporations and small businesses
> Advertising agencies
> Architectural firms
> Web design consulting firms

Available At:

The following programs are just a sampling of the opportunities that are available to students interested in animation. Visit the websites of schools in your area to see if they offer study options in the field.

Bergen Community College
400 Paramus Road, Paramus, NJ 07652
201/447-7195
admsoffice@bergen.edu
http://www.bergen.edu/ecatalog/
programview.asp?program.cbn=10&semester.rm=1
Degrees available: Associate degree

Brooks College
Animation Program
4825 East Pacific Coast Highway, Long Beach, CA 90804
866/746-5711
http://www.brookscollege.edu/animation.asp
Degrees available: Associate degree

Macomb Community College
Media & Communication Arts Program
14500 East 12 Mile Road, Warren, MI 48088
586/445-7435
answer@macomb.edu
http://www.macomb.edu/ProgramDescriptions/
MediaCommunicationArt.asp#Art
Degrees available: Certificate, associate degree

Madison Area Technical College
Art Department
3550 Anderson Street, Madison, WI 53704
608/246-6002
http://matcmadison.edu/matc/ASP/showprogram.asp?ID=2908
Degrees available: Associate degree

Mohawk Valley Community College
Art Department
1101 Sherman Drive, Utica, NY 13501
315/792-5446
http://www.mvcc.edu/acdmcs/dprtmnts/art/dgtlmtn.cfm
Degrees available: Associate degree

Moraine Valley Community College
Art Department
9000 West College Parkway, Palos Hills, IL 60465-0937
708/974-4300
http://www.morainevalley.edu/programs/program_list.htm
Degrees available: Associate degree

New Hampshire Technical Institute
31 College Drive, Concord, NH 03301-7412
603/271-7757
info@nhti.edu
http://nhti.edu/academics/academicprograms/degaggp.html
Degrees available: Associate degree

Santa Ana College
Department of Fine and Performing Arts
1530 West 17th Street, Santa Ana, CA 92706
714/564-5600
http://www.sac.edu/degrees/sac/Art-3-D_Animation.htm
Degrees available: Certificate

For More Information:

International Animated Film Society
721 South Victory Boulevard, Burbank, CA 91502
818/842-8330
info@asifa-hollywood.org
http://www.asifa-hollywood.org

Animation World Network
http://www.awn.com

Aquaculture

Aquaculture is similar to agriculture, but instead of growing crops or raising typical farm livestock, fish and shellfish are raised. The study of aquaculture is growing in popularity for a number of reasons: the rise in demand for seafood by health-conscious consumers, the need to combat overfishing in the wild, and the need to find economical and efficient ways of providing food sources for the world's burgeoning population. Most fish raised through aquaculture are for human consumption or are used to stock ponds, rivers, and lakes for recreational fishing. Catfish, salmon, trout, tilapia, crayfish, and shrimp are just some of the many species that are cultivated through aquaculture. The fish are typically raised in pens not only in coastal areas, but inland as well, by utilizing natural or man-made water structures. Students interested in aquaculture can focus on the biological, technical, or managerial aspects of the industry. Aquaculture is practiced all over the world and is expected to provide new employment opportunities in the near future.

Typical Courses:

> Introduction to Fisheries Management
> Aquatic Ecology
> Diseases of Fish
> Nutrition of Fish
> Fish Reproduction
> Introduction to Computer Concepts and Applications
> Aquacultural Organisms
> Aquacultural Laboratory Techniques
> Aquacultural Field Techniques
> Aquacultural Management Practices

Potential Employers:

> Commercial fisheries
> Aquariums
> Colleges and universities
> State or federal organizations (such as the United States Fish and Wildlife Service)

Available At:

The following programs are just a sampling of the opportunities that are available to students interested in aqaculture. Visit http://www. was.org for more aquaculture programs. .

Bristol Community College
777 Elsbree Street, Fall River, MA 02720
508/678-2811
http://www.bristolcommunitycollege.edu/catalog/ca2/certificate/ ca2_aquc.html
and
http://www.bristolcommunitycollege.edu/catalog/ca5/certificate/ ca5_aqtc.html
Degrees available: Certificates

Did You Know?

18

Aquaculture in the United States has grown from a $45-million industry in 1974 to a nearly $1-billion dollar industry today, according to the U.S. Department of Agriculture.

College of Southern Idaho
315 Falls Avenue, PO Box 1238, Twin Falls, ID 83303-1238
800/680-0274
http://www.csi.edu/ip/Ag/CSI_AG_Programs/CSI_Aquaculture/ csi_aquaculture.html
Degrees available: Certificate, associate degree

Delaware Technical and Community College-Owens Campus
PO Box 610, Georgetown, DE 19947
302/855-5929
http://www.dtcc.edu/owens/programs
Degrees available: Certificate

Hillsborough Community College-Brandon Campus
Aquaculture Program
10414 East Columbus Drive, Tampa, FL 33619-7856
813/253-7802
http://www.hccfl.edu/by/aquaculture
Degrees available: Certificate, associate degree

Morrisville State College
Environmental Sciences Department
214 Charlton Hall, Morrisville, NY 13408
315/684-6106
http://www.morrisville.edu/Academics/Ag_NRC/NRC/html/
AquacultureAAS.htm
Degrees available: Associate degree

For More Information:

American Fisheries Society
5410 Grosvenor Lane, Bethesda, MD 20814-2199
301/897-8616
main@fisheries.org
http://www.fisheries.org

World Aquaculture Society (U.S. Branch)
143 J.M. Parker Coliseum
Louisiana State University, Baton Rouge, LA 70803
225/578-3137
wasmas@aol.com
http://www.was.org

Aquaculture Network Information Center
http://aquanic.org

Automobile Engineering Technology

If you have a passion for cars, and an aptitude for engineering, a degree in automotive engineering technology might be right up your alley. While your in-class work will focus on design, development, and testing of all kinds of motorized vehicles, most programs will also require a significant amount of time getting practical, hands-on experience in a variety of settings. Of the career paths available to automotive engineers, all require an interactive, people-focused personality—you'll be working daily with customers and personnel from other departments. Careers in automotive engineering are plentiful; most graduates find jobs with major automotive manufacturers.

Typical Courses:

> Calculus
> Statistics
> DC Circuits
> Computer-Aided Drafting
> Material Processing and Metallurgy
> Automotive Drivability and Diagnosis
> Fluid Power Systems
> Automotive Thermodynamics and Engine Design
> Industrial and Construction Safety
> Automotive Technology and Systems

Potential Employers:

> Automotive manufacturers
> Engineering firms

Available At:

Macomb Community College-South Campus
14500 12 Mile Road, R-124, Warren, MI 48088
586/445-7435
engineeringtech@macomb.edu
http://www.macomb.edu/academics/departments/drvd/default.asp
Degrees available: Associate degree

For More Information:

American Society for Engineering Education
1818 N Street, NW, Suite 600, Washington, DC 20036-2479
202/331-3500
http://www.asee.org

Junior Engineering Technical Society, Inc.
1420 King Street, Suite 405, Alexandria, VA 22314
703/548-5387
info@jets.org
http://www.jets.org

Aviation Management

Aviation management prepares students to work in the airline industry in management, marketing, finance, sales, personnel, public relations, and other related areas. Programs can often have different areas of emphasis, based on the department in which they are housed. Some programs are designed for students interested in a curriculum containing a strong engineering science and analysis component, while others are for those who prefer a liberal arts background and a broader base of social sciences or business management principles. Some programs require actual flight training, while others do not.

Typical Courses:

> Introduction to Aviation Management
> National Airspace Systems
> Air Traffic Control
> Aviation Law
> Airport Planning
> Airport Management
> Airline Management
> Airline Marketing
> General Aviation Operations
> Aviation Industry Regulation
> Aviation Management Writing and Communication
> Aviation Management Practices and Processes
> Air Transport Labor Relations
> Fiscal Aspects of Aviation Management
> Aviation Industry Career Development

Potential Employers:

> Airlines
> Commercial service airports (e.g., Chicago O'Hare International, Detroit Metro, and Los Angeles International)
> General aviation and reliever airports (e.g., Teterboro Airport, New Jersey, or DuPage Airport, Illinois)
> Federal Aviation Administration
> Transportation Security Administration

> Aviation/aerospace manufacturers (e.g., Lockheed-Martin, B.F. Goodrich Aerospace, Bell Helicopters-Textron, and The Boeing Company)
> General aviation companies (e.g., Cessna Aircraft Company, Signature Flight Support)

Available At:

The following list of aviation management programs is not exhaustive. Check with academic institutions near you to determine if majors, minors, certificates, or concentrations are available in aviation management.

Cecil Community College
Department of Transportation and Logistics
One Seahawk Drive, North East, MD 21901
410/287-1000
information@cecilcc.edu
http://www.cecilcc.edu/programs/programs-05-07/
transportation-logistics/aviation-management.asp
Degrees available: Certificate, associate degree

23

Fun Fact

According to the Federal Aviation Administration, there are a total of 19,576 airports in the United States—of which, 510 are commercial service.

Community College of Allegheny County-South Campus
1750 Clairton Road, Route 885, West Mifflin, PA 15122-3097
412/469-4301
http://www.ccac.edu/default.aspx?id=137380
Degrees available: Associate degree

Community College of Baltimore County
Business Department
800 South Rolling Road, Baltimore, MD 21228
410/455-4157
http://www.ccbcmd.edu/bsswe/aviation/aviation_degrees.html
Degrees available: Associate degree

Miami Dade College (multiple campuses)
https://sisvsr.mdc.edu/ps/sheet.aspx
Degrees available: Associate degree

Oakland Community College
Department of Business, Management, and Law
2480 Opdyke Road, Bloomfield Hills, MI 48304
248/341-2000
http://www.oaklandcc.edu/FutureStudents/DegreePrograms.asp
Degrees available: Associate degree

For More Information:

Air Transport Association of America
1301 Pennsylvania Avenue, NW, Suite 1100, Washington, DC 20004
202/626-4000
ata@airlines.org
http://www.airlines.org

Federal Aviation Administration
800 Independence Avenue, SW, Washington, DC 20591
866/835-5322
http://www.faa.gov

24

Beacon College

Beacon College serves students with language-based learning disabilities, auditory and visual processing differences, reading/writing disabilities, expressive/receptive language deficits, math disabilities, and ADD/ADHD. It is the only accredited college in the United States with a program exclusively for students with learning disabilities that offers a bachelor of arts degree. Students can choose to earn an associate of arts degree or a bachelor of arts degree in human services, liberal studies, or computer information systems. The College strives to provide every student with the tools and support necessary to succeed in school, and features a strong Educational Support Services program. Other programs include the Field Placement Program, which allows students to gain valuable work experience in their chosen field while still in school; and the Cultural Studies Abroad Program, which offers students the option to study abroad in several countries. Students have previously taken advantage of this program to visit England, France, Germany, Ireland, Italy, Spain, and Switzerland. The school has several clubs and student organizations, such as the Book Club, Poets and Writers Club, and Fishing Club.

Available Fields of Study:

> Human Services
> Liberal Studies
> Computer Information Systems

For More Information:

Beacon College
105 East Main Street, Leesburg, FL 34748
352/787-7660
http://www.beaconcollege.edu
Degrees available: Associate degree, bachelor's degree

Bioinformatics

If you are interested in computer science and biology, then the new field of bioinformatics might be for you. Bioinformatics can be generally described as the application of cutting-edge computer science to analyze and manage biological information. Bioinformatics played a significant role in the Human Genome Project, and it has also helped shorten the research and development time for pharmaceuticals. Experts predict that bioinformatics will be used in the future to create designer drugs and treatments that will be much more effective for individual patients. Bioinformatics is sometimes known as biostatistics. Advanced degrees are typically required for the best positions in the field.

Typical Courses:

> Fundamentals of Biology
> Genetics
> Cell and Molecular Biology
> Biochemistry
> Bioinformatics
> Bioethics
> Computer Science
> Database Design
> Fundamentals of Chemistry
> Organic Chemistry
> Calculus
> Statistics
> Data Structures
> Discrete Mathematics
> Algorithms

Potential Employers:

> Pharmaceutical companies (such as Aventis, Bristol-Myers Squibb, Merck & Co., Pfizer, and Wyeth)
> Research laboratories
> Colleges and universities
> Government agencies
> Software companies

Available At:

Howard Community College
10901 Little Patuxent Parkway, ILB 239, Columbia, MD 21044
410/772-4114
http://www.howardcc.edu/business/BioinformaticsAADegree.htm
Degrees available: Associate degree

For More Information:

American Association for the Advancement of Science
1200 New York Avenue, NW, Washington, DC 20005
202/326-6400
http://www.aaas.org

Biotechnology Industry Organization
1225 Eye Street, NW, Suite 400, Washington, DC 20005
info@bio.org
202/962-9200
http://www.bio.org

Biomedical Equipment Technology

Students who are mechanically inclined may enjoy working in the field of biomedical equipment technology. *Biomedical equipment technicians* are responsible for the maintenance and repair of important medical equipment such as lasers, x-ray equipment, and machines used to perform tests such as EKGs, CT scans, and MRIs. They may also be responsible for the modification or operation of some medical instruments or equipment. They may work in laboratories and hospitals, medical equipment manufacturers, and in other locations that use medical equipment. Biomedical equipment technicians must be able to think quickly and work effectively under pressure, as they may be called to repair lifesaving equipment in time-sensitive situations. In addition to being mechanically inclined, workers in the field of biomedical equipment technology should also have good computer skills and communication skills. Demand for biomedical equipment technicians is expected to grow about as fast as the average for other occupations, according to the U.S. Department of Labor.

Typical Courses:

> Algebra and Trigonometry
> AC and DC Circuit Analysis
> Physiological Transducers
> Biomedical Instrumentation and Systems
> Biomedical Equipment Laboratory
> Computer Calculations for Electronics
> Analytic Geometry & Calculus
> Medical and Clinical Equipment
> Medical Technology Management
> Medical Equipment Troubleshooting
> Microprocessor Systems

Potential Employers:

> Hospitals
> Shared service organizations
> Other medical facilities

Available At:

Only two institutions that offer programs in biomedical equipment technology are accredited by the Technology Accreditation Commission for the Accreditation Board for Engineering and Technology: Cincinnati State Technical and Community College and Pennsylvania State University.

Cincinnati State Technical and Community College
3520 Central Parkway, Cincinnati, OH 45223
513/861-7700
http://www.cinstate.cc.oh.us/FutureStudent/Academics/
AcademicDivisions/EngineeringTechnologies/BMET.htm
Degrees available: Associate degree

Pennsylvania State University-New Kensington Campus
3550 Seventh Street Road, New Kensington, PA 15068-1765
724/334-6712
http://www.nk2.psu.edu/bet/index.html
Degrees available: Associate degree

The following schools offer training in biomedical equipment technology, but are not accredited by the Technology Accreditation Commission for the Accreditation Board for Engineering and Technology.

Delaware County Community College
Admissions Office
Main Campus Room 3545
901 South Media Line Road, Media, PA 19063-1094
610/359-5050
admiss@dccc.edu
http://www.dccc.edu/catalog/
career_programs.html#biomedical_equip
Degrees available: Associate degree

Delgado Community College-City Park Campus
615 City Park Avenue, New Orleans, LA 70119
800/377-7285
enroll@dcc.edu
http://www.dcc.edu/programs/programlist.htm
Degrees available: Associate degree

Howard Community College
Science and Technology Division
10901 Little Patuxent Parkway, Columbia, MD 21044
410/772-4827
http://www.howardcc.edu/process.cfm?page_id=1551
Degrees available: Certificates

Texas State Technical College-Waco
3801 Campus Drive, Waco, TX 76705
254/867-4885
http://www.waco.tstc.edu/bet/index.php
Degrees available: Associate degrees

For More Information:

American Society for Healthcare Engineering
One North Franklin, 27th Floor, Chicago, IL 60606
ashe@aha.org
http://www.ashe.org

Association for the Advancement of Medical Instrumentation
1110 North Glebe Road, Suite 220, Arlington, VA 22201-4795
703/525-4890
http://www.aami.org

Medical Equipment and Technology Association Board
contact@mymeta.org
http://www.mymeta.org

Interview: Myron Hartman

Myron Hartman is an instructor and the program coordinator for Pennsylvania State University's Biomedical Engineering Technology program, one of only two programs of its kind in the nation to be accredited by the Technology Accreditation Commission for the Accreditation Board for Engineering and Technology. He discussed his program and the field of biomedical engineering technology (BET) with the editors of *They Teach That in Community College!?*

Q. Tell us about your program.

A. The BET program at Penn State University, New Kensington campus is a two-year associate program. The major prepares the BET graduates who, during the first few years of professional practice, will be able to:

1. Perform preventive maintenance and assurance and safety inspections on a wide range of medical devices.

2. Understand use, application, and operation on a wide range of medical equipment and systems, with normal/abnormal outcomes/measurements.

3. Demonstrate a broad knowledge of electrical and electronic engineering technology fundamentals, components, and circuits.

4. Apply basic mathematical and scientific principals to identify, analyze, and solve technical problems on a wide range of medical equipment and systems.

5. Understand use and application of applicable test equipment, simulators, and tools required to [perform] preventive maintenance and service medical equipment and systems.

6. Be aware of, understand, and apply codes, standards, and regulations regarding medical equipment support.

7. Perform and assist with application design, installation, and acceptance testing for medical equipment and systems.

8. Work with fellow technicians, clinical professionals, and other related professionals by functioning effectively on committees and teams, and by independent work.

9. Properly document actions and follow required procedures, policies, and regulatory requirements.

10. Communicate effectively with fellow technicians, clinical professionals, and other related professionals.

11. Continue professional development by participating in education and training on medical equipment and systems.

12. Participate in quality improvement programs that support medical equipment and systems.

13. Participate in recognizing, reporting, and monitoring improvements to medical equipment and the related profession, as required by regulation and on a professional voluntary basis.

31

Q. What classes should high school students take to prepare for postsecondary BET programs?

A. For high school students preparing to enter any technical program, the following courses are essential: math (algebra and trigonometry), English, physics, chemistry, and any other science-related studies.

Q. What qualities do students need to be successful in their careers?

A. The number one skill to be successful in the BET field is customer skills. You must be able to work well with other people, and able to communicate, empathize with people's situations, understand the who-what-where-when-why of situations, and have a good attitude and smile. You also must be a self starter and be able to work independently, as most BMETs set their priorities for each work day and to what must be completed. Next would be the technical ability of problem solving—the ability to use electronic test equipment, computers, software, and tools to diagnose, dissemble, repair, calibrate, and test medical equipment. One additional skill would be creativity in problem solving. Many problems must be solved in short time frames, so being able to think quickly, know your resources, read technical manuals, contact and communicate with technical support departments, and solve the problem to meet the needs of the customer [are key].

Q. What is the future employment outlook for biomedical equipment technicians?

A. I think the employment opportunity is the best it has ever been. With only two ABET-accredited schools in the nation and fewer BET programs in general, there are fewer qualified people entering the profession. Individuals who started in the field in the late 70s are approaching retirement age, with some advancing to management and other related positions. Some hospitals have hired individuals with electronics or computer science degrees, but these individuals do not have the necessary fundamentals to be proficient as a BMET. Since I have been at Penn State, the employment placement is close to 100 percent. Graduates make good starting salaries, and advancement normally happens within a year or so after employment.

One of the biggest problems in getting more people interested in the field is that very few know it exists. Guidance counselors, high school teachers, and the public in general are not even aware of the profession. It is so specific, with very few schools offering programs, it is the best-kept secret for a rewarding field. Most people discover the program through a neighbor or relative who works in the field. But for those who do discover it, it is a very rewarding professional career. If you have good people skills, a good attitude, are open to relocation, and have passing grades and fairly good technical skills, you will get a job in this profession.

Biomedical Photography

Students who are interested in the biological sciences and photography may want to learn more about careers in biomedical photography. Students in biomedical photography programs explore the field by learning more about digital and traditional photography and their uses in science, medicine, technology, and industry. Classroom topics include black and white and color photography, close-up and high-magnification photography, lighting, ophthalmic photography, imaging technologies, desktop publishing software, computer graphics, techniques for biomedical news and public relations photography, equipment and techniques for magnified images, and planning, executing and presenting a professional portfolio. Some colleges, such as the Ohio Institute of Photography & Technology, offer specialized areas of concentration such as photography of the patient for medical documentation, public relations, standardization of lighting in the studio, close-up photography, photomicrography, digital imaging, and video and audio-visual presentation. Only two colleges offer associate degrees in biomedical photography: the Ohio Institute of Photography & Technology and Randolph Community College.

Typical Courses:

> Black and White Photography
> Color Photography
> Biomedical Photography
> Photography and the Microscope
> Digital Media
> Biology
> Desktop Publishing
> Creating a Portfolio

Potential Employers:

> Hospitals
> Colleges and universities
> Medical publishers
> Medical examiners' offices
> Forensic laboratories
> Pharmaceutical companies
> Health care and medical research centers

> Ophthalmic practices
> Producers of multimedia and web publishing

Available At:

Ohio Institute of Photography & Technology
2029 Edgefield Road, Dayton, OH 45439
800/932-9698
http://www.oipt.com/biomedical_photography.html
Degrees available: Associate degree

Randolph Community College
629 Industrial Park Avenue, Asheboro, NC 27204-1009
336/633-0200
info@randolph.edu
http://www.randolph.cc.nc.us/edprog/curr/bioph.html
Degrees available: Associate degree

For More Information:

34

BioCommunications Association, Inc.
220 Southwind Lane, Hillsborough, NC 27278
919/245-0906
office@bcz.org
http://www.bca.org

Health and Science Communications Association
39 Wedgewood Drive, Suite A, Jewett City, CT 06351
860/376-5915
http://www.hesca.org

Biotechnology

The Biotechnology Industry Organization defines biotechnology as the use of cellular and molecular processes to solve problems or make products, such as vaccines, diagnostic tests, disease-resistant crops, and so forth. Since the anthrax attacks of 2001, which made the general public aware of the threat of bioterrorism, the biotech field has gained attention. Biotech workers, after all, are the ones who work on developing ways of detecting the presence of infectious diseases as well as developing the antidotes to save us. Of course, not every biotech worker walks around in a contamination suit passing out vaccines. Areas of the industry include research and development, clinical research, manufacturing, and quality control. Since many specialties exist in biotechnology, there are many ways to train for the field. For example, scientists working in research and development may have a Ph.D. in a science field, an M.D., or both. Others who work in research and development may include laboratory assistants, research assistants, and plant breeders. These workers do not need advanced degrees such as a Ph.D. In fact, many may have technical certificates or associate degrees in biotechnology. Workers in clinical research, which involves working with patients, usually have science or nursing degrees. Those in administrative positions may have more advanced degrees. Engineers in manufacturing and quality control need at least a bachelor's degree in their specialty; technicians need associate degrees.

Typical Courses:

> General Biology
> General Biology Laboratory
> Cell Biology
> Molecular Biology
> Immunology
> Microbiology
> High Performance Computing for Bioinformatics
> Ethical Issues in Medicine and Biology
> Genetic Engineering
> Genomics
> Bioinformatics

Potential Employers:

> Biotechnology companies
> Agriculture industry
> Food industry
> Pharmaceutical industry
> Government agencies
> Health care industry
> Research institutes at colleges and universities
> Crime laboratories

Available At:

The following list of biotechnology programs is not exhaustive. Check with academic institutions near you to determine if majors, minors, certificates, or concentrations are available in biotechnology.

Camden County College
200 North Broadway, Camden, NJ 08102-1185
856/227-7200
http://www.camdencc.edu/departments/biotechnology/index.htm
Degrees available: Associate degree

Community College of Allegheny County-Allegheny Campus
808 Ridge Avenue, Pittsburgh, PA 15212-6097
412/237-4600
http://www.ccac.edu/default.aspx?id=142083
Degrees available: Certificate, associate degree

Community College of Baltimore County
Biotechnology Program
800 South Rolling Road, Baltimore, MD 21228
410/455-6942
http://www.ccbcmd.edu/math_science/biotech_degree.html
Degrees available: Certificate, associate degree

Delaware Technical and Community College (multiple campuses)
400 Stanton-Christiana Road, Newark, DE 19713
302/453-3784
http://www.dtcc.edu/stanton/biochem
Degrees available: Associate degree

Housatonic Community College
900 Lafayette Boulevard, Bridgeport, CT 06604
203/332-5200
http://www.hcc.commnet.edu/academics/programs/dynamic/
progDetail.asp?keyCode=EA98
Degrees available: Associate degree

Houston Community College
Biotechnology Department
3100 Main at Elgin, Houston, TX 77002
713/718-5253
http://www.hccs.edu/discipline/Bitc/bitc.html
Degrees available: Certificate, associate degree

Hudson Valley Community College
Biology Department
80 Vandenburgh Avenue, Troy, NY 12180
518/629-7453
https://www.hvcc.edu/las/biotech/index.html
Degrees available: Associate degree

Ivy Tech Community College of Indiana (multiple campuses)
50 West Fall Creek Parkway North Drive, Indianapolis, IN 46208
888/489-5463
http://www.ivytech.edu/programs/btn
Degrees available: Associate degree

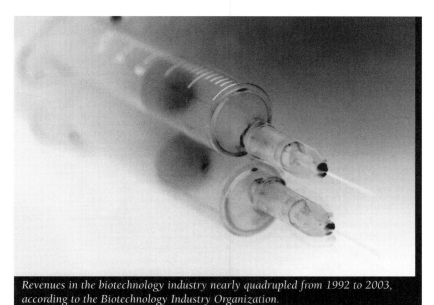

Revenues in the biotechnology industry nearly quadrupled from 1992 to 2003, according to the Biotechnology Industry Organization.

Macomb Community College
14500 East 12 Mile Road, Warren, MI 48088
866/622-6621
answer@macomb.edu
http://www.macomb.edu/ProgramDescriptions/
MolecularBiotechAS.asp
Degrees available: Associate degree

Monroe Community College
1000 East Henrietta Road, Rochester, NY 14623
http://www.monroecc.edu/etsdbs/MCCatPub.nsf/
AcademicPrograms?OpenPage
Degrees available: Associate degree

Montgomery College
Biotechnology Program
20200 Observation Drive, Germantown, MD 20876
http://www.mc.cc.md.us/Departments/biotechnology
Degrees available: Certificate, associate degree

Moorpark College
7075 Campus Road, Moorpark, CA 93021
http://www.moorparkcollege.edu/catalog
Degrees available: Certificate, associate degree

New Hampshire Community Technical College-Stratham
277 Portsmouth Avenue, Stratham, NH 03885-2231
http://ms.nhctc.edu/NHCTC/Stratham/Programs/Associate/
BIOTECH.htm
Degrees available: Certificate, diploma, associate degree

Northern Virginia Community College
4001 Wakefield Chapel Road, Annandale, VA 22003-3796
703/323-3000
http://www.nvcc.vccs.edu/curcatalog/programs/sci1.htm
Degrees available: Associate degree

Palm Beach Community College
4200 Congress Avenue, Lake Worth, FL 33416
561/207-5072
biotechnology@pbcc.edu
http://www.pbcc.edu/biotech
Degrees available: Associate degree

Pima County Community College
Department of Science and Engineering
4905 East Broadway Boulevard, Tucson, AZ 85709-1010
520/206-6763
infocenter@pima.edu
http://www.pima.edu/program/health-professions/biotech
Degrees available: Certificate

Portland Community College-Rock Creek Campus
17705 Northwest Springville Road, Building 7, Room 202
Portland, OR 97280-0990
866/922-1010
biotech@pcc.edu
http://www.pcc.edu/pcc/pro/progs/bit
Degrees available: Associate degree

Salt Lake Community College
Jordan Campus
Biotechnology Technicians Program
3491 West 9000 South, West Jordan, UT 84088
801/957-2851
http://www.slcc.edu/pages/1253.asp
Degrees available: Associate degree

Santa Fe Community College
Biotechnology Laboratory Technology Program
3000 Northwest 83rd Street, Building W, Room 002
Gainesville, FL 32606-6200
352/395-5650
biotech@sfcc.edu
http://inst.sfcc.edu/~btn/index.htm
Degrees available: Associate degree

Southern Maine Community College
2 Fort Road, South Portland, ME 04106
207/741-5500
http://www.smccme.edu/catalog/2005-2006/
index.php?section=5&navid=98&docid=0
Degrees available: Associate degree

Tallahassee Community College
444 Appleyard Drive, Tallahassee, FL 32304
850/201-6200
http://www.tcc.fl.edu/catalog/064-090.pdf
Degrees available: Associate degree

For More Information:

Biotechnology Industry Organization
1225 Eye Street, NW, Suite 400, Washington, DC 20005
202/962-9200
info@bio.org
http://www.bio.org

National Center for Biotechnology Information
National Library of Medicine
Building 38A, Bethesda, MD 20894
301/496-2475
info@ncbi.nlm.nih.gov
http://www.ncbi.nlm.nih.gov

BioWorld Online
http://www.bioworld.com

Interview: Dr. Thomas Burkett

Dr. Thomas Burkett is the program coordinator of the biotechnology program at the Community College of Baltimore County (Maryland). He discussed his program and the education of biotechnology students with the editors of *They Teach That in Community College!?*

Q. Please tell us about your program.

A. The biotechnology program at the Community College of Baltimore County is designed to provide students with the hands-on skills and knowledge base that they need to enter the field of biotechnology. Students have the option of obtaining a degree (A.A.S.) or a certificate as a biotechnology laboratory technician. The certificate option may be completed in as little as three semesters of evening courses. Students graduating from the program are ready for jobs in academic and industrial research and development labs as well as biomanufacturing (vaccines, biopharmaceuticals) positions.

Q. What high school subjects/activities should students focus on to be successful in this major?

A. A solid foundation in the sciences and good writing skills are important for success in this field. High school students interested in biotechnology should take chemistry, biology, physics, and math classes available to them. Also, don't forget English composition classes.

High school students may want to take part in any science clubs at their school, enter local science fairs, volunteer in a local college laboratory, or get a part-time job in a hospital laboratory. Even a job washing glassware will allow students to see how the things they learn in their classes are put into practice.

Q. What are the most important personal and professional qualities for biotechnology students?

A. I think the most important thing is to be excited about the field of biotechnology and always be willing to learn more about the various aspects of the field. If you're interested in research and

40

development, then curiosity and inquisitiveness are necessary; laboratory and manufacturing operations demand an eye for detail and some mechanical aptitude. A willingness to dive in and try new things (within reason) would serve one well in a research environment, and the ability to work independently is desired in almost all areas of the industry.

Q. What educational level is typically required for biotechnology graduates to land good jobs in the industry?

A. Biotechnology jobs are available at all education levels. Although it used to be that a person needed an advanced college degree to work in this area, that is no longer true. In fact, some of the greatest demand is for people with an associate degree or technical certificate. As with many other fields, the more education you have and the greater the number of skills you can bring to the job, the greater your employment and advancement opportunities. Remember that your degree and training just gets you in the door. It's important that you continue your education, either through training offered by your employer or through classes at the local college or university. In many cases your employer will offer tuition reimbursement plans, allowing you to finish your degree at a greatly reduced expense.

41

Q. Where do biotechnology graduates find employment?

A. Biotechnology graduates are in demand in a number of places. For instance, university and public/private research institutes often hire new college graduates to serve as laboratory technicians. A growing number of hospital laboratories are using biotechnology-based tests, and crime labs perform DNA isolations and DNA fingerprinting techniques. Biotechnology companies employ college graduates in R&D laboratories, in testing laboratories, and in biomanufacturing plants.

As employees gain more experience and knowledge, they may move into a supervisory capacity or move into fields that require an understanding of the scientific process but do not entail actual laboratory work. These fields include quality control and assurance, regulatory affairs, and business operations such as sales and marketing.

Bowling Industry Management

Training in all phases of bowling center operations—from sales and marketing to pinsetter maintenance—makes a degree in bowling industry management a unique investment. In today's exceedingly competitive recreational industry, such highly specialized training programs position the future bowling industry manager ahead of the crowd. Vincennes University is the only college in the United States to offer a degree in bowling industry management. Erie Community College offers a bowling management track as part of its recreation leadership degree.

Typical Courses:

> Lane and Pinsetter Maintenance
> Marketing
> Business English
> Pro Shop Operations
> Management

Potential Employers:

> Bowling alleys
> Equipment manufacturers
> Pro shops

Available At:

Erie Community College-South Campus
4041 Southwestern Boulevard, Orchard Park, NY 14127
http://ecc.edu/academic
Degrees available: Associate degree

Vincennes University
1002 North First Street, Vincennes, IN 47591
812/742-9198
http://www.vinu.edu
Degrees available: Associate degree

For More Information:

Professional Bowlers Association
719 Second Avenue, Suite 701, Seattle, WA 98104
http://www.pba.com

Interview: Gary Sparks

Gary Sparks is the director of the Bowling Lanes Management Program at Vincennes University in Vincennes, Indiana. He is also the coach of the Vincennes University bowling program and a member of the National Junior College Athletic Association's Hall of Fame. Mr. Sparks discussed his program and the education of students in the field with the editors of *They Teach That in Community College!?*

Q. Tell us about your program.

A. The program offers either an AS or AAS degree in Bowling Industry Management, depending on what level of some of the general education classes that are taken. The degree itself is a comprehensive program that goes through all aspects of the operation of a bowling center, including mechanics, maintenance, and the "core" operations of building lineage and leagues, including dealing with employees and all the financial obligations that go with running a business.

Q. What are the most important personal and professional qualities for bowling industry management majors?

A. Good bowling center managers are those who have good "people" skills. A good personality, the ability to work and interact with others, leadership qualities, and decision-making qualities are all strong components of being a successful center manager.

Q. Where do bowling industry management graduates find employment?

A. Graduates have many opportunities in the entire bowling industry field for potential employment. The "management" side is still the biggest core, getting directly into managing a center or being an assistant manager for a time before moving up. But we also place many graduates into sales, marketing, and technical positions within the industry. Some graduates have went out into the pro shop business area, so that becomes a potential area as well.

43

Computer and Digital Forensics

A new field of study is emerging from two hot career areas—computers and forensics. Computer and digital forensics combines computer know-how with the meticulous methods of forensic science. Due to the prevalence of computers in society today, many criminal activities utilize computers—creating a need for the *computer and digital forensic specialist*. Computer and digital forensic specialists work to find evidence of such things as the tampering, destruction, or copying of files, email, or instant messages. They also track such things as Internet usage and the use of restricted programs or databases. In many cases they must be careful to extract the sought-after computer data without destroying the original version, and to preserve the data in question in such a way that it will hold up in a court of law.

Typical Courses:

> Analysis of Digital Media
> Investigative Interviewing
> Computer Forensics
> Criminal Investigation
> Introduction to Statistics
> Computer and Network Security
> Financial Accounting
> Forensic Accounting
> Criminal Law
> Preserving/Documenting Evidence

Potential Employers:

> Law enforcement agencies
> Government agencies/U.S. military
> Corporations
> Law firms
> Accounting firms

Available At:

The following list of colleges and universities that offer programs in computer and digital forensics is not exhaustive. Visit the website of the

American Academy of Forensic Sciences (http://www.aafs.org) for a complete list of schools that offer training in computer forensics and other forensics-related specialties. Visit http://www.e-evidence.info/education.html for additional schools with developing programs in computer forensics and/or courses and minors in computer forensics.

Butler County Community College
PO Box 1203, Butler, PA 16003-1203
http://bc3.cc.pa.us/academics/technology/compforensics.htm
Degrees available: Associate degree

Champlain College
163 South Willard Street, West Hall, Room 12, Burlington, VT 05401
http://digitalforensics.champlain.edu
Degrees available: Certificate, associate degree, bachelor's degree

Community College of Beaver County
One Campus Drive, Monaca, PA 15061
http://www.ccbc.edu
Degrees available: Associate degree

Iowa Lakes Community College-Estherville Campus
300 South 18th Street, Estherville, IA 51334
http://www.iowalakes.edu/programs_study/social_human/criminal_justice/computer_forensics.htm
Degrees available: Associate degree

Lake Washington Technical College
11605 132nd Avenue, NE, Kirkland, WA 98034-8506
http://lwtchost.ctc.edu/programs2/CSNT/cfor/index.asp
Degrees available: Certificate, associate degree

Lehigh Carbon Community College
4525 Education Park Drive, Schnecksville, PA 18078
http://www.lccc.edu/default.aspx?pageID=415&degree=22
Degrees available: Associate degree

Redlands Community College
1300 South Country Club Road, El Reno, OK 73036-5304
http://www.redlandscc.edu
Degrees available: Associate degree

Tompkins Cortland Community College
PO Box 139, Dryden, NY 13053
http://www.tc3.edu/academic/forensic/main.asp
Degrees available: Associate degree

For More Information:

American Academy of Forensic Sciences
410 North 21st Street, Colorado Springs, CO 80904-2798
http://www.aafs.org

IEEE Computer Society
1730 Massachusetts Avenue, NW, Washington, DC 20036
http://www.computer.org

National Association of Forensic Accountants
2455 East Sunrise Boulevard, Suite 1201, Fort Lauderdale, FL 33304
http://www.nafanet.com

National Center for Forensic Science
PO Box 162367, Orlando, FL 32816-2367
http://ncfs.ucf.edu/home.html

Interview: Patricia Riola

Patricia Riola is an associate professor of computer science and the coordinator of the Department of Computer Science at Lehigh Carbon Community College (LCCC) in Schnecksville, Pennsylvania. She discussed its computer and digital forensics program and the education of students in this field with the editors of *They Teach That in Community College!?*

Q. Please tell us about your program.

A. LCCC's Computer Forensics program is a combination of criminal justice, computer networking, and computer forensics and security. The student learns about criminal law, court procedures, constitutional law, search and seizure, personal computer technician (A+) certification, criminal psychology, accounting, computer ethics, computer forensics, and computer security. It is expected that the student is comfortable with criminal law and investigations as well as computer repair and diagnostics. The student will be prepared to work as either a digital detective in law enforcement or as a security manager in the corporate computing environment. As a digital detective, the graduate may be called upon as an expert witness and will likely hold certifications as a crediting factor. As a security manager, the graduate will set up computer security policies and manage the network from a security perspective.

Q. What high school subjects/activities should students focus on to be successful in this major?

A. A student would do well if he or she were exposed to computer networking basics, accounting, statistics, and criminal justice. The student will be using these skills in more advanced courses in the computer forensics program at the college level. It will also give the student an idea of whether the skill is a good match for the student.

Q. Where do computer forensics graduates find employment?

A. Computer forensics graduates will find employment in both the public sector and the private sector. In the public sector, the graduate may be employed in law enforcement as a digital detective or as a computer analyst. In the private sector, the student will likely work as a computer security specialist.

Q. What is the future employment outlook for computer and digital forensics?

A. Computer forensics and security is one of the fastest-growing fields. As computing usage continues to increase worldwide, so too does computer crime.

Interview: Ken Whitener

Ken Whitener is an assistant professor of computer forensics in the Criminal Justice Department at Iowa Lakes Community College in Esterville, Iowa. He discussed its computer forensics program and the education of students in this field with the editors of *They Teach That in Community College!?*

Q. Please tell us about your program.

A. The Computer Forensics program at Iowa Lakes Community College trains students in the techniques and methodologies of performing forensic analysis of computer systems. We start the students off with general computer and criminology coursework: hardware, networking, information systems, and criminal justice, and gradually move into the complex world of file systems, operating systems, and data recovery. The students are required to purchase, build, and configure their own workstation which they in turn use for the remainder of the program. Manual forensic techniques are employed prior to utilizing the automated suites of computer forensic software such as: EnCase, Forensic Toolkit, and X Ways. We currently offer a 73-credit associate of science degree in computer forensics and a 19-credit certificate. In addition to this we have conducted one-day seminars in digital crime scene processing for local law enforcement.

Q. What are the most important personal and professional qualities for computer forensics students?

A. Excellent written and verbal communications skills are a must for professionals in this area. Many times highly technical terms and processes must be explained to laymen in a comprehensible manner. These explanations are delivered in both formal written reports and via verbal legal proceedings: discovery, jury trials, and expert witness testimony. Personally, students need to be highly motivated and addicted to learning as this field is in a constant state of flux and those with complacency will be left behind. Obviously technical proficiency is a must as well. Knowledge of programming, computer science, and math helps tremendously.

Q. How will the field change in the future?

A. This field changes daily. With the advanced state of telecommunications the world is shrinking rapidly. The sheer numbers of proprietary devices that enable humans to communicate create obstacles to the forensic investigator. It is common to encounter devices with which you are not familiar and whose technical specifications are not published. The data still needs to be retrieved and analyzed in a forensically sound manner. Another factor is the dramatic increase in digital storage capabilities. An enormous amount of data can now be stored on relatively small devices. This really increases the time necessary to perform a forensically sound analysis and may end up changing the foundations of computer forensic methodology.

Computer and Internet Security

Computer systems of all sizes and complexity are vulnerable. They are vulnerable to the threat of hackers who may have devious intentions—to access highly confidential data, to steal money electronically, or to infect a system with a destructive virus. In today's computerized world, businesses—small and large—need to be protected against such threats. The computer and internet security professional's job is to keep computer systems secure at all times. They must stay on top of the latest high-tech advancements in order to always be one step ahead of the latest virus, worm, or hacker. Individuals who enter this field should have a strong interest in math and computer programming, with a desire to be lifelong problem solvers. Security situations can change without notice, and computer and internet security professionals must periodically update and execute strategies to ensure safe networks for companies. This individual's position is increasingly important as our world continues to become more and more dependent on computerized records in all areas of business.

Typical Courses:

> Linux/UNIX Fundamentals
> Managing Network Security
> Managing Web Servers
> Network Security Design
> Internet Connectivity
> Introduction to Routers
> IT and Data Assurance
> IT Hardware Essentials
> IT Operating Systems
> Managing LAN Hardware
> Security Awareness
> High Technology Crime

Potential Employers:

> Corporations and small businesses
> Government agencies
> Schools and university systems
> Computer networking consulting firms

Available At:

The following list of computer and Internet security programs is not exhaustive. Check with academic institutions near you to determine if majors, minors, certificates, or concentrations are available in computer and Internet security.

Macomb Community College
14500 East 12 Mile Road, Warren, MI 48088
888/622-6621
answer@macomb.edu
http://www.macomb.edu/ProgramDescriptions/
InformationTechnology.asp#Security
Degrees available: Associate degree

Moraine Valley Community College
Information Management Systems Department
9000 West College Parkway, Palos Hills, IL 60465-0937
708/974-4300
http://www.morainevalley.edu/programs/
2005-2006/2005-2006_fall/1420_course.htm
Degrees available: Certificate, associate degree

Washtenaw Community College
PO Box D-1, Ann Arbor, MI 48106
734/973-3300
http://www.wccnet.edu/academicinfo/creditofferings/programs/
atoz/atoz2.php?code=APCSS
Degrees available: Certificate, associate degree

For More Information:

CERT Coordination Center
Software Engineering Institute
Carnegie Mellon University, Pittsburgh, PA 15213-3890
412/268-4793
cert@cert.org
http://www.cert.org

Computer Security Institute
600 Harrison Street, San Francisco, CA 94107
csi@cmp.com
http://www.gocsi.com

Computer Game Development

In the days of Pong and Pac-Man in the 1970s and 1980s, kids could only dream of designing their own computer games. Since then, computer games have grown from a novelty to a multi-billion-dollar industry. The Entertainment Software Association estimates that approximately 60 percent of the U.S. population plays computer and video games, and this growing interest has created a demand for computer game developers, programmers, and other professionals. And in addition to use as entertainment, computer and video games are being used in a variety of industries including advertising, law enforcement, health care, and corporate training. In 1994, DigiPen Institute of Technology became the first school in North America to offer a two-year degree in video game programming. Today, the Institute offers associate and bachelor's degrees. In addition to DigiPen, a growing number of community colleges offer courses or degrees in game design and development.

Typical Courses:

> Introduction to Game Design and Production
> Algebra and Trigonometry
> Linear Algebra and Geometry
> Calculus and Planar Analytic Geometry
> Computer Graphics
> Game Implementation Techniques
> Discrete Math and Combinatorics
> 2D Computer Animation Production
> 3D Computer Animation Production
> High Level Programming
> Advanced Animation and Modeling

Potential Employers:

> Computer game companies
> Educational publishers
> Any industry that requires computer simulations

Available At:

The following list of colleges that offer degrees in computer and video game development is not exhaustive. For a complete list of schools that offer computer and video game development degrees and certificates, visit http://www.igda.org/breakingin/resource_schools.php or http://www.gamasutra.com/education.

Art Institutes International (locations nationwide)
888/624-0300
http://www.artinstitutes.edu
Degrees available: Associate degree, bachelor's degree

Austin Community College
High Technology Institute
5930 Middle Fiskville Road, Austin, TX 78752-4341
512/223-7000
http://www.austincc.edu/techcert/Video_Games.html
Degrees available: Certificate, associate degree

Bellevue Community College
Digital Gaming Program
3000 Landerholm Circle Southeast, Mailstop N212
Bellevue, WA 98007-6484
425/564-2140
http://www.bcc.ctc.edu/gaming
Degrees available: Certificate, associate degree

Bristol Community College
Game Development and Game Programming
777 Elsbree Street, Fall River, MA 02720
508/678-2811
http://www.bristolcommunitycollege.edu/catalog/ca4/degree/ca4_gamcr.html
and
http://www.bristolcommunitycollege.edu/catalog/ca4/degree/ca4_gampr.html
Degrees available: Associate degrees (two separate programs)

Community College of Baltimore County-Essex Campus
7201 Rossville Boulevard, Baltimore, MD 21237
410/918-4045
http://www.ccbcmd.edu/sait/programs/immtdegsim.html
Degrees available: Associate degree

Delaware County Community College-Marple Campus
Information Technology Department
901 South Media Line Road, Media, PA 19063-1094
610/359-5050
http://www.dccc.edu/catalog/
career_programs.html#game_development
Degrees available: Associate degree (in IT with a concentration in Game Development)

Did You Know?

The best-selling video game genres in 2005 were Action (30.1 percent of all units sold), Sports (17.8 percent), Shooters (9.6 percent), and Children & Family Entertainment (9.5 percent), according to the NPD Group/NPD Funworld.

DigiPen Institute of Technology
5001-150th Avenue, NE, Redmond, WA 98052
425/558-0299
info@digipen.edu
http://www.digipen.edu/main.html
Degrees available: Associate degree, bachelor's degree, master's degree

53

Edmonds Community College
20000 68th Avenue W, Lynnwood, WA 98036
425/640-1902
gamedev@edcc.edu
http://gamedev.edcc.edu
Degrees available: Certificate

Houston Community College Southwest-West Loop Center of the Southwest Campus
Digital Gaming and Simulation Department
5601 West Loop South, Houston, TX 77081
713/718-5728
http://swc2.hccs.edu/digigame
Degrees available: Certificates, associate degrees

Montgomery College-Rockville Campus
51 Mannakee Street, Rockville, MD 20850
301/279-5000
http://www.montgomerycollege.edu/ca/gaming/degree.html
Degrees available: Certificate, associate degrees

New Hampshire Technical Institute
31 College Drive, Concord, NH 03301-7412
603/271-6484
info@nhti.edu
http://www.nhti.edu/academics/academicprograms/degaggp.html
Degrees available: Associate degree

Piedmont Community College-Caswell County Campus
PO Box 1150, Yanceyville, NC 27379
336/694-5707
http://www.piedmontcc.edu
Degrees available: Associate degree

Sanford-Brown College-St. Charles
100 Richmond Center Boulevard, St. Peters, MO 63376
636/949-2620
http://www.sbcstcharles.com/programs/computer-game-design.asp
Degrees available: Associate degree

For More Information:

Entertainment Software Association
575 7th Street, NW, Suite 300, Washington, DC 20004
esa@theesa.com
http://www.theesa.com

International Game Developers Association
870 Market Street, Suite 1181, San Francisco, CA 94102-3002
415/738-2104
info@igda.org
http://www.igda.org

Interview: Deborah Solomon

Deborah Solomon is a professor in the Computer Applications Department at Montgomery College (Rockville Campus) in Rockville, Maryland. She discussed the program and the education of computer game development students with the editors of *They Teach That in Community College!?*

Q. Tell us about your program.

A. Computer gaming and simulation is part of a rapidly growing and exciting new industry. Gaming is not only the fastest-growing segment of the technology industry but also the fastest-growing segment of the entertainment industry.

Gaming is not just about entertainment; game technology is increasingly being applied in a variety of settings, from medical and corporate training to advocacy, advertising, and emergency response simulation.

At Montgomery College, where I have been teaching for the past five years, we offer an interdepartmental AA degree in Computer Gaming and Simulation. We also offer a shorter certificate that is focused on web game development. The degree has three tracks: game programming, game production, and game graphic design.

Our degree presents students with an introduction to the skills needed to explore this emerging technology area. Students are exposed to core game development skills and theory, gaming and computer simulation technology applications, and computer graphics technology. More details about the program can be found at http://www.studygaming.com. Students can take classes about the game industry, level design, 2D and 3D modeling, computer graphics, and programming. They can even study "serious games"—games that are not just focused on entertainment, but also have a serious purpose like training, advertising, military recruitment, or crime scene reconstruction.

Our newest class in Exergaming and Health Games will cover the cutting-edge topic of health and fitness games, from movement games like Dance Dance Revolution and Kinetic to games that reduce pain for cancer patients, help kids manage diabetes, treat autism and ADHD, and educate about topics like drug addiction, AIDS prevention, immunology, and nutrition.

After graduating with the AA degree in Gaming, qualified students can transfer to the University of Baltimore to complete their junior and senior years for a four-year degree in game development.

Q. What high school subjects/activities should students focus on to be successful in this major?

A. To be successful in the game degree program, students should have experience playing a variety of digital games from different genres, not just their favorite genres. That is probably not too unpleasant a task for most high school stu-

55

dents! However, they should play analytically—asking themselves what makes the game fun? What was frustrating? Were there any bugs? How is this game similar to or different from other games in the same genre? And how could they change the game design to improve the playing experience?

Students may also want to try creating mods and levels, using the free tools that ship with many major game titles. For example, level editing tools come free with *Unreal, Half-Life, Far Cry, Elder Scrolls,* and many other popular game series.

Students need to take their high school education seriously. Game development is a very challenging and competitive field. Students won't succeed without solid skills.

Specific subjects/activities to focus on depend on the student's interest. There are many different career paths in gaming, such as programming, 2D art/animation, 3D art/animation, audio, script writing, etc. For more information about these different career paths, I suggest that students take a look at the website of the International Game Developers Association, http://www.igda.org/breakingin.

Q. What are the most important personal and professional qualities for computer gaming students?

A. As mentioned above, game development is a challenging, rapidly evolving field. Students should be detail oriented, intelligent, able to rapidly learn new software and techniques, and able to communicate and work in a team environment.

Q. What educational level is typically required for computer gaming graduates to land good jobs in the industry?

A. It varies. Some game professionals landed their first job based on creating a great mod, without any academic training at all. Mods and levels are still very effective as samples to have in one's portfolio. The level of skill and education required varies widely depending on the career path. For example, someone who wants to be able to program a game engine or write complex artificial intelligence algorithms might need graduate degree-level skills. On the other hand, a texture artist might be OK with a two-year or four-year degree program. My advice to students is to think about their specific career goals and to research typical education requirements for that career path in the gaming industry.

We hope to prepare students so they can go on to succeed in advanced gaming studies and entry-level game industry careers. We strongly encourage students to continue on to a four-year program because gaming skill sets are becoming more specialized, and having a four-year degree will give them better flexibility in their careers.

Q. Where do computer gaming graduates find employment?

A. Maryland has been called the "East Coast hub of the gaming industry." People are often surprised to find out how many game companies are based in Maryland, particularly in Montgomery County and Baltimore County. Because we are so close to the federal government and biotechnology industry, there are also a lot of "serious game" and simulation companies in the neighborhood. Students graduating with game development skills can look to all of these companies for employment opportunities.

Students graduating with an AA degree could be prepared for a number of entry-level jobs after graduation—particularly in art, 2D animation, web games, web development, game testing, and basic level design. Game testers and texture artists are probably the most common entry-level positions in the industry. However, as explained above, we do strongly encourage most of our students to continue on to a four-year degree program.

In addition to opportunities in entertainment gaming and serious gaming, students may find that their technical and team-based skills open doors in other converging industries like film and cartoon production, web and software development, and database design.

Q. How will the field of computer gaming change in the future?

A. An interesting question. There are many possible answers, and of course, it is difficult to predict the future. But change is apparent on many different layers:

57

Hardware: For example, next generation consoles like the XBOX 360 and the upcoming PlayStation 3 and Nintendo Revolution are changing player expectations of game appearance and quality. New types of controllers like the Eyetoy camera, the Revolution controller, and the guitars used in Harmonix's Guitar Hero game can bring new players to the marketplace and make games more immersive.

Development costs: There are a number of forces making games more expensive to produce (larger teams, more content, Hollywood voice-over talent, licensing of intellectual property, etc.). However it is still sometimes possible to achieve success with a small independent game project.

Software and content: Faced with rising development costs, game developers are looking into content and gameplay that is either generated procedurally (created dynamically during the game by the game engine) or created by users (or some combination of the two). Also, more games will likely be able to dynamically measure the player's skill level and adjust difficulty accordingly.

Serious Games: Many industries are beginning to see how gaming technologies can be used in the workplace—to train employees, to simulate complex molecular interactions, to increase awareness of safety issues, and so on. I expect that the field of serious games will grow exponentially over the next decade.

Did You Know?

Forty-two percent of the most frequent game players played their games online, according to the Entertainment Software Association. Fifty-six percent of all online game players are male.

Interview: Paula Hindman

Paula Hindman is the program director for the Digital Effects and Animation Technology Program at Piedmont Community College in Yanceyville, North Carolina. She discussed the school's program and the education of students in this field with the editors of *They Teach That in Community College!?*

Q. Please tell us about your program.

A. The Digital Effects and Animation Technology Program at Piedmont Community College is intended to provide students with the skills and knowledge needed to begin an entry-level position in a career in animation and graphics for television, film, or electronic games. Students who complete the program successfully are awarded an associate of applied science in digital effects and animation technology. The curriculum was developed with advice from a number of professionals in the industry, which included Red Storm Entertainment. Our advisory committee meets annually to make recommendations to keep our program relevant.

Q. What high school subjects/activities should students focus on to be successful in this major?

A. If students want to concentrate their efforts on the art side of animation, they should spend as much time as possible in whatever art classes are offered learning about drawing, painting, and design with traditional materials. Next on the list would be any classes that teach computer basics and computer programming. Other classes that contribute to success in the field could include photography, stage design and lighting, speech and communication, and art history.

Q. What types of internship opportunities do you provide?

A. Internships are considered very important to our program. The program requires completion of an internship to graduate. Students can learn more from an internship than any class. Often this is their first foray into the job-seeking world.

All students are encouraged to seek an internship that mirrors the type of work environment they would like to achieve. Therefore, some find jobs in game companies and others with local independent film companies or television stations like UNCTV. We also recommend that students become affiliated with appropriate professional organizations: Siggraph, GDC, or E3. Each year a number of our students attend Siggraph as volunteers, and some have displayed art work in the Siggraph Student Show.

Q. What advice would you offer computer game development majors as they graduate and look for jobs?

A. Our guest speakers and those that present at Siggraph explain that it is a very tough industry to break into. Many job announcements mention the need to have a published game under your belt just to apply. One of my students achieved this by contributing to a game over a summer internship and by working on props for a company during the school year via email. I also recommend that students break in via the game testing route. It goes without saying that students should work very hard on developing their portfolios while in school. Our school offers 24/7 access to the computer labs. I recommend that students take advantage of the lab while they are in school in order to develop projects for their portfolios.

Q. Where do computer game development graduates find employment?

A. Our graduates have attained jobs at companies such as nSpace, Inc., Mad Doc Software, NASA Stennis Space Center, Fox 50/Durham, and Out of Our Minds Studios.

Q. What does the future hold for your department at Piedmont Community College?

A. Piedmont Community College has just built a new building to house our Film Program and the Digital Effects and Animation Technology Program. We are moving into it in May 2006. We hope to continue serving about 40 students (20 first-year and 20 second-year).

Construction Management

Every building, big or small, that makes up the skyline of your town or city has been constructed under the vision and management of a few key individuals—the *construction manager* among them. Construction managers work with architects, building owners, contractors, and tradesworkers to oversee the development of a variety of projects, including residential housing, commercial construction such as stores and shopping malls, skyscrapers, transportation systems, municipal services, and utilities. College degree programs in construction management typically include many industry-specific courses, combined with business courses in operations, finance, and marketing.

Typical Courses:

> Building the Human Environment
> Construction Methods
> Concrete and Concrete Form Systems
> Surveying and Building Layout
> Structural Steel Systems
> Construction Estimating and Bidding
> Electrical Systems
> Soil Mechanics
> Construction Safety and Risk Management
> Heavy Civil and Highway Construction
> Field Work Experience

Potential Employers:

> General contractors
> Specialty contractors such as mechanical, plumbing, and electrical
> Architectural firms
> Engineering firms
> Governmental agencies

Available At:

Only nine construction management programs in the U.S. and Canada are accredited by the American Council for Construction Education (http://www.acce-hq.org). These include:

Albuquerque Technical-Vocational Institute
TVI Technologies
525 Buena Vista Drive, SE, Building A, Room 102
Albuquerque, NM 87106
505/224-3340
http://tech.tvi.edu/Programs/
Construction_Management_Technology/programhome.html
Degrees available: Associate degree

Cincinnati State Technical & Community College
Engineering Technologies Division
3520 Central Parkway, Cincinnati, OH 45223
513/861-7700
http://www.cinstate.cc.oh.us
Degrees available: Associate degree

Columbus State Community College
Construction Sciences Department
Columbus, OH 43215
614/287-5030
construct@cscc.edu
http://www.cscc.edu/cs/const.htm
Degrees available: Associate degree

Jefferson State Community College
Department of Building Science Technology
2601 Carson Road, Birmingham, AL 35215-3098
http://www.jeffstateonline.com/manufacturing_center/
curriculum/building_science_tech/default.htm
Degrees available: Associate degree

John A. Logan College
Department of Applied Technologies
Carterville, IL 62918
618/985-2828
http://www.jal.cc.il.us/applied_technology/const_mgmt/
Degrees available: Associate degree

North Lake College
Construction Management and Technology
5001 North MacArthur Boulevard, Irving, TX 75038
http://www.northlakecollege.edu/academics/ConTech/conmgt.htm
Degrees available: Certificate, associate degree

Santa Fe Community College
Department of Industrial Technology
3000 NW 83rd Street, Gainesville, FL 32602
352/395-5252
http://inst.sfcc.edu/~bcn
Degrees available: Associate degrees

Saskatchewan Institute of Applied Science and Technology-Palliser Campus
Saskatchewan Street and 6th Avenue, NW, PO Box 1420
Moose Jaw SK S6H 4R4 Canada
http://www.siast.sk.ca/palliser
Degrees available: Diploma

State University of New York College of Technology at Delhi
Construction Technology Program
Technology Division
Delhi, NY 13753
800/96-DELHI
http://www.delhi.edu/academics/techdivision/
programs_of_study_construction_technology.asp
Degrees available: Associate degree

Other colleges that offer certificates and degrees in construction management include:

College of DuPage
Business and Technology Division
425 Fawell Boulevard, Glen Ellyn, IL 60137-6599
630/942-2331
http://www.cod.edu/dept/architecture/arch_cm.htm
Degrees available: Associate degree

63

Erie Community College-City Campus
121 Ellicott Street, Buffalo, NY 14203
716/842-2770
http://www.ecc.edu/academics/constructionmanage.asp
Degrees available: Associate degree

Edmonds Community College
Construction Management Department
20000 68th Avenue West, Lynnwood, WA 98036
425/640-1026
const@edcc.edu
http://const.edcc.edu
Degrees available: Certificate, associate degree

Florida Community College at Jacksonville
501 West State Street, Jacksonville, FL 32202
904/633-8295
info@fccj.edu
http://www.fccj.org/prospective/programs/data05_06/2234.html
Degrees available: Associate degree

Ivy Tech Community College of Indiana (multiple campuses)
50 West Fall Creek Parkway North Drive, Indianapolis, IN 46208
888/489-5463
http://www.ivytech.edu/programs/bcm
Degrees available: Associate degree

Kirkwood Community College
6301 Kirkwood Boulevard, SW, Cedar Rapids, IA 52404
800/363-2220
info@kirkwood.cc.ia.us
http://www.kirkwood.edu/site/index.php?d=125&p=856&t=2
Degrees available: Associate degree

New York City Technical College
Department of Construction Civil Engineering Technology
300 Jay Street, Voorhees Hall 433 (V-433), Brooklyn, NY 11201-2983
718/260-5575
http://www.citytech.cuny.edu/academics/deptsites/
constructiontech/index.shtml
Degrees available: Certificate, associate degrees

Northern Virginia Community College
Brault Building
4001 Wakefield Chapel Road, Annandale, VA 22003-3796
703/323-3000
http://www.nvcc.vccs.edu/curcatalog/programs/conman.htm
Degrees available: Associate degree

State Fair Community College
Department of Applied Science and Technology
Fielding Technical Center
3201 West 16th Street, Sedalia, MO 65301-2199
660/530-5800
http://www.sfcc.cc.mo.us/pages/206.asp
Degrees available: Associate degree

Triton College
School of Technology
2000 Fifth Avenue, River Grove, IL 60171-1995
708/456-0300
triton@triton.edu
http://www.triton.edu/cgi-bin/r.cgi/
department_detail.html?SESSION=k1vDG2eZxv&ContentID=126
Degrees available: Associate degree

For More Information:

American Council for Construction Education
1717 North Loop 1604 East, Suite 320, San Antonio, TX 78232
acce@acce-hq.org
http://www.acce-hq.org

Court and Real-Time Reporting

Court reporters use stenotype machines to record legal proceedings in courtrooms. *Real-time reporters* combine shorthand machine reporting with computer-aided transcription to provide real-time testimony in courtrooms and other settings. Other professionals help people with hearing disabilities by creating closed captions for television shows, Webcasting, and movies, as well as in classrooms, meetings, and other settings. An associate degree in court reporting is recommended to work in the field.

Typical Courses:

> Theory
> Introduction to Computer-Aided Transcription
> Speed Development
> Realtime Reporting Punctuation and Proofreading
> Realtime Concepts
> Introduction to Transcription Preparation
> Technical Dictation
> Principles of Captioning/CART
> Captioning/CART Technology
> Medical Terminology and Anatomy
> Legal Terminology

Potential Employers:

> Courts
> Law firms
> Broadcasting companies
> Organizations that provide services to the deaf
> Corporations

Available At:

The following list of colleges that offer degrees in court reporting is not exhaustive. Visit the National Court Reporters Association's website http://www.ncraonline.org/education/schools/index.shtml for a list of more than 65 programs approved by the Association.

Academy of Court Reporting
(six campuses in Michigan, Ohio, and Pennsylvania)
http://www.acr.edu
Degrees available: Associate degree

Did You Know?

Approximately 18,000 court reporters are employed in the United States, according to the U.S. Department of Labor. Approximately 60 percent work for state and local governments.

66

Alfred State College
215 EJ Brown Hall, Alfred, NY 14802
800/4-ALFRED
http://www.alfredstate.edu
Degrees available: Associate degree

Alvin Community College
3110 Mustang Road, Alvin, TX 77511
281/756-3757
CourtReporting@alvincollege.edu
http://www.alvincollege.edu/Current/Court_Reporting.cfm
Degrees available: Certificate, associate degree

Chattanooga State Technical College
4501 Amnicola Highway, Chattanooga, TN 37406-1097
423/697-4402
http://www.chattanoogastate.edu
Degrees available: Associate degree

Community College of Allegheny County
808 Ridge Avenue, Pittsburgh, PA 15212-2748
412/237-4600
http://www.ccac.edu
Degrees available: Associate degree

Cuyahoga Community College
700 Carnegie Avenue, Parma, OH 44115
http://www.tri-c.edu/ccr/Default.htm
Degrees available: Associate degree

Gadsden State Community College
PO Box 227, Gadsden, AL 35902-0227
256/549-8200
http://www.gadsdenstate.edu
Degrees available: Associate degree

GateWay Community College
108 North 40th Street, Phoenix, AZ 85034
602/286-8000
info@gatewaycc.edu
http://business.gatewaycc.edu/Programs/
RealTimeClosedCaptioning/default.htm
Degrees available: Certificate, associate degree

Green River Community College
12401 SE 320th Street, Auburn, WA 98092
253/833-9111
http://www.greenriver.edu/ProgramInformation/
ComputerReportingTechnologies_CourtReporting.htm
and
http://www.greenriver.edu/ProgramInformation/ComputerReport
ingTechnologies_Captioning.htm
Degrees available: Certificate, associate degrees

Hinds Community College-Raymond Campus
501 East Main Street, PO Box 1100, Raymond, MS 39154-1100
800/HINDS-CC
http://www.hinds.cc.ms.us
Degrees available: Associate degree

Huntington Junior College
900 Fifth Avenue, Huntington, WV 25701
304/697-7550, 800/344-4522
admissions@huntingtonjuniorcollege.com
http://www.huntingtonjuniorcollege.com/
Real-timeReporting.htm
Degrees available: Associate degree

Key College
225 East Dania Beach Boulevard, Dania, FL 33004
954/923-4440
admissions@keycollege.edu
http://www.keycollege.edu/page9.html
Degrees available: Associate degree

Las Vegas College
170 North Stephanie Street, Suite 125, Henderson, NV 89074
888/741-4270
http://lasvegas-college.com
Degrees available: Associate degree

Lenoir Community College
231 Highway 58 South, PO Box 188, Kinston, NC 28502-0188
252/527-6223
http://www.lenoircc.edu/nsite/academicprogs/crt/courtreport.html
Degrees available: Associate degree

Madison Area Technical College
3550 Anderson Street, Madison, WI 53704
608/246-6368
http://matcmadison.edu/matc/ASP/showprogram.asp?ID=3055
Degrees available: Associate degree

Midlands Technical College
Information Systems Technology Department
PO Box 2408, Columbia, SC 29202
803/738-8324, 800/922-8038
http://www.midlandstech.edu/edu/ed/ISM/CPT/programs/crp.htm
Degrees available: Certificate

Oakland Community College
2480 Opdyke Road, Bloomfield Hills, MI 48304
248/341-2000
http://www.oaklandcc.edu/FutureStudents/DegreePrograms.asp
Degrees available: Certificate, associate degree

South Suburban College
Court Reporting Program
15800 South State Street, South Holland, IL 60473-1200
708/596-2000
http://www.ssc.cc.il.us/acad/career/depts/legalstudies/courtreport.htm
Degrees available: Associate degree

West Kentucky Community and Technical College
4810 Alben Barkley Drive, PO Box 7380, Paducah, KY 42002
270/554-9200
http://business.westkentucky.kctcs.edu/legal
Degrees available: Diploma, associate degree

For More Information:

National Court Reporters Association
8224 Old Courthouse Road, Vienna, VA 22182-3808
800/272-6272
msic@ncrahq.org
http://www.verbatimreporters.com

National Verbatim Reporters Association
207 Third Avenue, Hattiesburg, MS 39401
601/582-4345
nura@nvra.org
http://www.nvra.org

Interview: Janice McElhaney

Janice McElhaney is the director of the court reporting and captioning program at Lenoir Community College in Kinston, North Carolina. She discussed the program and the education of court reporting and captioning students with the editors of *They Teach That in Community College!?*

Q. Please tell us about your program.

A. The Lenoir Community College Court Reporting and Captioning Curriculum is designed to provide specialized training in accepted court reporting and conference procedures such as recording court proceedings in a computer-integrated courtroom, depositions, business and convention meetings, and real-time captioning activities.

Coursework includes training in real-time machine short-hand theory, real-time computer software and technology, word processing, legal and medical terminology, specialized vocabularies, court procedures, dictation, and transcription.

Graduates should qualify for employment as an official court reporter, freelance reporter, television and video captioner, stenointerpreter, conference reporter, stenographer, or transcriptionist.

Q. What high school subjects/activities should students focus on to be successful in college and in their careers?

A. Court reporting encompasses all subject areas. The main subjects students should focus on include English grammar and punctuation; human anatomy and physiology; history; geography; keyboarding; finance; computer science; and languages. Activities and clubs that would assist students would include book clubs and language clubs.

Q. What are the most important personal and professional qualities for court reporting majors?

A. The most important personal qualities are intelligence quotient, determination, stamina, motivation, finger dexterity, and the ability to concentrate for extended periods of time.

The professional qualities for court reporting would include ethics, organizational skills, critical thinking, presentation, and quality control.

Q. How will the field of court reporting change in the future?

A. The field of court reporting will change as it continues to strive to be an integral part of new technology, through continuing education, by providing reasonable access to the deaf and hard-of-hearing through real-time writing of the spoken word in judicial, educational, and communications settings.

Did You Know?

Court reporters earned salaries that ranged from less than $23,370 to $78,840 or more in November 2004, according to the U.S. Department of Labor. The following states (in descending order) employed the highest number of court reporters: Pennsylvania, Indiana, Louisiana, and Montana.

70

Interview: Carol Adams

Carol Adams is an instructor in the Real-Time Reporting Program at Huntington Junior College in Huntington, West Virginia. She discussed the program and the education of real-time reporting students with the editors of *They Teach That in Community College!?*

Q. Please tell us about your program.

A. Huntington Junior College offers an associate degree in real-time reporting. Students can specialize in Judicial Reporting or Captioning/CART. Judicial Reporting focuses on the legal profession. Graduates can become official reporters, those who work in the courtroom, or freelance reporters, reporters taking pretrial testimony for attorneys. Captioning/CART graduates focus on providing text for television programming or other live events for the deaf and hard-of-hearing community.

Q. What high school subjects should students focus on to be successful in college and in their careers?

A. High school students today have such a grasp on computers, and that's important as our profession is very high-tech. Our profession is all about words: hearing them, processing them, preparing written transcripts. Vocabulary, spelling, and punctuation are extremely important subjects.

Q. What are the most important personal and professional qualities for court reporting majors?

A. Perseverance and willingness to work hard. There's a lot of homework involved in this program, as you are training to transform the spoken word into text instantaneously. Completing exercises once or twice is not enough: repetition is the key to eliminate hesitation when performing this skill. Maturity is also important: dealing with hard-to-work-with-attorneys and deadlines can be stressful!

71

Did You Know?

The National Court Reporters Association offers the following professional certifications: Registered Professional Reporter, Registered Merit Reporter, Registered Diplomate Reporter, Certified Realtime Reporter, Certified Broadcast Captioner, Certified CART Provider, Certified Legal Video Specialist, Certified Reporting Instructor, Master Certified Reporting Instructor, and Certified Manager of Reporting Services.

Q. Where do real-time reporting graduates find employment?

A. Judicial reporters work in the courtroom as an official reporter or as freelance reporters for court reporting firms or on their own, taking depositions of witnesses involved in lawsuits before trial. Captioners/CART providers work for captioning companies providing text for live television, or they can be self-employed providing text for deaf and hard-of-hearing consumers at live events.

Q. How will the field of court reporting change in the future?

A. This profession continues to explore and implement new technology to benefit the legal community and the sdeaf and hard-of-hearing community. Court reporting and captioning jobs are expected to grow. In the judicial field, a third party will always be necessary to record legal proceedings to ensure impartiality. In the captioning/CART field, captioners are in demand due to a federal mandate that all new live programming must be captioned.

Deep Springs College

A two-year liberal arts education for free? The catch: students at Deep Springs College—a 26-student, male-only institution with a working cattle ranch and alfalfa farm—must perform manual labor in exchange for their tuition (a $35,000 value). Duties might include milking cows, baling hay, cooking breakfast, scrubbing toilets, or mopping floors. Classes—typically one or two a day—are usually held in the morning with work done in the early morning (before classes) and in the afternoon. Deep Springs College is highly selective (the average SAT score of students is 1450) and rarely accepts more than 15 percent of applicants. It has an excellent reputation for preparing students for work and life in general; many of its graduates go on to pursue bachelor's degrees at top schools such as Harvard, Yale, Stanford, Columbia, Oxford, University of California-Berkeley, and Cornell. Deep Springs College was founded by Lucien Lucius Nunn, a mining magnate, in 1917. Its founding principles are academics, labor, and self-governance. The average class size at Deep Springs College is four!

Available Fields of Study:

Instruction is offered in the humanities, in the social sciences, and in the natural sciences and mathematics. Students are free to choose coursework from any of these areas but are required to take composition and public speaking.

For More Information:

Deep Springs College
HC72 Box 45001, Dyer, NV 89010-9803
760/872-2000
http://www.deepsprings.edu
Degrees available: Associate degree

Diagnostic Medical Sonography

While many of us may instinctively think of ultrasound as a means to determining the sex of a fetus, the technology of sonography is used for diagnostic purposes for a variety of medical problems associated with the female reproductive system, liver, kidneys, gallbladder, spleen, pancreas, brain, and eyes. *Diagnostic medical sonographers* are the professionals who explain the procedure to patients, take medical histories, operate the transducer which transmits sound waves, and take the photographs to show to the physician. While it is the physician who makes the medical diagnosis, sonographers must possess the knowledge of which photographs to take—which angles best show healthy versus unhealthy images of the organs. The field is experiencing growth due to an aging population and the increased popularity of sonography over radiologic diagnostic procedures. While certificate programs are widespread in this field, students should be aware that individuals entering a certificate program must generally first possess an associate degree.

Typical Courses:

> General Sonography: Abdomen
> Obstetric & Gynecologic Sonography
> Sonographic Physics
> Sonographic Instrumentation
> Anatomy and Physiology
> Medical Terminology
> Sonographic Cross Sectional Anatomy
> Clinical Experience

Potential Employers:

> Hospitals
> Physicians' offices
> Clinics

> Diagnostic imaging centers
> Public health facilities
> Laboratories
> Other medical settings

Available At:

The following list of colleges that offer degrees in diagnostic medical sonography (DMS) is not exhaustive. Visit http://www.caahep.org/programs.aspx for a list of approximately 140 DMS programs that are accredited by the Commission on Accreditation of Allied Health Education Programs. Note: certificates offer professionals the opportunity to obtain advanced certifications (i.e., abdominal ultrasound), but are not alone a path to a job.

Bellevue Community College
3000 Landerholm Circle Southeast, Bellevue, WA 98007-6484
425/564-1000
http://www.bcc.ctc.edu/catalog/degrees/dutec
Degrees available: Certificates, associate degree

Broward Community College
111 East Las Olas Boulevard, Fort Lauderdale, FL 33301
http://www.broward.edu/ext/ProgramOverview.jsp?A012
Degrees available: Certificate, associate degree

Bunker Hill Community College
250 New Rutherford Avenue, Boston, MA 02129-2925
http://www.bhcc.mass.edu
Degrees available: Associate degrees

Cincinnati State Technical and Community College
3520 Central Parkway, Cincinnati, OH 45223
513/861-7700
http://www.cinstate.cc.oh.us
Degrees available: Certificate, associate degree

Community College of Allegheny County-Boyce Campus
595 Beatty Road, Monroeville, PA 15146-1396
http://www.ccac.edu/default.aspx?id=138709
Degrees available: Associate degree

Cuyahoga Community College
700 Carnegie Avenue, Cleveland, OH 44115
http://www.tri-c.edu/dms/Pages/Home.htm
Degrees available: Associate degree

75

Did You Know?

The U.S. Department of Labor estimates that employment opportunities for diagnostic medical sonographers will grow much faster than the average for all other occupations through 2014.

Delaware Technical and Community College-Stanton/Wilmington Campus
333 Shipley Street, Wilmington, DE 19801
302/571-5355
http://www.dtcc.edu/wilmington/ah/dms.html
Degrees available: Associate degree

Lansing Community College
PO Box 40010, Lansing, MI 48901-7210
800/644-4522
selectiveadmissions@lcc.edu
http://www.lcc.edu/health/sonography
Degrees available: Certificate, associate degree

Montgomery College-Takoma Park/Silver Spring Campus
Department of Diagnostic Medical Sonography
7977 Georgia Avenue, Health Science Center, Room 426
Silver Spring, MD 20910
301/562-5563
http://www.mc.cc.md.us/dms
Degrees available: Certificate, associate degree

Oakland Community College
2480 Opdyke Road, Bloomfield Hills, MI 48304
248/341-2000
http://www.oaklandcc.edu/FutureStudents/DegreePrograms.asp
Degrees available: Associate degree

Palm Beach Community College
4200 Congress Avenue, Lake Worth, FL 33461
866/576-7222
enrollmt@pbcc.edu
http://www.pbcc.edu/Sonography
Degrees available: Certificate, associate degree

Valencia Community College-West Campus
Department of Health Sciences, HSB Room 200
1800 South Kirkman Road, Orlando, FL 32811
407/582-1565
http://www.valencia.cc.fl.us/departments/west/health
Degrees available: Associate degree

For More Information:

Society of Diagnostic Medical Sonography
2745 Dallas Parkway, Suite 350, Plano, TX 75093-8730
800/229-9506
http://www.sdms.org

Interview: Patty Braga

Patty Braga is program director for the sonography program at Palm Beach Community College in Lake Worth/Gardens Campus, Florida. She is a registered diagnostic medical sonographer in abdomen and OB/GYN, as well as a registered vascular sonographer and registered diagnostic cardiac sonographer, who has worked in the field for 30 years. She discussed the school's program and the education of students in this field with the editors of *They Teach That in Community College!?*

Q. Please tell us about your program.

A. Palm Beach Community College offers an associate of science degree and certification in sonography. It is a career-oriented college-level program consisting of classroom, lab, and clinical experience. The mission of the program is to graduate students with entry-level employment skills required of a sonographer. Two tracks of completion are available for the sonography program. For students who wish to earn a certificate, documentation of previous program completion is required. For students who wish to earn an associate of science degree in sonography, general education courses are also required, in addition to previous patient care program completion. The program has a 14-month, competency-based curriculum which includes practical experience in local hospitals and is designed to develop technical proficiency through extensive clinical exposure. The program is designed to begin in the summer term each year, and requires a full-time commitment beginning in the fall term.

Q. What high school subjects/activities should students focus on to be successful in this major?

A. A sonographer must have an exceptional understanding of human anatomy and an artistic, creative, self-directed approach. Therefore, health-related classes, leadership programs, and volunteer work at local hospitals should be the focus for high school students.

Q. What are the most important personal and professional qualities for sonography students?

A. Using independent judgment and systematic problem-solving methods to produce high-quality diagnostic information to optimize patient care is extremely important. Students should adhere to the accepted professional ethical standards, provide patient care without bias and with respect for everyone, and communicate effectively with patients and other health care professionals.

Q. Where do sonography graduates find employment?

A. Sonographers and vascular technologists can choose to work in clinics, hospitals, private practice physician offices, public health facilities, laboratories, and other medical settings performing examinations in their areas of specialization. They can work as staff personnel, per-diem for more flexibility or as agency sonographers with the opportunity to work all over the country.

Career advancement opportunities exist in education, administration, and research, and in commercial companies as education/application specialists, sales representatives, and technical advisors.

Q. How will the field of sonography change in the future?

A. Sonography is a dynamic profession that has grown significantly over the past 20 years. With rapidly developing new technologies and increased use of diagnostic ultrasound procedures, growth is projected to continue in the future with employment opportunities for qualified sonographers in both urban and rural areas nationwide. According to the U.S. Department of Labor, employment of diagnostic medical sonographers is expected to grow faster than the average for all occupations through 2012 as the population grows and ages, increasing the demand for diagnostic imaging and therapeutic technology.

Digital Media

Turn on your television and you will be unable to escape a barrage of advertisements for the latest cellular phone—and it probably shoots videos, sends email, and more. This is just one example of emerging digital media. Ten years ago there would have been those among us who had never used the Internet, and the idea of digital radios, televisions, or cameras was just a dream. Digital media is commonplace in today's modern world. As a result, colleges across the country have been developing degree programs in this emerging field. After all, someone needs to be skilled in producing the content for all forms of existing and emerging digital media! Prospective students should have a desire for a truly multidisciplinary course of study. Courses housed in the departments of art, communications, engineering, and computer science are required. If developing digital media for DVDs, CD-ROMs, and the Internet; creating video projects; and capturing and manipulating video, image, and audio files sounds fun to you, then a degree in digital media studies will be the first step into this fast-growing field.

Typical Courses:

> Digital Video Art
> Interactive Art and Design
> Digital Design Concepts
> Field Production and Editing
> Web Building and Site Management
> Web Application Development
> Telecommunication and Internet Law
> Technical Foundations of Digital Media
> Digital Animation
> 2D and 3D Design

Potential Employers:

> Advertising agencies
> Graphic design firms
> Film and television companies
> Game design firms
> Book and publishing companies
> Corporate art and graphic design departments

Available At:

The following list of digital media programs is not exhaustive. Check with academic institutions near you to determine if majors, minors, certificates, or concentrations are available in digital media.

Borough of Manhattan Community College-City University of New York
199 Chambers Street, New York, NY 10007
212/220-1476
http://www.bmcc.cuny.edu/computer/multimedia/MMP.html
Degrees available: Associate degree

Bristol Community College
135 County Street, Attleboro, MA 02703
508/678-2811
http://www.bristolcommunitycollege.edu/catalog/ca4/degree/ca4_mul.html
and
http://www.bristolcommunitycollege.edu/catalog/ca4/certificate/ca4_mulc.html
Degrees available: Certificate, associate degree

Broward Community College-South Campus
7200 Pines Boulevard, Pembroke Pines, FL 33024
954/201-8967
http://www.broward.edu/ext/ProgramOverview.jsp?A018
Degrees available: Certificates, associate degree

Columbus State Community College
PO Box 1609, Columbus, OH 43216-1609
800/621-6407
http://www.cscc.edu/DOCS/intermediacurr.htm
Degrees available: Certificates, associate degree

Community College of Baltimore County (multiple campuses)
410/918-4045
http://www.ccbcmd.edu/sait/programs/immt.html
Degrees available: Certificates, associate degrees

Delaware Technical and Community College-Terry Campus
100 Campus Drive, Dover, DE 19904
302/857-1312
http://www.dtcc.edu/terry/program_pdfs/multimedia_design.pdf
Degrees available: Associate degree

Florida Community College-Jacksonville-South Campus
11901 Beach Boulevard, Jacksonville, FL 32246
904/646-2239
info@fccj.edu
http://www.fccj.org/prospective/programs/data05_06/2135.html
Degrees available: Certificate, associate degree

Gibbs College-Norwalk
10 Norden Place, Norwalk, CT 06855-1436
800/845-5333
http://www.gibbsnorwalk.edu/digital.asp
Degrees available: Associate degree

Montgomery College-Rockville Campus
51 Mannakee Street, Rockville, MD 20850
301/279-5000
http://www.montgomerycollege.edu/curricula/descriptions/
cdcommunications.htm#digital
Degrees available: Certificate

Portland Community College-Cascade Campus
705 North Killingsworth, Terrell Hall, Portland, OR 97280-0990
503/978-5672
multimed@pcc.edu
http://www.pcc.edu/pcc/pro/progs/mm
Degrees available: Certificate, associate degree

Seminole Community College
100 Weldon Boulevard, Sanford, FL 32773-6199
407/708-4722
http://www.scc-fl.edu/digitalmedia
Degrees available: Associate degree

Southern Maine Community College
2 Fort Road, South Portland, ME 04106
207/741-5500
http://www.smccme.edu/catalog/2005-2006/
index.php?section=5&navid=117&docid=0
Degrees available: Associate degree

Tallahassee Community College
444 Appleyard Drive, Tallahassee, FL 32304
850/201-8352
http://www.tcc.fl.edu
Degrees available: Associate degree

Valencia Community College
Department of Digital Media Technology
PO Box 3028, Orlando, FL 32802-3028
http://valenciacc.edu/IToptions/job_digitalmedia.asp
and
http://valenciacc.edu/asdegrees/as.asp#entertainment
Degrees available: Associate degree

West Georgia Technical College
303 Fort Drive, LaGrange, GA 30240
706/837-4231
http://www.westgatech.edu/academics/DigitalMedia/
DigitalMedia.htm
Degrees available: Certificate, associate degree

For More Information:

International Digital and Media Arts Association
Ball State University
CICS, BC221, Muncie, IN 47306
765/285-1889
http://www.idmaa.org

Interview: Troy Johnson

Troy Johnson is the Instructional Program Manager for the
Digital Media Arts program at Florida Community College in
Jacksonville, Florida. He discussed the school's program and the
education of students in this field with the editors of *They Teach
That in Community College!?*

Q. What is digital media?

A. Digital media is the production of everything you see—from
entertainment, games, broadcasting, and advertising, to corporate presentations and 3-D animations. Digital media is
part of our everyday experience and will continue to become
an increasing part of our everyday lives.

Q. What high school subjects/activities should students
focus on to be successful in this major?

A. Art, television production and computer science courses tend
to be the most common high school courses offered today.

Q. What are the most important personal and professional qualities for digital media students?

A. Students should consider themselves artistic, self-motivated,
and patient.

Q. Where do digital media graduates find employment?

A. Students find employment in all sorts of settings and industries—medical, corporate, broadcasting, game design, digital
production houses, and more.

Q. How will the field of digital media change in the
future?

A. Digital media is an ever-evolving field of technology. Through
the ever-increasing convergence of technology, digital media
has already entered our lives from television, cable, broadcasting, and radio to computers, cell phones, PDAs, and
other forms of mobile media such as mp3 players and iPod
pod casting. Digital media is everywhere, and in the future as
the Internet, telecommunications (telephones, cell phones),
cable, and broadcasting technology and services continue to
merge, the science fiction of today's movies will be tomor-
row's digital media.

Electronic Commerce

Online retailing has become big business—an essential component in every retailer's sales plan. What critics once thought would never catch on—has. Consumers around the world have gotten over their fear of giving out their personal information electronically and continue to make the Internet an ever-expanding marketplace. There is hardly anything that you CAN'T purchase online today. Purchasing items while sitting at your computer, in the comfort of your own home, is indeed now a part of life that marketers, retailers, and business owners have to study. As a result, programs focused on this new e-commerce phenomenon have sprung up, attracting more and more students into this new field. While all programs combine core courses in business and technology, students with a particular interest in one or the other should be aware that some programs are more business-based—that is, they focus on how to attract online customers and expand online sales—while others are technologically based, focusing on the engineering fundamentals that make it possible to buy a car at the click of a mouse button.

Typical Courses:

> E-Commerce Website Engineering
> Data Communications
> Object Oriented Modeling
> Technical Fundamentals of Distributed Information
> Intranets and Portals
> Internet Supply Chain Management
> Secure Electronic Commerce
> Internet Marketing
> Software Project Development and Management
> Java Programming

Potential Employers:

> Internet-based or communications-related businesses
> Traditional product/service companies using electronic commerce
> Consulting companies in the virtual or actual marketplace

Available At:

The following list of electronic commerce programs is not exhaustive. Check with academic institutions near you to determine if majors, minors, certificates, or concentrations are available in electronic commerce.

Brevard Community College
1519 Clearlake Road, Cocoa, FL 32922
321/632-1111
http://www.brevard.cc.fl.us
Degrees available: Certificate

Bunker Hill Community College
250 New Rutherford Avenue, Boston, MA 02129-2925
617/228/2422
http://www.bhcc.mass.edu/AR/ProgramsOfStudy/
Programs2005.php?programID=7
Degrees available: Certificate

Columbus State Community College
PO Box 1609, Columbus, OH 43216-1609
800/621-6407
http://www.cscc.edu/DOCS/mktgcurr.htm
Degrees available: Certificates, associate degree

Community College of Allegheny County-Allegheny Campus
808 Ridge Avenue, Pittsburgh, PA 15212-6097
http://www.ccac.edu/default.aspx?id=146023
Degrees available: Certificate

Community College of Baltimore County
800 South Rolling Road, Catonsville, MD 21228
http://www.ccbcmd.edu/sait/programs/ebus.html
Degrees available: Certificates, associate degrees

Cuyahoga Community College-Western Campus
Business, Math & Technology Department, C-251
11000 Pleasant Valley Road, Parma, OH 44130
216/987-5007
http://www.tri-c.edu/ebusiness
Degrees available: Associate degree

Delaware County Community College-Marple Campus
Information Technology Department
901 South Media Line Road, Media, PA 19063-1094
610/359-5050
http://www.dccc.edu/catalog/career_programs.html#e_commerce
Degrees available: Certificate, associate degree

Delaware Technical and Community College (multiple campuses)
333 Shipley Street, Wilmington, DE 19801
302/888-5296
http://www.dtcc.edu/wilmington/busadmin/ebus.html
Degrees available: Associate degree

Gibbs College-Norwalk
10 Norden Place, Norwalk, CT 06855-1436
800/761-8285
http://www.gibbsnorwalk.edu/digital.asp
Degrees available: Associate degree

University of Hawaii/Kapiolani Community College
Business Education Department
4303 Diamond Head Road, Kopiko 201, Honolulu, HI 96816
808/734-9140
http://ebus.kcc.hawaii.edu
Degrees available: Associate degree

Hudson Valley Community College
80 Vandenburgh Avenue, Troy, NY 12180
518/629-7309
https://www.hvcc.edu/programs.html
Degrees available: Associate degree

Milwaukee Area Technical College (multiple campuses)
700 West State Street, Milwaukee, WI 53233-1443
http://mktgcamp.matc.edu/ecommerce/index.aspx
Degrees available: Associate degrees

Montgomery College-Rockville Campus
51 Mannakee Street, Rockville, MD 20850
301/279-5000
http://www.montgomerycollege.edu/curricula/descriptions/
cdcommunications.htm#digital
Degrees available: Certificate

Moraine Valley Community College
9000 West College Parkway, Palos Hills, IL 60465-0937
708/974-4300
http://www.morainevalley.edu/programs/program_list.htm
Degrees available: Certificate

Pellissippi State Technical Community College
10915 Hardin Valley Road, Knoxville, TN 37933-0990
865/694-6400
http://www.pstcc.edu/community_relations/catalog/ctp/
programs/emarke.html
Degrees available: Associate degree

Piedmont Community College-Caswell County Campus
Business Administration Department
PO Box 1150, Yanceyville, NC 27379
336/694-5707
http://www.piedmontcc.edu
Degrees available: Associate degree (concentration)

Seminole Community College
100 Weldon Boulevard, Sanford, FL 32773-6199
407/708-2372
http://www.scc-fl.edu/e-business
Degrees available: Certificates, associate degrees

Sheridan College
Computer Web Development and Internet Business Program
3059 Coffeen Avenue, Sheridan, WY 82801
307/674-6446
http://www.sheridan.edu/programs/ecommerce.asp
Degrees available: Associate degree

Tulsa Community College-Southeast Campus
Business and Information Technology Division
10300 East 81st Street, Tulsa, OK 74133
918/595-7639
http://www.tulsacc.edu/page.asp?durki=4058&site=85&return=3543
Degrees available: Associate degree

Washtenaw Community College
PO Box D-1, Ann Arbor, MI 48106
734/973-3300
http://www.wccnet.edu/academicinfo/creditofferings/programs/
atoz/atoz2.php?code=CTEBF
Degrees available: Certificate

For More Information:

Information Technology Association of America
1401 Wilson Boulevard, Suite 1100, Arlington, VA 22209
703/522-5055
http://www.itaa.org

Interview: Tom Walker

Tom Walker is the program manager of the e-business technology program at Seminole Community College in Sanford, Florida. He discussed the school's program and the education of students in this field with the editors of *They Teach That in Community College!?*

Q. Tell us a little about e-business and your program at Seminole Community College.

A. E-business is the use of the Internet (World Wide Web) to promote, market, and sell products to consumers, industry, and government. Our curriculum at Seminole Community College consists of one 64-credit AS degree with four separate majors or specializations: Business, Software, Network Technology and Network Security. Each degree has associated certificates (21-24 credit hours). Software has two elective tracks: Database and Web Design. Network Technology has two tracks: Microsoft and UNIX.

Q. What high school subjects/activities should students focus on to be successful in this major?

A. Students should have a strong computer-based background for the software, networking, and security specializations. Business specialization students should possess a strong entrepreneurial personality as this specialization is designed for people who want to create a home-based, business-to-consumer (B2C) business.

Q. Where do e-business graduates find employment?

A. Our Business Specialization is designed for people wishing to create a home-based business. All companies need people with security skills. Network security is also the highest paying area since so few people possess these skills.

Q. How will the field of e-business change in the future?

A. B2C sales have increased from $75 billion to $150 billion in just four years. Online sales for B2C represent nearly 10 percent of all retail sales. Online purchasing will only continue to increase, and this will change retailing forever because of the convenience of online buying. B2B sales are measured in the trillions of dollars.

Enology and Viticulture

Harvesting grapes, trucking them to the winery, loading them into the crushers, and supervising the aging, racking, and blending of wine is what students studying viticulture and enology experience as part of their hands-on internship experience. A select few colleges in the United States offer programs in the specialized fields of viticulture, the science of wine-grape growing, and enology, the science of wine-making. Students in these disciplines study the scientific principles that are involved in growing grapes and manufacturing wine.

Typical Courses:

> Organic Chemistry
> Plant Propagation
> Viticulture and Small Fruits
> Chemistry and Biochemistry of Fruit and Wine
> Vineyard and Winery Systems
> Advanced Horticultural Crop Physiology
> Viticulture-Enology Interface
> Varietal wines (international and domestic)
> Winery production practices
> Must and wine analysis

Potential Employers:

> Wineries
> Distribution and retail businesses

Did You Know?

✔ Grapes are grown in 40 U.S. states.
✔ U.S. wine industry revenue more than tripled in 15 years, from $955 million in 1985 to almost $3 billion in 2000.
✔ The top wine-producing states are California, New York, Washington, and Oregon.
✔ Approximately 556,000 people are employed in the U.S. wine industry.

Source: American Wine Society

Chardonnay grapes hang on a vine in a vineyard.

Available At:

Chemeketa Community College
4000 Lancaster Drive Northeast, PO Box 14007, Salem, OR 97309
503/399-5066
http://www.chemeketa.edu/exploring/areas/careers/ag.html
Degrees available: Certificate, associate degree

Shawnee Community College
8364 Shawnee College Road, Ullin, IL 62992
618/634-3216
http://www.shawneecc.edu/courses/viticulture.asp
and
http://www.shawneecc.edu/courses/enology_asst.asp
Degrees available: Certificate

Viticulture and Enology Science and Technology Alliance
Missouri State University-Mountain Grove
9740 Red Spring Road, Mountain Grove, MO 65711-2229
http://vesta-usa.org
Degrees available: Certificate, associate degree
This is a partnership between Missouri State University,
Northeast Iowa Community College, Shawnee Community
College in Illinois, and the Mid-America Viticulture and Enology
Center, along with state agricultural agencies, to create a collabo-
rative program of study in the fields of viticulture and enology.

Walla Walla Community College
Walla Walla Institute for Enology and Viticulture
500 Tausick Way, Walla Walla, WA 99362
877/992-9922
http://www.wwcc.edu/programs/proftech/wine/index.cfm
Degrees available: Certificates, associate degree

University of Washington
Department of Horticulture and Landscape Architecture
PO Box 646414, Pullman, WA 99164-6414
509/335-9502
http://www.wineducation.wsu.edu/enology
and
http://www.wineducation.wsu.edu/viticulture
Degrees available: Certificates, bachelor's degree

For More Information:

American Society for Enology and Viticulture
PO Box 1855, Davis, CA 95617-1855
530/753-3142
society@asev.org
http://www.asev.org

American Wine Society
PO Box 3330, Durham, NC 27702
919/403-0022
http://www.americanwinesociety.com

Entrepreneurship

To own one's own business and work for oneself is for many people a significant step towards achieving their version of the American Dream. Whether the goal is to start a small, modest company that will provide enough income to live on comfortably or a company for which the goal is to become the next Wal-Mart of its industry—the dominant presence in the marketplace—becoming an entrepreneur requires a certain amount of business savvy, book smarts, and risk taking. It also requires high levels of independence and responsibility, along with the realization that the traditional work week will probably exceed 40 hours. After all, the success of your business comes from what you put into it. Most businesses, particularly in the early stages of start-up, require a significant time commitment. If your American Dream is such that through hard work you will attain a level of independent financial prosperity while pursuing a passion that is all your own, becoming your own boss—an entrepreneur—might be the right direction for you.

Typical Courses:

> Accounting/Finance
> Marketing and Advertising
> Business Communications
> Business Law
> Management
> Business Planning
> Entrepreneurship
> International Trade and Exports
> Salesmanship
> Macroeconomics and Microeconomics

Potential Employers:

> Self-employment

Available At:

The following list of entrepreneurship programs is not exhaustive. Check with academic institutions near you to determine if majors, minors, certificates, or concentrations are available in entrepreneurship.

Alfred State College
10 Upper College Drive, Alfred, NY 14802
800/425-3733
admissions@alfredstate.edu
http://www.alfredstate.edu/alfred/
Entrepreneurship_AAS.asp?SnID=281006888
Degrees available: Certificate, associate degree

Borough of Manhattan Community College-City University of New York
199 Chambers Street, New York, NY 10007
212/220-8205
http://www.bmcc.cuny.edu/business/SBE/sbe.html
Degrees available: Associate degree

Bristol Community College
Business Administration Department
777 Elsbree Street, Fall River, MA 02720
508/678-2811
http://www.bristolcommunitycollege.edu/catalog/ca2/degree/
ca2_ent.html
Degrees available: Associate degree

Cincinnati State Technical and Community College
3520 Central Parkway, Cincinnati, OH 45223
http://www.cinstate.cc.oh.us/FutureStudent/Academics/
AcademicDivisions/BusinessTechnologies/etrpc.htm
Degrees available: Certificate

93

Did You Know?

Approximately two-thirds of students surveyed by Students in Free Enterprise hope to become entrepreneurs at some point in their careers.

Community College of Philadelphia
1700 Spring Garden Street, Philadelphia, PA 19130
215/751-8010
http://www.ccp.edu/site/academic/degrees/management.php
Degrees available: Associate degree (concentration)

Cuyahoga Community College-Western Campus
Business, Math, and Technology Department
11000 Pleasant Valley Road, Parma, OH 44130
http://www.tri.edu/programs/docs/Program%20PDFs/
Small%20Business%20(rev).pdf
Degrees available: Associate degree

Delaware County Community College-Marple Campus
901 South Media Line Road, Media, PA 19063-1094
610/359-5050
http://www.dccc.edu/catalog/career_programs.html#small_business
Degrees available: Certificate, associate degree

Flathead Valley Community College-Kalispell Campus
777 Grandview Drive, Kalispell, MT 59901
406/756-3860
http://www.fvcc.edu/academics
Degrees available: Certificate, associate degree

Fort Belknap College
PO Box 159, Harlem, MT 59526
406/353-2607
http://www.fbcc.edu/html/business_entre.html
Degrees available: Associate degree

Housatonic Community College
900 Lafayette Boulevard, Bridgeport, CT 06604
203/332-5200
http://www.hcc.commnet.edu/academics/programs/dynamic/
progDetail.asp?keyCode=EA89
Degrees available: Associate degree

J. Sargeant Reynolds Community College
PO Box 85622, Richmond, VA 23285-5622
804/371-3000
http://www.jsr.vccs.edu/curriculum/programs/
Entrepreneurship%20in%20Small%20BusinessCSC.htm
Degrees available: Certificate

Johnson County Community College
12345 College Boulevard, Overland Park, KS 66210-1299
913/469-8500
http://www.jccc.net/home/catalog/default/toccareerprograms/
careerprograms/AAS-ENTREP
and
http://www.jccc.net/home/catalog/default/toccareerprograms/
careerprograms/VC-ENTREP
Degrees available: Certificate, associate degree

Kingsborough Community College-City University of New York
2001 Oriental Boulevard, Brooklyn, NY 11235
718/368-5555
businessdept@kbcc.cuny.edu
http://www.kingsborough.edu/apdegree/Kcccentrp.htm
Degrees available: Certificate

Mohawk Valley Community College
1101 Sherman Drive, Utica, NY 15501
315/792-5348
http://www.mvcc.edu/acdmcs/dprtmnts/bit/smbsnsmngtc.cfm
Degrees available: Certificate

New Hampshire Community Technical College-Nashua
505 Amherst Street, Nashua, NH 03063
603/882-6923
nashua@nhctc.edu
http://www.nashua.nhctc.edu/Academic%20Programs/
Small%20Business%20Mgmt%20Cert.htm
and
http://www.nashua.nhctc.edu/Academic%20Programs/
Small%20Business.htm
Degrees available: Certificate, associate degree

New Hampshire Technical Institute
31 College Drive, Concord, NH 03301-7412
603/271-8880
info@nhti.edu
http://www.nhti.edu/academics/academicprograms/
certsmbusmgmt.html
Degrees available: Certificate

Northeast Community College
801 East Benjamin Avenue, PO Box 469, Norfolk, NE 68702-0469
402/371-2020
http://www.northeastcollege.com/PS/PDF/Degree_Offerings/
BM_Entrepreneurship_AAS.pdf
Degrees available: Associate degree

Southern Maine Community College
2 Fort Road, South Portland, ME 04106
207/741-5500
http://www.smccme.edu/catalog/2005-2006/
index.php?section=5&navid=110&docid=276
Degrees available: Certificate

Spokane Falls Community College
3410 West Fort George Wright Drive, Mail Stop 3011
Spokane, WA 99224-5288
888-509/7944
http://tech.spokanefalls.edu/SmallBus/default.asp?page=Outline
Degrees available: Associate degree

Washtenaw Community College
PO Box D-1, Ann Arbor, MI 48106
734/973-3300
http://www.wccnet.edu/academicinfo/creditofferings/programs/
atoz/atoz2.php?code=CTENT
Degrees available: Certificate

Williston State College
1410 University Avenue, PO Box 1326, Williston, ND 58802
888/863-9455
http://www.wsc.nodak.edu/academics/programs.htm
Degrees available: Certificate, associate degree

For More Information:

International Franchise Association
1350 New York Avenue, NW, Suite 900, Washington, DC 20005
202/628-8000
ifa@franchise.org
http://www.franchise.org

Students in Free Enterprise
1959 East Kerr Street, Springfield, MO 65803-4775
417/831-9505
sifehq@sife.org
http://www.sife.org

U.S. Small Business Administration
409 Third Street, SW, Washington, DC 20416
800/U-ASK-SBA
http://www.sba.gov

Equestrian Studies

According to a recent study by the American Horse Council, the equine, or horse, industry adds $102 billion to our economy and offers more than 1.4 million full-time jobs. Colleges have responded to our love of all things equine by creating a variety of equestrian studies programs. Majors may include equine administration or equine business, which offer training for people who are interested in becoming instructors, trainers, equine managers, riders, equine insurance adjusters, bloodstock agents, race track administrators, farm managers, and equine product salespersons, and equestrian science, which offers training to those interested in becoming trainers, equine managers, instructors, and riders.

Typical Courses:

> Anatomy, Movement, and Farrier Methods
> Theory of Equine Nutrition
> Stable Management
> Equine Care
> Equine Health and First Aid
> Techniques of Horse Management
> Horse Industry Overview
> Horse Show and Event Management
> Entrepreneurship
> Principles of Management

Potential Employers:

> Racetracks
> Stables
> Breeding and racing organizations
> Bloodstock agencies
> Equine publications
> Horse show facilities
> Horse show management firms
> Feed companies
> Sales industry
> Insurance industry

Available At:

The following list of schools offering programs in equestrian studies is not exhaustive. For a complete list of programs, visit http://www.horseschools.com.

College of Southern Idaho
315 Falls Avenue, PO Box 1238, Twin Falls, ID 83303-1238
208/732-6414
info@csi.edu
http://www.csi.edu/ip/Ag/CSI_AG_Programs/CSI_Horse_Mgt/csi_horse_mgt.html
Degrees available: Associate degree

Dawson Community College
300 College Drive, PO Box 421, Glendive, MT 59330
800/821-8320
http://www.dawson.edu/academics/Catalog/DCCAASDegreePlansofStudy.asp#Agri2
Degrees available: Associate degree

Ellsworth Community College
3702 South Center Street, Marshalltown, IA 50158
641/752-4645
http://www.iavalley.cc.ia.us/Catalog05-06/VocTech/VTEquineManagement.htm
Degrees available: Associate degree

J. Sargeant Reynolds Community College
PO Box 85622, Richmond, VA 23285-5622
804/371-3000
http://www.jsr.vccs.edu/curriculum/programs/Equine%20ManagementCSC.htm
Degrees available: Certificate

Kirkwood Community College
6301 Kirkwood Boulevard, SW, Cedar Rapids, IA 52404
319/398-5617
info@kirkwood.cc.ia.us
http://www.kirkwood.edu/site/index.php?d=120&p=984&t=2
Degrees available: Associate degree

Morrisville State College
College of Agriculture and Technology
Marshall Hall, Morrisville, NY 13408
315/684-6586
admissions@morrisville.edu
http://www.morrisville.edu/Academics/Ag_NRC/Equine_Science
Degrees available: Associate degrees, bachelor's degrees

Northeastern Junior College
Equine Management Program
100 College Avenue, Sterling, CO 80751
http://www.njc.edu/agriculture/equinemgmt.html
Degrees available: Associate degree

Pikes Peak Community College
5675 South Academy Boulevard, Colorado Springs, CO 80906
http://www.ppcc.cccoes.edu/CatalogSchedule/Programs/
Programs.cfm?Program=FaSp
Degrees available: Certificate

For More Information:

American Horse Council
1616 H Street, NW, 7th Floor, Washington, DC 20006
AHC@horsecouncil.org
http://www.horsecouncil.org

American Riding Instructors Association
28801 Trenton Court, Bonita Springs, FL 34134-3337
aria@riding-instructor.com
http://www.riding-instructor.com

American Youth Horse Council
6660 #D-451 Delmonicom Colorado Springs, CO 80919
info@ayhc.com
http://www.ayhc.com

Interview: Dr. Christopher Nyberg

Dr. Christopher Nyberg is the chair of the Equine Science
Department at Morrisville State College in Morrisville, New
York. The College awards both associate and bachelor's degrees
in equine science. Dr. Nyberg discussed the school's program
and the education of students in this field with the editors of
They Teach That in Community College!?

Q. Please tell us about your program.

A. There are currently 14 faculty and staff members in the
Equine Department at Morrisville State College, with a wide
range of academic backgrounds and tremendous industry
experience. The program has been in existence in some form
since the late '60s but has had a large increase in size in the
past few years. It is one of the most diverse equine programs

in the country with equine opportunities in breeding, training (western, huntseat, and draft horses), and racing (standard-bred harness racing and thoroughbred racing). We currently have three indoor arenas, a half-mile harness training track, and four stables with a total of 182 permanent stalls. We also have a new equine rehabilitation and racing facility designed that will be entering the fund-raising stage this spring.

Q. What type of internship programs are offered in your program?

A. We have two internships available to students. One is a four-credit-hour elective that students can take over the summer by finding an employment opportunity in any equine field. The second is a mandatory 15-credit hour internship required for the bachelor of technology degree in which students must find an employment opportunity in the area of the equine industry in which they are specializing.

Q. What advice would you offer equine science majors as they graduate and look for jobs?

A. Our students' success is due to their strong work ethic, knowledge of the industry they are entering, and a level of responsibility consistent with what is expected of them in terms of a commitment to the animals in their care, and the ability to problem solve and work well with others. It is these skills and abilities along with equestrian skills that truly help them succeed.

Q. Where do equine science graduates find employment?

A. Equine science graduates from Morrisville State College are finding employment in all aspects of the equine industry. They are working in traditional equine farm and management positions as well as for businesses that revolve around the traditional horse careers. They are working all over the country—on breeding and training farms, for bloodstock agencies, equine publications, horse show facilities, horse show management firms, and feed companies. Others are pursuing higher degrees in veterinary school and graduate school.

Fashion Design

Are you obsessed with the latest fashions? Do you have a creative side that manifests itself in the unique clothes you wear? If so, perhaps a career in the fast-paced world of fashion design would be a perfect fit. But, don't be fooled into thinking fashion design is all glamour and no work. The recent Tommy Hilfiger-hosted fashion reality television show, *The Cut,* proved how cutthroat the world of fashion design can be. However, there is plenty of room for professionals in the industry who don't attain pop star-like fame by creating their own lines of clothing. A degree in fashion design prepares students to work as designers, pattern makers, illustrators, fabric buyers, sewers, and sample makers, and each of these positions plays a vital role in the developmental process of creating a line of clothing. Individuals well suited for careers in fashion design are those who thrive under pressure, are resourceful, are original thinkers, and enjoy some level of risk taking.

Typical Courses:

> Concept Development
> Drawing Fundamentals
> 3D Design
> Fashion History, Culture, and Society
> Fashion Drawing
> Computer-Aided Design
> Shoe Design
> Studio Methods
> Current Issues in the Global Fashion Industry
> Flat Pattern/Draping

Potential Employers:

> Fashion studio owners
> Textile and apparel manufacturers
> Retailers
> Department stores
> Fashion magazines and other publications
> Fashion houses

Available At:

The following list of schools offering programs in fashion design is not exhaustive. For a complete list of programs, visit the following website, http://fashionschools.com.

Bauder College
384 Northyards Boulevard, NW, Atlanta, GA 30313
800/241-3797
http://www.bauder.edu/Programs/FashionDesign.aspx
Degrees available: Associate degree

Brooks College
4825 East Pacific Coast Highway, Long Beach, CA 90804
866/746-5711
http://www.brookscollege.edu/fashion-design.asp
Degrees available: Associate degree

College of DuPage
425 Fawell Boulevard, Glen Ellyn, IL 60137-6599
630/942-2619
http://www.cod.edu/academic/acadprog/occ_voc/fashion
Degrees available: Certificate, associate degree

Fashion Institute of Technology
Seventh Avenue at 27th Street, Building B, Room 701
New York, NY 10001-5992
212/217-7667
http://www.fitnyc.edu/aspx/Content.aspx?menu=Future:Schools
AndPrograms:ArtAndDesign:FashionDesign
Degrees available: Associate degree, bachelor's degree

University of Hawaii-Honolulu Community College
874 Dillingham Boulevard, Honolulu, HI 96817
808/845-9129
http://tech.honolulu.hawaii.edu/ft/index.html
Degrees available: Certificates, associate degree

Houston Community College-Central College
1300 Holman, PO Box 7849, Houston, TX 77270-7849
713/718-6152
http://www.hccs.edu/discipline/Fshd/fshd.html
Degrees available: Certificates, associate degree

Pasadena City College
Department of Business and Computer Technology
1570 East Colorado Boulevard, Pasadena, CA 91106
626/585-7123
http://www.pasadena.edu/divisions/business-computertech
Degrees available: Associate degree

San Joaquin Delta College
Family, Consumer & Health Sciences Division
5151 Pacific Avenue, Stockton, CA 95207
209/954-5516
http://www.deltacollege.edu/div/fchs/fashion.html
Degrees available: Certificate

Santa Ana College
1530 West 17th Street, Santa Ana, CA 92706-3398
http://www.sac.edu/degrees/sac/
Fashion_Design_and_Custom_Clothing.htm
Degrees available: Certificate, associate degree

Santa Monica College
Fashion Design and Merchandising Department
1900 Pico Boulevard, Santa Monica, CA 90405
http://homepage.smc.edu/mobasheri_fereshteh/fm
Degrees available: Certificates, associate degrees

Sierra College
College of Liberal Arts
5000 Rocklin Road, Rocklin, CA 95677
916/781-0588
http://www.sierra.cc.ca.us/ed_programs/divisions.htm
Degrees available: Associate degree

103

For More Information:

American Apparel and Footwear Association
1601 North Kent Street, Suite 1200, Arlington, VA 22209
http://www.apparelandfootwear.org

Council of Fashion Designers of America
1412 Broadway, Suite 2006, New York, NY 10018
http://www.cfda.com

Fashion Group International, Inc.
8 West 40th Street, 7th Floor, New York, NY 10018
http://www.fgi.org

International Association of Clothing Designers and Executives
835 Northwest 36th Terrace, Oklahoma City, OK 73118
http://www.iacde.com

National Association of Schools of Art and Design
11250 Roger Bacon Drive, Suite 21, Reston, VA 20190-5248
http://nasad.arts-accredit.org

Careerthreads.com
http://www.careerthreads.com

Fashion Merchandising and Management

If last winter's hottest trend was tucking your jeans into colorful, furry boots, no doubt this winter it will be a fashion no-no. Yet, 10 years from now, the look may reappear—with a new twist. Black is in. Brown is out. Flats are in, heels are out. The world of fashion is indeed one of constant, evolutionary change. The "business" behind the "trends" is no different. Those who enter the field are generally those who strive to always stay a step ahead of the crowd with the latest styles. They have an aptitude for business and people, and a sincere dedication to a career that promises to never become stagnant! Students' studies will focus on the areas of retailing, merchandising, marketing, and management. They'll explore topics such as consumer influence, global economics, and emerging technology as they relate to the business of fashion. Professionals with degrees in fashion merchandising may become managers of stores, departments or areas within stores, or groups of stores. Others go on to manage special events such as fashion shows, design store window displays, or purchase lines of clothing for department stores. Entrepreneurial-minded students open their own boutiques.

Typical Courses:

> Clothing Adornment and Human Behavior
> Textile and Apparel Economics
> Textile Science
> Merchandising Promotion
> Merchandising Systems
> Social-Psychological Aspects of Clothing
> Historic Textiles
> Retail Sales and Customer Strategies

Potential Employers:

> Retailers
> Wholesalers

Available At:

The following list of schools offering programs in fashion merchandising and management is not exhaustive. For a complete list of programs, visit http://fashionschools.com.

Bauder College
384 Northyards Boulevard, NW, Atlanta, GA 30313
800/241-3797
http://www.bauder.edu/Programs/FashionMerchandising.aspx
Degrees available: Associate degree

Brookdale Community College
765 Newman Springs Road, Lincroft, NJ 07738
732/224-2345
http://www.brookdalecc.edu/fac/marketing/fashion/index.html
Degrees available: Associate degree

Brooks College
4825 East Pacific Coast Highway, Long Beach, CA 90804
866/746-5711
http://www.brookscollege.edu/fashion-merchandising.asp
Degrees available: Associate degree

College of DuPage
425 Fawell Boulevard, Glen Ellyn, IL 60137-6599
630/942-2619
http://www.cod.edu/academic/acadprog/occ_voc/fashion
Degrees available: Certificate, associate degree

Houston Community College-Central College
1300 Holman, PO Box 7849, Houston, TX 77004
713/718-6152
http://www.hccs.edu/discipline/Fshn/fshn.html
Degrees available: Certificates, associate degree

Kirkwood Community College
6301 Kirkwood Boulevard, SW, Cedar Rapids, IA 52404
800/363-2220
info@kirkwood.cc.ia.us
http://www.kirkwood.edu/site/index.php?d=135&p=1193&t=2
Degrees available: Certificate, associate degree

Madison Area Technical College-Truax Campus
3550 Anderson Street, Madison, WI 53704
608/246-6551
http://matcmadison.edu/matc/ASP/showprogram.asp?ID=2953
Degrees available: Associate degree

San Joaquin Delta College
Family, Consumer & Health Sciences Division
5151 Pacific Avenue, Stockton, CA 95207
209/954-5516
http://www.deltacollege.edu/div/fchs/fashion.html
Degrees available: Certificate

Santa Ana College
1530 West 17th Street, Santa Ana, CA 92706-3398
714/564-6000
http://www.sac.edu/degrees/sac/
Fashion_Design_and_Custom_Clothing.htm
Degrees available: Certificate, associate degree

Santa Monica College
Fashion Design and Merchandising Department
1900 Pico Boulevard, Santa Monica, CA 90405
310/434-4000
http://homepage.smc.edu/mobasheri_fereshteh/fm
Degrees available: Certificates, associate degrees

Sierra College
College of Liberal Arts
5000 Rocklin Road, Rocklin, CA 95677
916/781-0588
http://www.sierra.cc.ca.us/ed_programs/divisions.htm
Degrees available: Associate degree

Spokane Falls Community College
3410 West Fort George Wright Drive, Mail Stop 3011
Spokane, WA 99204-5288
509/533-3699
http://tech.spokanefalls.edu/Management/default.asp?page=Man
Degrees available: Associate degree

For More Information:

American Apparel and Footwear Association
1601 North Kent Street, Suite 1200, Arlington, VA 22209
800/520-2262
http://www.apparelandfootwear.org

American Purchasing Society
PO Box 256, Aurora, IL 60506
630/859-0250
support@american-purchasing.com
http://www.american-purchasing.com

International Association of Clothing Designers and Executives
835 Northwest 36th Terrace, Oklahoma City, OK 73118
405/602-8037
newyorkiacde@cox.net
http://www.iacde.com

National Retail Federation
325 7th Street, NW, Suite 1100, Washington, DC 20004
800/673-4692
http://www.nrf.com

Careerthreads.com
http://www.careerthreads.com

Fire Science Technology

Whether you want to be out in the field fighting fires and serving as a member of a rescue team, behind the scenes conducting inspections to determine property value or loss, or speaking to the public about fire safety, a degree in fire science technology prepares you for a fascinating public service career. You can expect to study not only the fundamentals of fire prevention and suppression, but also the evolving technologies that make a degree in fire science technology so necessary for today's firefighters. Individuals should possess an aptitude for science and math as well as physical strength and mental stamina. In many programs, you'll develop leadership skills, become an effective communicator, and be introduced to the business of managing and operating a successful fire department. And in this business, success means more than achieving a business goal—it is often a matter of life or death. Students can expect to enter the field with the necessary skills to save lives and make a lasting impact on the communities in which they live.

Typical Courses:

> Building Construction
> Physics
> Hazardous Toxic Materials
> Water Supply Hydraulics
> Codes and Standards
> Fire Suppression
> Business Technology Report Writing
> Fundamentals of Fire Prevention and Inspection
> Organization and Management of Fire Departments
> Fire Investigation
> Sprinklers and Fixed Extinguishing Systems
> Hazardous Materials Operations
> Emergency Medical Care

Potential Employers:

> Fire departments
> Public and private fire protection organizations
> State and federal organizations such as the Federal Emergency Management Agency, the Department of Homeland Security, and the Bureau of Alcohol, Tobacco, Firearms, and Explosives

> Fire engineering firms
> Fire investigation firms
> Insurance companies
> Industrial firms

Available At:

The following list of fire science technology programs is not exhaustive. Check with academic institutions near you to determine if majors, minors, certificates, or concentrations are available in fire science technology.

Brevard Community College
1519 Clearlake Road, Cocoa, FL 32922
321/632-1111
http://www.brevard.cc.fl.us
Degrees available: Associate degree

Bristol Community College
777 Elsbree Street, Fall River, MA 02720
508/678-2811
http://www.bristolcommunitycollege.edu/catalog/ca7/degree/
ca7_fir.html
Degrees Available: Associate degree

Broward Community College
111 East Las Olas Boulevard, Fort Lauderdale, FL 33301
954/201-7400
http://www.broward.edu
Degrees available: Associate degree

Capital Community College
950 Main Street, Hartford, CT 06103
860/906-5000
http://www.ccc.commnet.edu/business/fire.htm
Degrees available: Associate degree

Chemeketa Community College
4000 Lancaster Drive Northeast, PO Box 14007, Salem, OR 97309
503/399-6241
http://www.chemeketa.edu/exploring/areas/careers/safety.html
Degrees available: Certificate, associate degree

College of DuPage
425 Fawell Boulevard, Glen Ellyn, IL 60137-6599
630/942-2107
http://www.cod.edu/FireSci
Degrees available: Certificates, associate degree

Delaware Technical and Community College-Stanton Campus
400 Stanton-Christiana Road, Newark, DE 19713
302/454-3976
http://www.stanton.dtcc.edu/stanton/fet/info.html
Degrees available: Diploma, associate degrees

Did You Know?

Fire departments in the United States responded to 1,550,500 fires in 2004, according to the National Fire Protection Association. These fires caused 3,900 civilian fire fatalities, 17,785 civilian fire injuries, and approximately $9,794,000,000 in direct property loss.

Eastern Maine Community College
354 Hogan Road, Bangor, ME 04401
207/974-4600
admissions@emcc.edu
http://www.emcc.edu/programs/fireScience.htm
Degrees available: Certificate, associate degree

Erie Community College-South Campus
4041 Southwestern Boulevard, Orchard Park, NY 14127
716/851-1003
http://ecc.edu/studentlife/student_acad_fpt.php3
Degrees available: Associate degree

Lansing Community College
PO Box 40010, Lansing, MI 48901-7210
800/644-4522
welcome@lcc.edu
http://www.lcc.edu/publicservice/fire_science
Degrees available: Certificate, associate degrees

Macomb Community College
14500 East 12 Mile Road, Warren, MI 48088
866/622-6621
http://www.macomb.edu/ProgramDescriptions/FireScience.asp
Degrees available: Certificates, associate degree

Madison Area Technical College
3550 Anderson Street, Madison, WI 53704
608/246-6911
http://matcmadison.edu/matc/ASP/showprogram.asp?ID=2957
Degrees available: Associate degree

Monroe Community College-Brighton Campus
1000 East Henrietta Road, Rochester, NY 14623
585/292-2000
http://www.monroecc.edu/etsdbs/MCCatPub.nsf/AcademicProgr
ams?OpenPage
Degrees available: Associate degree

Moraine Valley Community College
9000 West College Parkway, Palos Hills, IL 60465-0937
708/974-4300
http://www.morainevalley.edu/programs/program_list.htm
Degrees available: Certificates, associate degree

New Hampshire Community Technical College-Laconia
379 Belmont Road, Laconia, NH 03246
800/357-2992
http://www.laconia.nhctc.edu/programs/
FIRE%20SCIENCE%20Profile2%2004-05.htm
Degrees available: Associate degrees

Northern Virginia Community College
4001 Wakefield Chapel Road, Annandale, VA 22003-3796
703/323-3000
http://www.nvcc.vccs.edu/curcatalog/programs
Degrees available: Associate degrees

111

Palm Beach Community College
4200 Congress Avenue, Lake Worth, FL 33461
561/868-3772
http://www.pbcc.edu/fire/index.asp
Degrees available: Certificates, associate degree

Sierra College
5000 Rocklin Road, Roseville, CA 95677-3397
916/781-6250
http://www.sierra.cc.ca.us/ed_programs/public_safety/index.html
Degrees available: Certificates, associate degrees

Southern Maine Community College
2 Fort Road, South Portland, ME 04106
207/741-5500
http://www.smccme.edu/catalog/2005-2006/
index.php?section=5&navid=120&docid=0
Degrees available: Associate degree

For More Information:

International Association of Arson Investigators
12770 Boenker Road, St. Louis, MO 63044
314/739-4224
http://www.firearson.com

National Fire Protection Association
1 Batterymarch Park, PO Box 9101, Quincy, MA 02269-9101
617/770-3000
http://www.nfpa.org

Interview: Tennis Tollefson

Tennis Tollefson is an instructor of fire technology in the Fire
Technology and Health Sciences Department at Sierra College in
Rocklin, California. Mr. Tollefson has 33 years in the fire service
and has also been teaching for almost 20 years. He discussed the
school's fire technology program and the education of students
in this field with the editors of *They Teach That in Community
College!?*

Q. Please tell us about your program.

A. Sierra College offers an associate in arts or an associate in science degree in fire technology, depending on what general
education course the student follows. We also offer a certificate program for students who desire to acquire vocational
skills. The certificate track is not equivalent to an A.A. or A.S.
degree. In addition to these tracks, we offer a regional
Firefighter I academy accredited by the California State Fire
Marshal, and courses for Fire Officer and Chief Officer certification through the California State Fire Marshal's office. We
also offer a variety of wildland firefighting, hazardous materi-
al, and rescue classes.

Q. What type of internship programs are offered in your
program?

A. We offer an internship class for our fire technology students.
Students can earn between .5 and four units per semester
based on the hours they work at an on-site location. We
assist in placing students with area fire departments to work
and learn additional areas of work within the fire service that
they would not normally be exposed to in a classroom setting. This class may be taken four times.

Q. What educational level is typically required for fire technology graduates to land good jobs in the industry?

A. For individuals to advance within the fire service, bachelor's degrees and graduate degrees are now the standard for those individuals who want to climb the career ladder. However, in California the typical minimal educational requirement for a starting firefighter is a high school diploma or equivalent, EMT certification, and completion of an accredited regional fire academy. To further increase employment opportunities, a student may want to consider completing paramedic training. I would advise college graduates in fire technology to be willing to relocate. There are many job opportunities for work in both public and private organizations for individuals willing to relocate. I would also advise them to continue with their education after they begin their careers.

Q. Where do fire technology graduates find employment?

A. Most fire technology students look for employment in various local, state, or federal fire departments. There are also employment opportunities with private fire departments, fire engineering firms, and fire protection system companies.

Q. What does the future hold for your program and fire technology graduates?

A. We see our program growing in the future. Most jurisdictions expect their prospective employees to be highly motivated and trained. Due to enhanced retirement programs, the California fire service is expecting upwards of 30 percent of its current workforce to retire within the next five years. The aging demographics of the nation and an increased expectation of advanced emergency medical services to be provided by fire departments will require future firefighters to be more highly skilled, and it will require larger numbers of firefighters. Homeland security and dealing with potential terrorism is also becoming more of a focus for the fire service, and we will expand and meet these expectations and needs.

Interview: Jeffrey Huber

Jeffrey Huber is a professor of fire science in the Public Service and Careers Department at Lansing Community College in Lansing, Michigan. He has 30 years of fire fighting experience, holds a master's of science in fire and emergency services management administration, has published a book on the executive fire officer, and has been teaching for four years. He discussed the school's fire science program and the education of students in this field with the editors of *They Teach That in Community College!?*

Q. Please tell us about your program.

A. Lansing Community College (LCC) provides two associate degrees and one certificate program. LCC has an associate degree in fire science technology that has three options to choose from. The degree consists of approximately 63 credit hours of study. We offer an associate degree in fire science/basic EMT, which is approximately 60 credit hours of study. The Regional Fire Academy is a certificate program that is 19 credit hours long or one semester. This program provides fire fighter I & II, haz-mat awareness, and haz-mat operations certifications through the Michigan Fire Fighter's Training Council.

Q. What high school subjects/activities should students focus on to be successful in this major?

A. Students should concentrate on writing, math, and science courses. Math courses in trigonometry, geometry, and high levels of algebra are vital. Science courses in physics, chemistry, and biology are very important. Play sports and keep very active and in great shape.

Q. What are the most important personal and professional qualities for fire science majors?

A. Honesty, dedication, leadership, mechanical aptitude, and physical abilities are extremely important.

Forensic Science

If the terms DNA, body decay, blood splatter, and rigor mortis fascinate rather than repulse you, you might have a future in the forensic sciences. Popularized by television shows such as *CSI: Crime Scene Investigation*, *Crossing Jordan*, and *The X Files*, the forensic sciences are enjoying remarkable popularity on college campuses. Degrees, certificates, and classes are available in the following areas: Crime Scene Investigation, Forensic Science, Forensic Psychology, Forensic and Toxicological Chemistry, Forensic and Investigative Science, Forensic DNA Profiling, Forensic Anthropology, Forensic Biology, Forensic Pathology, and Forensic Accounting.

Typical Courses:

> Crime Scene Investigation
> Forensic Anthropology
> Survey of Forensic Science
> Death Investigation
> Firearms Evidence
> Forensic Entomology
> Medical Terminology
> Human Physiology
> Laboratory Measurements and Techniques
> Organic Chemistry
> Forensic Chemistry
> Biochemistry
> Statistics for Biomedical Sciences
> Criminology

Potential Employers:

> State and local law enforcement agencies
> Government agencies (i.e., the Drug Enforcement Administration; the Bureau of Alcohol, Tobacco, Firearms, and Explosives; the Federal Bureau of Investigation; the United States Postal Service; the Secret Service; the Central Intelligence Agency; and United States Fish and Wildlife Services)
> Hospitals
> Medical schools
> Medical examiners

Available At:

The following programs that offer certificates or degrees in forensic science or related subjects are accredited by the American Academy of Forensic Sciences (http://www.aafs.org).

Anne Arundel Community College
101 College Parkway, Arnold, MD 21012-1895
410/777-AACC
http://www.aacc.edu/criminaljustice/ForensicScience.cfm
Degrees available: Associate degree

Forsyth Technical Community College
2100 Silas Creek Parkway, Winston-Salem, NC 27103
336/723-0371
http://www.forsyth.tec.nc.us/degree/crimj_latent.pdf
Degrees available: Associate degree

Griffin Technical College
501 Varsity Road, Griffin, GA 30223
770/229-3487
http://www.griffintech.edu/pages/fstdex.html
Degrees available: Diploma, associate degree

Grossmont Community College
8800 Grossmont College Drive, El Cajon, CA 92020
619/644-7000
http://www.grossmont.edu/aoj/forensic.asp
Degrees available: Associate degree

Hudson Valley Community College
Fitzgibbons Hall, Room 010, Troy, NY 12180
518/629-7342
https://www.hvcc.edu/las/forensic/index.html
Degrees available: Associate degree

Kansas City Community College
7250 State Avenue, Kansas City, KS 66112
913/288-7631
http://www.kckcc.edu/mst/forensic
Degrees available: Associate degree

Keiser College (multiple campuses)
800/749-4456
http://www.keisercollege.edu/cst.htm
Degrees available: Associate degree

Phoenix College
Learning Center Building
1202 West Thomas Road, Phoenix, AZ 85013
602/285-7110
http://www.pc.maricopa.edu/cassdept/evidencetechnology.html
Degrees available: Certificates, associate degree

Other colleges that offer certificates or degrees in forensic science or related subjects include:

University of Arkansas Community College-Hope
2500 South Main, PO Box 140, Hope, AR 71801
http://www.uacch.edu/lowcontent.cfm?page=academics/degrees/
aas_crime&res=low
and
http://www.uacch.edu/lowcontent.cfm?page=academics/degrees/
crime_tc&res=low
Degrees available: Certificate, associate degree

Arkansas Northeastern College
2501 South Division Street, PO Box 1109, Blytheville, AR 72315
http://www.anc.edu/academics/academics.htm
Degrees available: Associate degree

Broward Community College
111 East Las Olas Boulevard, Fort Lauderdale, FL 33301
http://www.broward.edu/ext/ProgramOverview.jsp?21101
Degrees available: Associate degree

Community College of Baltimore County (multiple campuses)
http://www.ccbcmd.edu/media/academics/forensic.pdf
Degrees available: Associate degree

Georgia Perimeter College (multiple campuses)
3251 Panthersville Road, Decatur, GA 30034-3897
http://www.gpc.edu/~acadaff/cat/programs/AA_ForensicScience.html
Degrees available: Associate degree

For More Information:

American Academy of Forensic Sciences
410 North 21st Street, Colorado Springs, CO 80904-2798
719/636-1100
http://www.aafs.org

Society of Forensic Toxicologists
PO Box 5543, Mesa, AZ 85211-5543
480/839-9106
http://www.soft-tox.org

Funeral Services

Funerals have been held since the beginning of time to honor the dead and help the survivors deal with their grief. *Funeral services workers* are especially trained professionals who prepare the deceased for burial by embalming, arranging the burial and funeral services of the deceased, and providing the survivors with the emotional support they need to make it through a very difficult time in their lives. Funeral services workers, especially those who deal with the public such as *funeral directors,* must have compassion, empathy, tact, and good listening skills (especially when it comes to listening to their clients' wishes regarding the deceased). Funeral services workers also need physical strength and coordination in order to be able to lift and move the deceased in preparation for embalming and burial. Educational requirements for funeral services workers vary by state; contact your state's licensing board for more information on your state's requirements. According to the American Board of Funeral Service Education, most states require the completion of an associate degree (which should include 45 credits that focus specifically on funeral service). In addition, graduates typically serve an apprenticeship and pass a state licensing examination.

Typical Courses:

> Introduction to Funeral
> Embalming
> Restorative Art
> Funeral Directing
> Funeral Psychology/Sociology
> Funeral Services Law
> Funeral Merchandising
> Microbiology/Pathology
> Psychology of Grief and Death
> Funeral Service Counseling

Potential Employers:

> Funeral homes
> Mortuary schools
> U.S. military

Available At:

Fewer than 60 funeral service programs are accredited by the American Board of Funeral Service Education. Visit its website, http://www.abfse.org/html/dir-listing.html, for a complete list.

Arapahoe Community College
5900 South Santa Fe Drive, Littleton, CO 80160
303/797-5954
http://www.arapahoe.edu/deptprgrms/mor/index.html
Degrees available: Associate degree

University of Arkansas Community College-Hope
2500 South Main, PO Box 140, Hope, AR 71801
http://www.uacch.edu/lowcontent.cfm?page=academics/degrees/
aas_funeral&res=low
Degrees available: Associate degree

**Bishop State Community College-Baker-
Gaines Central Campus**
1365 Dr. Martin Luther King Avenue, Mobile, AL 36603
251/405-4435
http://www.bishop.edu/health/funeralserv.htm
Degrees available: Associate degree

Carl Sandburg College
2400 Tom L. Wilson Boulevard, Galesburg, IL 61401
877/236-1862, ext. 5229
http://www.sandburg.edu/Academic_Programs/Health/
Mortuary_Science/mortuary_science.html
Degrees available: Associate degree

University of District of Columbia-Van Ness Campus
4200 Connecticut Avenue, NW, Washington, DC 20008
202/274-5000
http://www.udc.edu/programs/arts_sciences/associates/
mortuary_science.htm
Degrees available: Associate degree

East Mississippi Community College-Scooba Campus
PO Box 158, Scooba, MS 39358
http://www.eastms.edu/academics/documents/
EMCCFinalCATALOG2005-2007.pdf
page 82
Degrees available: Associate degree

Ivy Tech Community College of Indiana (multiple campuses)
50 West Fall Creek Parkway North Drive, Indianapolis, IN 46208
http://www.ivytech.edu/programs/mor
Degrees available: Associate degree

John Tyler Community College
13101 Jefferson Davis Highway, Chester, VA 23831-5316
804/706-5121
http://www.jtcc.edu/file/2005_jtcc_catalog.pdf#page=47
Degrees available: Associate degree

Kansas City Kansas Community College
7250 State Avenue, Kansas City, KS 66112
913/334-1100
http://www.kckcc.edu/catalog/
kckcc_mcc_agreement_mortuary_sciecne.psp
Degrees available: Associate degree

Mercer County Community College
1200 Old Trenton Road, West Windsor, NJ 08550
609/586-4800
http://www.mccc.edu/programs_degree_funeral.shtml
and
http://www.mccc.edu/programs_degree_funeralprep.shtml
Degrees available: Associate degrees

Piedmont Technical College
620 North Emerald Road, Greenwood, SC 29648-1467
800/868-5528
http://www.ptc.edu/academic/Programs/
Associate_in_Business_Funeral_Services_Full.htm
Degrees available: Certificate, associate degree

Worsham College of Mortuary Science
495 Northgate Parkway, Wheeling, IL 60090
847/808-8444
info@worshamcollege.com
http://www.worshamcollege.com
Degrees available: Associate degree

For More Information:

American Board of Funeral Service Education
3432 Ashland Avenue, Suite U, St. Joseph, MO 645
816/233-3747
http://www.abfse.org

National Funeral Directors Association
13625 Bishop's Drive, Brookfield, WI 53005-6607
800/228-6332
nfda@nfda.org
http://www.nfda.org

Gallery Management

The *gallery manager* serves a vital role in the success of an art show or popularity of a special museum exhibit. An associate degree in gallery management will prepare you for a career in this exciting field. Your coursework will include exhibition design, proper handling of art pieces, and correct lighting and display, as well as the publicity and marketing of an exhibit. You will also learn Web-based applications for art media such as digital photography. Santa Fe Community College offers this degree as well as the chance for its students to get hands-on experience working within the confines of its onsite visual arts gallery.

Typical Courses:

> Art Criticism
> Connoisseurship/Art Collection Management
> Gallery Practices
> Introduction to Web Design
> Sales: The Art of the Deal
> Professional Framing/Matting
> Contemporary Art
> Digital Photography
> Photoshop
> Office Information Management

Potential Employers:

> Art galleries
> Museums

Available At:

Santa Fe Community College
6401 Richards Avenue, Santa Fe, NM 87508-4887
505/428-1501
http://www.sfccnm.edu/sfcc/pages/1052.html
Degrees available: Associate degree

For More Information:

Art Dealers Association of America
575 Madison Avenue, New York, NY 10022
212/940-8590
http://www.artdealers.org

Fine Art Dealers Association
PO Box D1, Carmel, CA 93921
http://www.fada.com

National Association of Schools of Art and Design
11250 Roger Bacon Drive, Suite 21, Reston, VA 20190-5248
703/437-0700
info@arts-accredit.org
http://nasad.arts-accredit.org

Gaming Industry

Casinos are found not just in Las Vegas and Atlantic City anymore; they are popping up all over the United States. Whether you love or hate casinos, it is clear that the gaming industry is playing an increasing role in the health of local economies across the United States. In addition to gambling entities on Native American reservations, commercial casinos can be found in Colorado, Illinois, Indiana, Iowa, Louisiana, Michigan, Mississippi, Missouri, Nevada, New Jersey, and South Dakota. Although educational requirements vary by casino, our nation's colleges are beginning to recognize the demand for training in "gambling-ology." Certificates and degrees are available in casino management, tribal gaming, and other areas.

Typical Courses:

> Introduction to Indian Gaming
> Introduction to Gaming Management
> Gaming Device Management
> Surveillance and Security
> Casino Industry Regulation
> Casino Resort Management Food and Beverage
> Marketing
> Mathematics and Statistics

Potential Employers:

> Commercial casinos
> Native American casinos

Available At:

The following list of gaming programs is not exhaustive. Check with academic institutions near you to determine if majors, minors, certificates, or concentrations are available in gaming.

Mohave Community College
1971 Jagerson Avenue, Kingman, AZ 86409
http://www.mohave.edu/pages/262.asp
Degrees available: Certificates

Commercial casinos are located in 11 states.

124

Morrisville State College
PO Box 901, Morrisville, NY 13408
http://www.morrisville.edu/Academics/Business/
Gaming_Casino/index.htm
Degrees available: Certificate, associate degree

Northeast Wisconsin Technical College
2740 West Mason Street, PO Box 19042, Green Bay, WI 54307
http://www.nwtc.tec.wi.us
and
http://www.nwtc.tec.wi.us/Programs/
PDFs05-06/Native_American_Gaming-Casino_Management.pdf
Degrees available: Associate degree

San Diego State University
College of Extended Studies
5250 Campanile Drive, San Diego, CA 92182-1925
http://www.ces.sdsu.edu/casino.html
Degrees available: Certificate

Sisseton Wahpeton College
Agency Village Box 689, Sisseton, SD 57262
http://www.swc.tc/Academic%20Programs%20Docs/
casinomgmt.pdf
and
http://www.swc.tc/Academic%20Programs%20Docs/
gamingcert.pdf
Degrees available: Certificate, associate degree

Did You Know?

According to the American Gaming Association , the top 10 casino markets (in descending order) by revenue in 2004 were: Las Vegas Strip, NV; Atlantic City, NJ; Chicagoland, IN/IL; Connecticut (Indian); Tunica/Lula, MS; Detroit, MI; Biloxi/Gulfport, MS; Reno/Sparks, NV; Lawrenceburg/Rising Sun/Elizabeth/Vevay, IN; and St. Louis, MO/IL.

Tulane University
A. B. Freeman School of Business
125 Gibson Hall, New Orleans, LA 70118
504/865-5555
choose@tulane.edu
http://www.tulane.edu/~choose/new_page_8.htm
Degrees available: Associate degree

For More Information:

American Gaming Association
555 13th Street, NW, Suite 1010 East, Washington, DC 20004-1109
202/637-6500
http://www.americangaming.org

National Indian Gaming Association
224 2nd Street, SE, Washington, DC 20003
202/546-7711
info@indiangaming.org
http://www.indiangaming.org

Geographic Information Systems

Geographic information systems technology is a computer-based system that allows users to gather any type of information about the Earth that has a spatial component. This information is used in planning and carrying out of countless tasks, from implementing precision farming; setting up branches or ATMs for banks; creating routes for emergency response teams; designing, building, and operating a public transportation system; assessing the environmental impact of a major construction project; mapping the outbreak of an infectious disease; assessing climate change; designing a cellular phone network; and managing entire cities. Students who are successful in this field have an interest in geography, computer science, statistics, and computers.

Typical Courses:

> Introduction to Geographic Information Systems (GIS)
> Geography
> Computer Information Systems
> Mathematics
> Statistics
> Acquiring GIS Data
> Elements of Cartography
> Elements of Photogrammetry
> GIS Software
> Advanced GIS Applications

Potential Employers:

> Government agencies such as the United States Geological Survey and the United States Forest Service
> Construction industry
> Banking industry
> Health care industry
> Transportation industry
> Insurance industry
> Energy industries
> Marketing research firms
> Telecommunications companies

> Environmental organizations
> Map and database publishers
> Timber companies
> Utilities

Available At:

The following list of geographic information systems programs is not exhaustive. Visit the Urban and Regional Information Systems Association's website, http://www.urisa.org/Career_center/college_certif_programs.htm, for more programs.

Columbus State Community College
PO Box 1609, Columbus, OH 43216-1609
800/621-6407
http://www.cscc.edu/DOCS/giscurr.htm
Degrees available: Certificate, associate degree

Moorpark College
7075 Campus Road, Moorpark, CA 93021
805/378-1459
http://www.moorparkcollege.edu/catalog
Degrees available: Associate degree

New Hampshire Community Technical College-Berlin
2020 Riverside Drive, Berlin, NH 03570
603/752-1113, ext. 2002
http://www.berlin.nhctc.edu/courses/gis.html
Degrees available: Associate degree

San Jacinto College-Central Campus
8060 Spencer Highway, Pasadena, TX 77505
281/476-1813
http://www.sjcd.edu/program/geographic_info.html
Degrees available: Certificate, associate degree

Texas State Technical College-Waco
Department of Geospatial Technology
3801 Campus Drive, Waco, TX 76705
254/867-4874
http://www.waco.tstc.edu/gis/index.php
Degrees available: Certificate, associate degrees

For More Information:

American Society for Photogrammetry and Remote Sensing
5410 Grosvenor Lane, Suite 210, Bethesda, MD 20814-2160
301/493-0290
http://www.asprs.org/career

Association of American Geographers
1710 16th Street, NW, Washington, DC 20009-3198
202/234-1450
http://www.aag.org

Urban and Regional Information Systems Association
1460 Renaissance Drive, Suite 305, Park Ridge, IL 60068
847/824-6300
info@urisa.org
http://www.urisa.org

GIS.com
http://www.gis.com

Goldsmithing/Jewelry Design

If you are good with your hands, have a creative disposition, and have excellent hand-eye coordination, than a career as a goldsmith/jewelry designer may be in your future. Flathead Valley Community College in Kalispell, Montana, offers a bench certificate in goldsmithing, a one-year certificate in ArtCam CAD/CAM, and an associate degree in professional goldsmithing. Students in these programs learn the latest techniques in jewelry repair, stone setting, wax modeling/casting, forging, and CAD/CAM design. Graduates can work as self-employed artisans, displaying their work in galleries, at art shows, and in other settings. Others go on to work for jewelry stores or manufacturers.

Typical Courses:

> Drawing
> Jewelry and Metalsmithing
> Forging and Smithing
> 3D Jewelry Design and Modeling
> Wax Modeling and Casting
> Surface Embellishments
> Marketing
> Entrepreneurship
> Business Mathematics
> Jewelry Repair

Potential Employers:

> Jewelry stores
> Jewelry manufacturing companies
> Self-employment

Available At:

Flathead Valley Community College-Kalispell Campus
777 Grandview Drive, Kalispell, MT 59901
http://www.fvcc.edu/academics/catalog/2005/
ProfessionalGoldsmithing.shtml
and
http://www.fvcc.edu/academics/catalog/2005/Goldsmithing.shtml
and
http://www.fvcc.edu/academics/catalog/2005/
3DJewelryComputerDesignandProductionOneYea.shtml
Degrees available: Certificates, associate degree

For More Information:

Jewelers of America
52 Vanderbilt Avenue, 19th Floor, New York, NY 10017
800/223-0673
info@jewelers.org
http://www.jewelers.org

Manufacturing Jewelers and Suppliers of America
45 Royal Little Drive, Providence, RI 02904
800/444-6572
mjsa@mjsainc.com
http://mjsa.polygon.net

Health Information Management

If you are interested in playing an integral role in the health care field, with little to no patient care involvement, you may be a perfect candidate for a career in health information management. *Health information technicians* are responsible for keeping detailed records of patient care. They document or code patient histories, procedures, and treatment outcomes. *Medical transcriptionists* listen to recordings made by physicians and transcribe them into special formats. It is even possible to work as a transcriptionist from a home-based business. Others work as *medical coders* who assign codes to patient information. This coded information is used by insurance companies in the processing of claims. Additional administrative office work may also be performed by the health information technician. Although the work is administrative in nature, these professionals must have a background in the health sciences since accuracy and understanding of medical terminology is exceptionally important in these careers. They must translate physician notes, spot any inconsistencies, and avoid errors at all costs. Being detailed oriented is a must for a career in health information management. The U.S. Department of Labor estimates that employment for health information technicians is expected to grow at a much faster than average rate through 2014.

Typical Courses:

> Human Anatomy, Physiology, and Pathology
> Health Data Management
> Biomedical Terminology
> Introduction to Pharmacology

Did You Know?

Approximately 159,000 medical records and health information technicians are employed in the United States, according to the U.S. Department of Labor.

> Clinical Classification Systems
> Clinical Data Analysis
> Legal and Qualitative Aspects of Health Information
> Principles of Management
> Medical Reimbursement
> Medical Transcription Practicum
> Medical Coding Practicum

Potential Employers:

> Hospitals
> Outpatient clinics
> Surgical centers
> Nursing homes
> Health care facilities
> Home-based self-employment

Available At:

132

The following list of colleges that offer certificates and degrees in health information management is not exhaustive. Visit the American Health Information Management Association's website, http://www.ahima.org/careers/college_search/search.asp for a list of other programs accredited and approved by the Association.

College of DuPage
Department of Health Information Technology
425 Fawell Boulevard, Glen Ellyn, IL 60137
http://www.cod.edu/academic/acadprog/occ_voc/HealthIn.htm
Degrees available: Certificates, associate degree

Columbus State Community College
PO Box 1609, Columbus, OH 43216-1609
800/621-6407
http://www.cscc.edu/DOCS/hlthcurr.htm
Degrees available: Certificates, associate degree

Community College of Allegheny County-Allegheny Campus
808 Ridge Avenue, Pittsburgh, PA 15212-6097
412/237-2511
http://www.ccac.edu/default.aspx?id=138717
and
http://www.ccac.edu/default.aspx?id=138728
Degrees available: Certificate, associate degree

Community College of Philadelphia
1700 Spring Garden Street, Philadelphia, PA 19130
http://www.ccp.edu/site/academic/degrees/health_information.php
Degrees available: Associate degree

Cuyahoga Community College-Metro Campus
2900 Community College Avenue, Cleveland, OH 44115
216/987-4247
http://www.tri-c.edu/HIM/default.htm
Degrees available: Certificate, associate degree

Did You Know?

Medical transcriptionists earned salaries that ranged from less than $20,360 to $40,880 or more in November 2004, according to the U.S. Department of Labor. Medical transcriptionists employed in general medical and surgical hospitals earned mean annual salaries of $29,860.

133

Erie Community College-North Campus
Division of Allied Health
6205 Main Street, Williamsville, NY 14221
http://www.ecc.edu/academics/healthinfo.asp
Degrees available: Associate degree

Florida Community College at Jacksonville
501 West State Street, Jacksonville, FL 32202
904/766-6663
http://www.fccj.org/prospective/programs/healthcare/index.html
Degrees available: Diploma, associate degree

Hudson Valley Community College
80 Vandenburgh Avenue, Troy, NY 12180
518/629-7225
business@hvcc.edu
https://www.hvcc.edu/bus/hit/index.html
Degrees available: Certificate, associate degree

Kirkwood Community College
Health Science Department
6301 Kirkwood Boulevard, SW, 221 Linn Hall
Cedar Rapids, IA 52404
800/332-2055
info@kirkwood.cc.ia.us
http://www.kirkwood.edu/site/index.php?t=2&d=2&p=58
Degrees available: Diploma, associate degree

Montgomery College-Rockville Campus
51 Mannakee Street, Rockville, MD 20850
301/562-5519
http://www.mc.cc.md.us/hit
Degrees available: Certificate, associate degree

National Park Community College
101 College Drive, Hot Springs National Park, AR 71913
501/760-4294
http://www.npcc.edu/Academics/health_sciences_hit.htm
Degrees available: Certificates, associate degree

San Jacinto College-North Campus
5800 Uvalde Road, S212, Houston, TX 77049
281/459-7117
http://www.sjcd.edu/program/health_mis.html
Degrees available: Certificate, associate degree

Other colleges that offer certificates and degrees in health information management include:

Chemeketa Community College
4000 Lancaster Drive Northeast, PO Box 14007, Salem, OR 97309
http://www.chemeketa.edu/exploring/areas/careers/business.html
Degrees available: Certificate, associate degree

Community College of Denver
PO Box 173363, Campus Box 250, Denver, CO 80217-3363
http://www.ccd.edu
Degrees available: Certificates

Flathead Valley Community College-Kalispell Campus
777 Grandview Drive, Kalispell, MT 59901
http://www.fvcc.edu/academics/catalog/2005/MedicalCoding.shtml
and
http://www.fvcc.edu/academics/catalog/2005/
MedicalTranscription.shtml
Degrees available: Certificates

Kilian Community College
300 East 6th Street, Sioux Falls, SD 57103-7020
http://www.kilian.edu/AcademicPrograms/MedicalCoding.htm
and
http://www.kilian.edu/AcademicPrograms/MedicalOfficePro.htm
and
http://www.kilian.edu/AcademicPrograms/MedicalTranscription.
htm
and
http://www.kilian.edu/AcademicPrograms/MedicalTranscriptionist.htm
Degrees available: Certificate, associate degree

Northeast Community College
801 East Benjamin Avenue, PO Box 469, Norfolk, NE 68702-0469
402/371-2020
http://www.northeastcollege.com/PS/PDF/Degree_Offerings/
Health_Info.pdf
Degrees available: Associate degree

North Idaho College
1000 West Garden Avenue, Coeur d' Alene, ID 83814
877/404-4536
http://www.nic.edu/programs/AppTech/MCA.htm
Degrees available: Associate degrees

Southern Maine Community College
2 Fort Road, South, Portland, ME 04106
207/741-5775
http://www.smccme.edu/catalog/2005-2006/
index.php?section=5&navid=103&docid=0
Degrees available: Associate degree

For More Information:

American Academy of Professional Coders
2480 South 3850 West, Suite B, Salt Lake City, UT 84120
info@aapc.com
800/626-2633
http://www.aapc.com

American Association for Medical Transcription
100 Sycamore Avenue, Modesto, CA 95354-0550
800/982-2182
aamt@aamt.org
http://www.aamt.org

American Health Information Management Association
233 North Michigan Avenue, Suite 2150, Chicago, IL 60601-5800
312/233-1100
info@ahima.org
http://www.ahima.org

MT Desk
http://www.mtdesk.com

Homeland Security/ Emergency Management

Since the terrorist attacks of September 11, 2001, the U.S. government has had the daunting task of protecting our nation from future attacks—whether on infrastructure such as bridges, power plants, and dams; our food and water supply; civilians; or other targets. In November 2002, Congress created the Department of Homeland Security (DHS) to protect our nation from terrorist threats. In response, two- and four-year colleges have developed or expanded curricula that aim to educate and train students to work for the DHS; other government agencies at the federal, state, and local level; and private security companies. Students in homeland security programs often have the opportunity to pursue a variety of tracks, including aviation safety and security, emergency medical services management, computer security, forensic sciences, public health and emergency management, telecommunications and national security, information security management, and computer fraud investigations. Students in each track take common core courses as well as general studies courses.

Typical Courses:

> Aviation Security
> Airline Transport Security
> Risk Management
> Terrorism, Counter Terrorism, and Terrorism Response
> Disaster Preparedness and Emergency Systems
> Emergency Response to Terrorism
> Cyberterrorism

Potential Employers:

> State and local government agencies
> Federal government agencies (such as the Department of Homeland Security; the Bureau of Alcohol, Tobacco, Firearms, and Explosives; and the Federal Bureau of Investigation)
> Private security companies
> Hospitals
> Airports
> Amusement parks

> Cruise industry
> Rail transportation industry

Available At:

Many community colleges are in the process of developing programs in homeland security. Some schools offer a concentration in homeland security, usually within their criminal justice departments. Check with institutions near you to determine if certificates, majors, minors, or concentrations are available in homeland security. You can also visit http://www.training.fema.gov/EMIWeb/edu/collegelist/ DHSASSOCIATE for a short list of programs.

Community College of Southern Nevada (multiple campuses)
admrec@ccsn.nevada.edu
http://www.ccsn.edu
Degrees available: Associate degree

Corinthian Colleges
888/741-4271
http://www.cci.edu
Degrees available: Associate degree, bachelor's degree
Note: Corinthian Colleges, Inc., one of the largest postsecondary education companies in North America, operating 96 colleges in 24 states in the U.S. and 33 colleges in seven provinces in Canada, offers degrees in Homeland Security at many of its campuses. Visit the organization's website for further information.

Fairmont State Community and Technical College
School of Health and Human Services
Homeland Security Program
315 Hardway Hall, Fairmont, WV 26554
304/367-4678
http://www.fairmontstate.edu/academics/
CTC_HomelandSecurity/default.asp
Degrees available: Associate degree

Pikes Peak Community College
5675 South Academy Boulevard, Colorado Springs, CO 80906
800/456-6847
http://www.ppcc.cccoes.edu/CatalogSchedule/Programs/
Programs.cfm?Program=HoSp
Degrees available: Associate degree

137

For More Information:

National Academic Consortium for Homeland Security
Program for International and Homeland Security
The Ohio State University
1501 Neil Avenue, Mershon Center, Columbus, OH 43201
614/688-3420
NACHS@osu.edu
http://homelandsecurity.osu.edu/NACHS

U.S. Department of Homeland Security
Washington, DC 20528
202/282-8000
http://www.dhs.gov/dhspublic

Interview: Les Boggess

Fairmont State Community and Technical College in Fairmont, West Virginia, created one of the first associate degree programs in homeland security in the United States. The editors of *They Teach That in Community College!?* discussed the program with Les Boggess, Program Coordinator.

Q. Please briefly describe your program.

A. Our program is a multitrack degree program. A student can choose to follow either criminal justice, aviation, safety, or emergency medical services tracks. There are common core classes and specific courses for the track, as well as general studies courses. At present, we are offering a two-year associate degree.

Q. What types of students enter your program? What are their career goals and interests?

A. Frequently, students who enroll in this program are also enrolled in the four-year Criminal Justice program. They can count the associate degree as their minor for criminal justice. Other students are planning a career strictly in homeland security, and major only in that field.

Q. What types of careers will students be able to work in upon completion of their degree?

A. There are all sorts of employment opportunities opening up at the federal level, but also in the private sector and among city, local, and county government agencies.

Q. What personal qualities should students have to be successful in your program and in their post-college career?

A. Motivation, a desire to help others and be part of a team, academic discipline, and a clean police record. They must also possess integrity, be a U.S. citizen, and be able to pass a background check.

Q. Does your school have any type of relationship with the Department of Homeland Security (DHS)?

A. Yes. I attended seminars this summer with the Department of Homeland Security and maintain close contact with representatives of the DHS. Our program is listed on the website maintained at http://www.training.fema.gov/EMIWeb/edu/ collegelist/dhsassociate.

Q. Is the DHS a logical career path for graduates of your program?

A. Yes. There will be many jobs created in the next few years that do not currently exist. Although it is unfortunate that these jobs are necessary, political reality suggests that we must of necessity become a more careful society, guarding against attacks both from outside and from within.

Hospitality Management

Many students get their introduction into the hospitality field when they work part-time jobs waiting tables or serving coffee to make a little extra money while they are in school. What many do not consider is that there are a whole plethora of careers in this field that do not require you to ask, "Would you like fries with that?" This consumer-driven field offers sales, marketing, and customer service opportunities with restaurants, hotels, and lodging facilities. Additionally, meeting planners and catering companies work together to create successful events for fundraisers, weddings, and corporate events in hotel ballrooms or large restaurants. Managerial roles also exist—you may aspire to become a district manager of a chain of restaurants or the CEO of a multinational hotel chain. You may even possess an entrepreneurial sprit and dream of opening your own business. The possibilities in the hospitality industry are endless, and a degree in hospitality management prepares students for what they will face when entering the job market in this competitive field.

Typical Courses:

> Food and Beverage Management
> Marketing & Sales in the Hospitality Industry
> Event, Meeting, and Convention Planning
> Food and Beverage Cost Control
> Catering and Banquets
> Foodservice Sanitation
> Hotel Front Office Procedures
> Hotel Administration
> Legal Issues for the Hospitality Industry
> Human Resources Management

Potential Employers:

> Restaurants
> Hotels
> Convention bureaus
> Meeting planning agencies
> Food regulatory agencies
> Catering companies
> Self-employment

Available At:

The following list of hospitality management programs is not exhaustive. Check with academic institutions near you to determine if majors, minors, certificates, or concentrations are available in hospitality management.

Brevard Community College
1519 Clearlake Road, Cocoa, FL 32922
321/632-1111
http://www.brevard.cc.fl.us
Degrees available: Associate degree

Broward Community College
111 East Las Olas Boulevard, Fort Lauderdale, FL 33301
954/201-7400
http://www.broward.edu/ext/ProgramOverview.jsp?A015
Degrees available: Associate degrees

Bunker Hill Community College
250 New Rutherford Avenue, Boston, MA 02129-2925
617/228/2422
http://www.bhcc.mass.edu
Degrees available: Certificate, associate degree

Cincinnati State Technical and Community College
3520 Central Parkway, Cincinnati, OH 45223
513/861-7700
http://www.cinstate.cc.oh.us/FutureStudent/Academics/
AcademicDivisions/BusinessTechnologies/BTDPrograms.htm
Degrees available: Associate degree

College of DuPage
425 Fawell Boulevard, Glen Ellyn, IL 60137-6599
630/942-2800
http://www.cod.edu/hospitalityadministration
and
http://www.cod.edu/academic/acadprog/occ_voc/Hotl_Occ.htm
Degrees available: Certificates, associate degrees (multiple)

College of Southern Idaho
315 Falls Avenue, PO Box 1238, Evergreen Building
Twin Falls, ID 83303-1238
800/680-0274, ext. 6407
info@csi.edu
http://www.csi.edu/l4.asp?hospitality
Degrees available: Associate degree

Community College of Baltimore County-Catonsville Campus
Business Department
800 South Rolling Road, Baltimore, MD 21228
410/455-6991
http://www.ccbcmd.edu/bsswe/hospitality/index.html
Degrees available: Certificates, associate degree

Community College of Philadelphia
1700 Spring Garden Street, Philadelphia, PA 19130
215/751-8010
http://www.ccp.edu/site/academic/degrees/
hospitality_management.php
Degrees available: Associate degree

Erie Community College-North Campus
6205 Main Street, Williamsville, NY 14221
716/634-0800
http://www.ecc.edu/academics/hotelmanage.asp
Degrees available: Associate degree

Ivy Tech Community College of Indiana (multiple campuses)
50 West Fall Creek Parkway North Drive, Indianapolis, IN 46208
888/489-5463
http://www.ivytech.edu/programs/hos
Degrees available: Certificate, associate degree

J. Sargeant Reynolds Community College
PO Box 85622, Richmond, VA 23285-5622
804/371-3000
http://www.jsr.vccs.edu/curriculum/programs/
Hospitality%20ManagementAAS.htm
Degrees available: Associate degree

Kirkwood Community College
Business and Information Technology Department
6301 Kirkwood Boulevard SW, Cedar Rapids, IA 52404
800/363-2220
info@kirkwood.cc.ia.us
http://www.kirkwood.edu/site/index.php?d=135&p=1181&t=2
Degrees available: Associate degree

Lansing Community College
PO Box 40010, Lansing, MI 48901-7210
800/644-4522
welcome@lcc.edu
http://www.lcc.edu/business/hosp_tourism
Degrees available: Associate degrees (multiple)

Monroe Community College-Brighton Campus
1000 East Henrietta Road, Rochester, NY 14623
585/292-2000
http://www.monroecc.edu/etsdbs/MCCatPub.nsf/
AcademicPrograms?OpenPage
Degrees available: Certificate, associate degree

Montgomery College-Rockville Campus
Hospitality Management Department
51 Mannakee Street, Technical Center, Suite 220
Rockville, MD 20850
301/279-5000
http://www.montgomerycollege.edu/Departments/hospitality
Degrees available: Certificates, associate degree

Morrisville State College
PO Box 901, Morrisville, NY 13408
800/258-0111
http://www.morrisville.edu/Academics/Business/hospitalitytech/index.htm
Degrees available: Associate degrees

Moraine Valley Community College
9000 West College Parkway, Palos Hills, IL 60465-0937
708/974-4300
http://www.morainevalley.edu/programs/program_list.htm
Degrees available: Certificates, associate degrees

New Hampshire Community Technical College-Concord
31 College Drive, Concord, NH 03301-7412
603/271-6484
info@nhti.edu
http://nhti.edu/academics/academicprograms/deghtladmin.html
and
http://nhti.edu/academics/academicprograms/certhoteladmin.html
Degrees available: Certificate, associate degree

Oakland Community College
27055 Orchard Lake Road, Farmington Hills, MI 48334-4579
248/522-3710
http://www.oaklandcc.edu/FutureStudents/DegreePrograms.asp
Degrees available: Certificate, associate degree (multiple)
Hospitality: Hotel/Restaurant

Palm Beach Community College
4200 Congress Avenue, Lake Worth, FL 33461
561/868-3353
http://www.pbcc.edu/programs/department.asp?dept_id=35
Degrees available: Associate degree

Pima County Community College
4905 East Broadway Boulevard, Tucson, AZ 85709-1010
800/860-7462
infocenter@pima.edu
http://www.pima.edu/program/hotel-restaurant/index.shtml
Degrees available: Associate degree

Southern Maine Community College
2 Fort Road, South Portland, ME 04106
207/741-5500
http://www.smccme.edu
Degrees available: Associate degree

Tidewater Community College
PO Box 9000, Norfolk, VA 23509-9000
757/822-1110
http://www.tcc.edu/academics/programs/curr/aas/index.htm
Degrees available: Associate degrees

Valencia Community College
PO Box 3028, Orlando, FL 32802
407/299-5000
http://www.valencia.cc.fl.us/hospitality
Degrees available: Associate degrees

For More Information:

**Educational Institute of the
American Hotel and Lodging Association**
800 North Magnolia Avenue, Suite 1800, Orlando, FL 32803
800/752-4567
info@ei-ahla.org
http://www.ei-ahla.org

**International Council on Hotel,
Restaurant and Institutional Education**
2810 North Parham, Suite 230, Richmond, VA 23294
804/346-4800
http://chrie.org

Landmark College

Landmark College in Putney, Vermont, is one of two colleges in the United States that offers an educational program designed exclusively for students with dyslexia, attention deficit hyperactivity disorder (ADHD), or other specific learning disabilities (LDs). The College offers an associate of arts degree in general studies that prepares students to transfer to bachelor's degree programs at four-year colleges and universities. It also offers an associate of arts degree in business studies. Landmark students can participate in six intercollegiate sports, including basketball, baseball, soccer, softball, cross-country, and golf. The College's Academic Resource Center has 30,000+ volumes, including an extensive LD/ADHD collection. Additionally, study abroad options are available in England, Ireland, Greece, Italy, and Spain.

Available Fields of Study:

> General Studies
> Business Studies

For More Information:

Landmark College
River Road South, Putney, VT 05346
802/387-6718
http://www.landmark.edu
Degrees available: Associate degree

Interview: Rob Bahny

The editors of *They Teach That in Community College!?* spoke with Rob Bahny, Associate Director of Admissions & Financial Aid at Landmark College, about his interesting college.

Q. Please briefly describe Landmark and the types of students it serves.

A. Landmark College is a small, residential, liberal arts college established in 1983 that offers associate degrees. Landmark exclusively serves students with ADHD and/or learning disabilities (dyslexia, disgraphia, reading disorder, disorder of written expression, etc.). We have 420 students and we are located in Putney, Vermont, which is a small town in the Connecticut River Valley in the southern part of the state. [By car], we are two hours from Boston, four hours from New York City, and three hours from Burlington, Vermont.

Q. What personal qualities should a student have to be successful at Landmark?

A. We are looking for students who are bright, mature, and motivated and who are not only interested in earning an associate degree, but who also have the desire to become more effective learners. A student coming to Landmark must be prepared to try many new things. Our professors are well versed in many different learning strategies, and they will ask students to try these strategies on a regular basis.

Q. What types of four-year colleges do students transfer to after earning their associate degrees?

A. Students go to any number of schools after Landmark. Many of our students continue at small, liberal arts colleges, some go to Ivy League schools, and some have gone overseas to continue their education. Some of our more popular destinations include: University of Vermont, University of Denver, American University, Bentley College, Savannah College of Art and Design, College of Santa Fe, and Sarah Lawrence College. A complete list of these colleges is available at www. landmark.edu/admissions/power_of_degree.html#colleges.

Q. What summer opportunities are available at your school?

A. Landmark has three different summer programs. We have a three-week program for current high school students where they take classes in areas such as writing, study skills, communications, or math. There is a High School to College Transition program that is two weeks long and is intended to help close the gap between high school and college.

Also, we have a four-week College Skills program for current college students in addition to credit courses for current Landmark students. This is intended to help college students who are struggling. The program aims to improve their skills in areas such as writing, communications, project/time management, etc.

All of these programs are intended for proactive and motivated students who can acknowledge that they need to improve their academic skills so that they can become better students. Each program is organized to serve the distinct and unique educational needs of students at that particular stage of their educational career.

Q. What does the future hold for Landmark?

A. The future for Landmark continues to look very bright. As more and more people become aware of our college and the uniqueness of what we do through our stepped-up recruiting efforts, we see our enrollment continuing to grow. We are able to become more selective and admit a student body that will be able to gain the most from our associate degree programs. Our student body continues to become more diverse, and our students continue to bring many different and exciting talents to our campus community.

147

Landscape Design

If you've ever admired a well-designed and beautiful park, playground, garden, college or high school campus, country club, shopping center, zoo, or even skate park, then you've seen the work of a landscape architect firsthand. Landscape architects analyze, plan, design, and manage outdoor spaces. They use computer-aided design software, computer mapping systems, and other tools to design outdoor spaces that not only serve practical needs, but also protect the environment. Employment prospects for landscape architects are excellent. The U.S. Department of Labor predicts that the career of landscape architect will grow faster than the average for all occupations through 2014. Approximately 30,000 landscape architects are employed in the United States, according to the American Society of Landscape Architects. For the best jobs in the industry, you will need to go on and earn a bachelor's or master's degree in the field.

Typical Courses:

> Landscape Design Methods
> Plans and Design
> Landscape Graphics
> Regional Landscape History
> Landscape Construction
> The Urban Landscape
> World Gardens
> Landscape Architectural Practice
> Drawing the Landscape

Potential Employers:

> Consulting firms
> Public agencies
> Landscape construction and nursery companies
> National Park Service
> U.S. Forest Service
> Bureau of Land Management
> Other governmental agencies
> Self-employment

Available At:

This list of schools offering programs in landscape design is not exhaustive. Check with academic institutions near you to determine if majors, minors, certificates, or concentrations are available in landscape design.

Delaware Technical and Community College-Owens Campus
PO Box 610, Georgetown, DE 19947
302/855-5929
http://www.dtcc.edu/programs
Degrees available: Certificate

Morrisville State College
Horticulture Department
PO Box 901, Morrisville, NY 13408
800/258-0111
http://www.morrisville.edu/Academics/Ag_NRC/Horticulture/
HTML/landscapearch.htm
Degrees available: Associate degree

New Hampshire Technical Institute
31 College Drive, Concord, NH 03301-7412
603/271-7122
info@nhti.edu
http://www.nhti.edu/academics/academicprograms/
certlanddesign.html
Degrees available: Certificate

Northern Virginia Community College
4001 Wakefield Chapel Road, Brault Building, Annandale, VA 22003
703/323-3000
http://www.nvcc.vccs.edu/curcatalog/programs/hortec1.htm
Degrees available: Associate degree

Did You Know?

If you like being your own boss, then a career in landscape architecture might be for you. According to the U.S. Department of Labor, more than 26 percent of all landscape designers are self-employed. That's more than three times the average for professionals in all fields.

Oakland Community College
2480 Opdyke Road, Bloomfield Hills, MI 48304
248/341-2000
http://www.oaklandcc.edu/FutureStudents/DegreePrograms.asp
Degrees available: Associate degree

Portland Community College
Rock Creek Campus
17705 Northwest Springville Road, Building 7, Room 202
Portland, OR 97229
503/614-7257
http://www.pcc.edu/academics/index.cfm/63,html
Degrees available: Certificates, associate degree

Tallahassee Community College
Division of Technology and Professional Programs
444 Appleyard Drive, Tallahassee, FL 32304
850/201-8352
http://www.tcc.fl.edu/dept/tpp/programs/aa_articulations/
aa_art_land_design.htm
Degrees available: Associate degree

For More Information:

American Society of Landscape Architects
636 Eye Street, NW, Washington, DC 20001-3736
202/898-2444
http://www.asla.org

LAprofession.org
http://www.laprofession.org

Legal Nurse Consultant

If you are interested in both nursing and the law, then you might be interested in learning more about the career of *legal nurse consultant.* Legal nurse consultants are registered nurses who have considerable experience and knowledge of the health care and legal industries. They use this knowledge to assist lawyers in health care-related cases. According to the American Association of Legal Nurse Consultants, the leading professional organization for the profession, legal nurse consultants offer support to the law profession in the following practice areas: personal injury, product liability, medical malpractice, workers' compensation, toxic torts, risk management, medical licensure investigation, criminal law, elder law, and fraud and abuse-compliance.

Typical Courses:

> Fundamentals of Law
> Principles of Legal Nurse Consulting
> Legal Research and Writing
> Computer Assisted Legal Research
> Paralegalism and Legal Procedure
> Elder Law
> Health Law
> Rules of Evidence
> Personal Injury and Product Liability
> Medical Ethics

Potential Employers:

> Law firms
> Insurance companies
> Corporations—such as pharmaceutical companies and medical equipment manufacturers—that deal with health-related products or services
> Government agencies
> Hospitals (in risk management departments)
> Forensic environments
> Consulting firms
> Health management organizations

Available At:

Bergen Community College
400 Paramus Road, Paramus, NJ 07652
201/447-7195
http://www.bergen.edu/ecatalog/
programview.asp?program.cbn=15&semester.rm=1
Degrees available: Associate degree

For More Information:

American Association of Legal Nurse Consultants
401 North Michigan Avenue, Chicago, IL 60611
877/402-2562
info@aalnc.org
http://www.aalnc.org

Maritime Technology

Marine services technicians maintain and repair marine vessels of all sizes, from motorboats to yachts to industrial fishing vessels. Educational programs are provided at community colleges throughout the United States, but most often in coastal areas or those located near other large bodies of water. Some maritime technology programs are general in nature, providing students with basic instruction in the repair of internal combustion engines and drive systems, electronics, and other maritime technology, as well as basic coursework in marina operations, boat safety, and boat handling. Others offer specialized training in boat design, boatbuilding, marine composites, marine mechanics, and other areas. There are 10,000 marine retailers in the United States and 1,500 boatyards that repair hulls and engines, according to *Boating Industry* magazine.

Typical Courses:

> Marine Technician Fundamentals
> Fundamentals of Electricity and Electronics
> Outboard Engine Service
> Inboard Engine Service
> Marine Drive Systems and Service
> Introduction to Boat Building
> Marine Gas & Diesel Systems
> Marine Hydraulics
> Fiberglass Technology and Repair
> Boat Handling
> Boatshop Safety
> Marina Operations

Potential Employers:

> Boat retailers
> Boatyards
> Boat repair shops
> Boat engine manufacturers
> Marinas
> Resorts
> State and federal agencies
> Businesses that are associated with marine science and research

Available At:

The following list of maritime technology programs is not exhaustive. Check with academic institutions near you to determine if majors, minors, certificates, or concentrations are available in maritime technology.

Cecil Community College
One Seahawk Drive, North East, MD 21901
http://www.cecilcc.edu/programs/programs-05-07/
transportation-logistics/yacht-design.asp
Degrees available: Certificate, associate degree

Honolulu Community College-University of Hawaii-
874 Dillingham Boulevard, Honolulu, HI 96817
http://tech.honolulu.hawaii.edu/marr/index.html
Degrees available: Associate degree

Kingsborough Community College-City University of New York
2001 Oriental Boulevard, Brooklyn, NY 11235
http://www.kingsborough.edu/apdegree/KCCMARIN.HTM
Degrees available: Associate degree

New Hampshire Community Technical College-Laconia
379 Belmont Road, Laconia, NH 03246
http://www.laconia.nhctc.edu
Degrees available: Certificate, associate degree

Northwest School of Wooden Boatbuilding
42 North Water Street, Port Hadlock, WA 98339
360/385-4948
http://www.nwboatschool.org
Degrees available: Diplomas, associate degrees

Washington County Community College-Calais Campus
One College Drive, Calais, ME 04619
http://www.wccc.me.edu/amtb.html
and
http://www.wccc.me.edu/dbt.html
and
http://www.wccc.me.edu/cmc.html
and
http://www.wccc.me.edu/cmm.html
and
Degrees available: Certificates, diploma, associate degree

For More Information:

National Marine Electronics Association
7 Riggs Avenue, Severna Park, MD 21146
http://www.nmea.org

Massage Therapy

Although not new, the field of massage therapy has steadily gained in popularity in recent years. Using soft-tissue manipulation techniques, massage therapists are able to provide medical benefits to their clients, treating disorders of the human body or helping them recover from injuries. Or massage therapists may simply promote relaxation or provide an energizing experience for their clients, depending upon the goal of the massage. Students enrolling in an accredited massage therapy program will likely take a survey of general massage therapy classes, then choose electives depending on which areas of massage therapy they wish to specialize in—reflexology, shiatsu, Swedish massage, and deep tissue massage are just a few of the options. Massage techniques are also geared towards different populations, such as sports massage for athletes, or massage specifically for infants, pregnant women, or the geriatric population. Because many therapists are self-employed, they need to know about the business and legal considerations of the career, and some massage therapy programs also offer classes to address those aspects of the profession. According to the U.S. Department of Labor, the need for massage therapists is likely to grow faster than average—providing a perfect opportunity for students who want a "hands-on" career, would like to help others, and desire the opportunity for self-employment.

Typical Courses:

> Introduction to Massage
> Massage Anatomy & Physiology
> Massage Techniques
> Massage Law and Business Principles
> Medical Ethics
> Massage Practicum
> Business Math
> Business Communications
> Special Topics in Massage
> Client Assessment

Potential Employers:

> Hospitals and clinics
> Chiropractor and doctor offices
> Wellness centers

> Fitness centers and salons
> Sports industry
> Corporate wellness programs
> Performing arts programs
> Private practice

Available At:

The following list of colleges that offer degrees in massage therapy is not exhaustive. Visit the following website for more programs: , http://massagetherapy.com/careers/training.php.

College of DuPage
Health, Social, and Behavioral Sciences Division
425 Fawell Boulevard, Glen Ellyn, IL 60137
http://www.cod.edu/academic/acadprog/occ_voc/TherMass.htm
Degrees available: Certificate, associate degree

Columbus State Community College
PO Box 1609, Columbus, OH 43216-1609
http://www.cscc.edu/DOCS/masscurr.htm
Degrees available: Certificate, associate degree

Community College of Allegheny County-Allegheny Campus
808 Ridge Avenue
Pittsburgh, PA 15212-6097
http://www.ccac.edu/default.aspx?id=138721
Degrees available: Certificate, associate degree

The Community College of Baltimore County
7201 Rossville Boulevard, CCBC Essex, J306, Baltimore, MD 21237
http://www.ccbcmd.edu/allied_health/massage_therapy.html
Degrees available: Associate degree

Community College of Denver
PO Box 173363, Campus Box 250, Denver, CO 80217-3363
http://www.ccd.edu/programs
Degrees available: Certificate

Community College of Vermont (multiple campuses)
inquire@ccv.edu
http://www.ccv.edu/massage
and
http://www.ccv.edu/massage-certificate.html
Degrees available: Certificate, associate degree

Cuyahoga Community College
Massotherapy Program
11000 Pleasant Valley Road, Parma, OH 44130
http://www.tri-c.edu/masso/default.htm
Degrees available: Associate degree

Florida Community College at Jacksonville
501 West State Street, Jacksonville, FL 32202
http://www.fccj.org/prospective/programs/data05_06/5700.html
Degrees available: Certificate

Ivy Tech Community College of Indiana-Fort Wayne Campus
3800 North Anthony Boulevard, Fort Wayne, IN 46805
http://www.ivytech.edu/programs/tma
Degrees available: Certificate, associate degree

Lansing Community College
PO Box 40010, Lansing, MI 48901-7210
welcome@lcc.edu
http://www.lcc.edu/health/massage
Degrees available: Certificate

Madison Area Technical College
3550 Anderson Street, Madison, WI 53704
http://matcmadison.edu/matc/ASP/showprogram.asp?ID=3026
Degrees available: Diploma

Monroe Community College-Brighton Campus
1000 East Henrietta Road, Rochester, NY 14623
http://www.monroecc.edu/etsdbs/MCCatPub.nsf/
AcademicPrograms?OpenPage
Degrees available: Associate degree

Moraine Valley Community College
9000 West College Parkway, Palos Hills, IL 60465-0937
http://www.morainevalley.edu/programs/
2005-2006/2005-2006_fall/1249_course.htm
Degrees available: Certificate

Morrisville State College
PO Box 901, Morrisville, NY 13408
http://www.morrisville.edu/Academics/Sci_Tech/nursing/html/
massagetherapy.htm
Degrees available: Associate degree

Oakland Community College
2480 Opdyke Road, Bloomfield Hills, MI 48304
http://www.oaklandcc.edu/FutureStudents/DegreePrograms.asp
Degrees available: Certificate, associate degree

Palm Beach Community College
4200 Congress Avenue, Lake Worth, FL 33461
561/862-4720
http://www.pbcc.edu/programs/programsheet.asp?id=88
Degrees available: Certificate

Pima County Community College-Northwest Campus
4905 East Broadway Boulevard, Tucson, AZ 85709-1010
520/206-2264
infocenter@pima.edu
http://www.pima.edu/program/therapeutic-massage/index.shtml
Degrees available: Certificate

Sanford-Brown College-St. Charles
100 Richmond Center Boulevard, St. Peters, MO 63376
636/949-2620
http://www.sbcstcharles.com/programs/massage-therapy.asp
Degrees available: Diploma

Williston State College
1410 University Avenue, PO Box 1326, Williston, ND 58802
888/863-9455
http://www.wsc.nodak.edu/academics/
career_tech%20programs/massage%20therapy/
massage%20therapy.htm
Degrees available: Certificate

For More Information:

American Massage Therapy Association
820 Davis Street, Suite 100, Evanston, IL 60201
847/864-0123
http://www.amtamassage.org

Associated Bodywork and Massage Professionals
1271 Sugarbush Drive, Evergreen, CO 80439-9766
800/458-2267
expectmore@abmp.com
http://www.abmp.com or http://www.massagetherapy.com

Interview: Theodora Welsh

Theodora Welsh is a certified massage therapist and the program coordinator for the School of Health Professions'massage therapy program at the Community College of Baltimore County-Essex in Baltimore, Maryland. She discussed the program and the education of students in this field with the editors of *They Teach That in Community College!?*

Q. Please tell us about your program.

A. The program is designed to prepare students to work as professional massage therapists in a variety of health settings and equip them with the additional skills required to be a holistically trained member of allied health and integrative medicine teams. Upon completion, the successful graduate will be prepared to immediately apply for national certification. Once they have obtained their certification, they may then apply to The State Board of Chiropractic Examiners for Maryland state licensure.

Q. What high school subjects/activities should students focus on to be successful in this major?

A. Successful therapists possess an extensive knowledge of human anatomy and physiology, creativity, critical thinking, and good communication and assessment skills. High school students should seek out classes that will foster these types of learning experiences.

159

Q. What types of internships are provided by your program?

A. The program houses a clinic in which Level II (Deep Tissue) and III (Advanced) students are required to participate, thus providing them real world experience before graduating. Level III students are also required to participate in a clinical experience through an established partnership with Franklin Square Medical Center in their Outpatient Oncology Clinic. Under the supervision of a preceptor, students provide massage to patients. This partnership is a very strong and profound learning experience for all involved.

Q. How will the field change in the future?

A. Massage will continue to grow in popularity and as research continues to document the therapeutic benefits of massage, this complimentary approach will become a natural extension of health care. Corporations, integrative heath care, and individuals have become more health conscious and recognize the value of massage therapy. After all, massage touches the "whole" person—body, mind, and spirit.

Motorsport Engineering

Are you a fan of auto racing? Do you like designing and building things? If so, the Motorsport Technology Program at Alfred State College may help you put the pedal to the metal when it comes to preparing for a career in motorsport engineering. Graduates of the program work as drive line specialists, tune-up specialists, crew foremen, chassis specialists, pit crew members, engine builders, and high-performance motorsports technicians. Program facilities include seven large repair shops and a newly renovated motorsports complex.

Typical Courses:

> Introduction to Motorsports
> Automotive Welding
> Brakes, Steering, and Suspension Systems
> Automotive Basic Electronics & Component Overhaul
> Tune Up, Electronic Engine Controls & Electrical Diagnosis
> Engine Service
> Motorsports Fabrication
> Racing Suspension Dynamics
> High Performance Tune-Up/Electronics
> High Performance Engine Building
> Motorsports Aerodynamics
> High Performance Steering/Brakes/Chassis

Potential Employers:

> Racing teams
> Automobile manufacturers
> NASCAR
> World of Outlaws
> Hot rod shops
> Professional dirt oval and paved oval race shops

Available At:

Alfred State College
School of Applied Technology Campus
Automotive Trades Department
South Brooklyn Avenue, Wellsville, NY 14895
http://www.alfredstate.edu
Degrees available: Associate degree

For More Information:

American Society for Engineering Education
1818 N Street, NW, Suite 600, Washington, DC 20036-2479
202/331-3500
http://www.asee.org

Junior Engineering Technical Society, Inc.
1420 King Street, Suite 405, Alexandria, VA 22314
http://www.jets.org

Society of Manufacturing Engineers
One SME Drive, PO Box 930, Dearborn, MI 48121
800/733-4763
http://www.sme.org

Interview: Cyril Merrick

Cyril Merrick is the chair of the Automotive Trades Department at Alfred State College's School of Applied Technology Campus in Wellsville, New York. He discussed its motorsports technology program and the education of students in this field with the editors of *They Teach That in Community College!?*

Q. Please tell us about the motorsports specialization.

A. The motorsports specialization includes 1,800 hours of practical experience and classroom training applicable to the motorsport field. The program includes brake systems, alignment procedures, electronic controls, engine overhaul, and transmission overhaul—all with racing modifications. Also, students receive training in arc, gas MIG, TIG, and spot welding that are practiced in the lab. A major emphasis in the program is to teach the students fabrication and set-up on various types of racing vehicles. Students graduate from our program with an associate in occupational studies degree.

Q. What high school subjects/activities should students focus on to become successful in this major?

A. Automotive advisors and employers from the industry stress that communication skills and writing skills are important areas that need more focus.

Q. What advice would you offer motorsports technology majors as they graduate and look for jobs?

A. Motorsports graduates must be prepared to put in long hours and be totally dedicated to their occupations. They must be prepared to move to an area where employment is available.

Q. Who employs your graduates?

A. Alfred State motorsports graduates have been successful in finding employment in almost every avenue they have chosen to take. Our graduates are working in hot rod shops and professional dirt oval and paved oval race shops. World of Outlaws and NASCAR are two of the major sanctioning bodies in which our graduates are working.

Q. What is the future employment outlook for motorsports technology?

A. Motorsports currently is the largest spectator sport in the world. The industry guarantees continued growth and expansion.

Music Business

The music business is much more than just the performers we hear on the radio and see in concert or in videos on TV. Who works behind the scenes to make the stars look good? Who engineers the recording of a hit song? Who promotes the band and its merchandise? Who books shows and plans entire concert tours? People with a love for music and a head for business work behind the scenes in this demanding, yet rewarding, industry. They handle all of the tasks mentioned above and more. Several schools across the United States now offer degrees that address the business side of music, preparing students for careers as music executives, sales representatives, music producers, music distributors, talent managers, recording engineers, sound technicians, booking agents, concert venue managers, music retailers, and more.

Typical Courses:

> Music Theory
> Music History
> Music Merchandising
> Accounting
> Principal Instrument/Voice
> Artist Management
> Music Copyright and Publishing
> Marketing and Advertising
> Basic or Choral Conducting
> Record Industry Operations
> Consumer Behavior
> Arts Administration and Venue Management

Potential Employers:

> Artist management agencies
> Music distributors
> Music production companies
> Music promoters
> Music publishers
> Music retailers
> Postsecondary institutions
> Professional symphonies and opera companies
> Recording studios

Available At:

The following list of schools offering programs in music business is not exhaustive. For more programs, visit the following websites: http://nasm.arts-accredit.org and http://www.meiea.org.

Bergen Community College
400 Paramus Road, Paramus, NJ 07652
201/447-7100
http://www.bergen.edu/ecatalog/programview.asp?program.cbn=
37&semester.rm=1
Degrees available: Associate degree

Harrisburg Area Community College
One HACC Drive, Harrisburg, PA 17110-2999
800/ABC-HACC
admit@hacc.edu
http://www.hacc.edu
Degrees available: Diploma, associate degree

McNally Smith College of Music
19 Exchange Street East, Saint Paul, MN 55101-2220
800/594-9500
info@mcnallysmith.edu
http://www.mcnallysmith.edu/music_business_degree.html
Degrees available: Associate degree, bachelor's degree

Northeast Community College
801 East Benjamin Avenue, PO Box 469, Norfolk, NE 68702-0469
402/371-2020
http://www.northeastcollege.com/PS/PDF/Degree_Offerings/
MusicBusinessAA.pdf
Degrees available: Associate degree

Shoreline Community College
16101 Greenwood Avenue North, Shoreline, WA 98133-5696
206/546-4101
http://www.shoreline.edu/musictech04.html
Degrees available: Associate degree

For More Information:

American Marketing Association
311 South Wacker Drive, Suite 5800, Chicago, IL 60606
800/262-1150
info@ama.org
http://www.marketingpower.com

American Society of Composers, Authors, and Publishers
One Lincoln Plaza, New York, NY 10023
212/621-6000
http://www.ascap.org

National Association of Schools of Music
11250 Roger Bacon Drive, Suite 21, Reston, VA 20190-5248
703/437-0700
info@arts-accredit.org
http://nasm.arts-accredit.org

Recording Industry Association of America
1330 Connecticut Avenue, NW, Suite 300, Washington, DC 20036
202/775-0101
http://www.riaa.com

Music Recording

Imagine yourself working with top recording artists and musicians, collaborating on their next album release, or perhaps the music video of their latest hit single. Does this sound like a dream job? You can make it into reality with the help of an associate degree in music recording. Your coursework and training will give you a competitive edge for entry-level positions at music studios or television stations, or with video or record producers. Many graduates use their associate degree as a stepping stone for advanced degrees in music, music recording, or music engineering. Some programs, such as the one offered at Ohio's Cuyahoga Community College, require their students to participate in work/study programs or internships at local and national music and recording facilities. Not only does this serve as important work experience, it allows the student to forge valuable industry contacts for the future.

Typical Courses:

> Introduction to Recording
> Audio Signal Processing
> Digital Audio Theory
> Location Recording
> Practicum in Radio Production
> Television Production
> Music/Multi-Track Recording
> Music Publishing
> The Internet for Musicians
> Pop & Commercial Music Theory

Potential Employers:

> Recording studios
> Music publishers
> Television studios
> Independent record labels

Available At:

The following list of colleges that offer degrees in music recording is not exhaustive. Visit htttp://www.aes.org for more programs.

Cayuga Community College-State University of New York
Electronic Media/Sound Recording/Telecommunications
197 Franklin Street, Auburn, NY 13021
315/255-1743
http://www.telcomcayuga.com/degrees2.htm
Degrees available: Associate degree

Cuyahoga Community College
700 Carnegie Avenue, Cleveland, OH 44115
216/987-4252
http://www.tri-c.edu/rat/default.htm
Degrees available: Associate degree

Finger Lakes Community College
Visual and Performing Arts Department
4355 Lakeshore Drive, Canandaigua, NY 14424-8395
http://www.fingerlakes.edu/academics/musicrecording/index.html
Degrees available: Associate degree

Houston Community College
Audio Recording and Film Campus
1060 West Sam Houston Parkway North, Houston, TX 77043
http://nwc.hccs.cc.tx.us/av/index.html
Degrees available: Associate degree

167

Nashville State Community College
120 White Bridge Road, Nashville, TN 37209
615/353-3390
http://www.nscc.edu/depart/music/index.html
Degrees available: Certificate

Northeast Community College
Audio/Recording Technology Department
801 East Benjamin Avenue, Norfolk, NE 68701
402/844-7365
http://www.northeastcollege.com/CS/Groups/
Audio_Recording_Technology/about.htm
Degrees available: Associate degree

Shoreline Community College
16101 Greenwood Avenue North, Shoreline, WA 98133-5696
206/546-4101
http://www.shoreline.edu/musictech01.html
Degrees available: Associate degrees

For More Information:

Audio Engineering Society
60 East 42nd Street, Room 2520, New York, NY 10165-2520
212/661-8528
http://www.aes.org

Recording Industry Association of America
1330 Connecticut Avenue, NW, Suite 300, Washington, DC 20036
202/775-0101
http://www.riaa.com

Society of Professional Audio Recording Services
9 Music Square South, Suite 222, Nashville, TN 37203
800/771-7727
spars@spars.com
http://www.spars.com

Musical Instrument Repair

Behind every top-performing professional symphony orchestra, high school band, and amateur musician lies the integral work of the music instrument repair technician. Although the musical instrument repair industry is small—6,100 U.S. workers—employment prospects are good for aspiring repairers willing to receive training via an apprenticeship or a formal music instrument repair program. Only five post-secondary institutions in the United States and Canada offer training in music instrument repair.

Typical Courses:

>   Introduction to Music
>   Introduction to Band Instrument Repair
>   Shop Practices and Safety for Band Instrument Repair
>   Dent Removal Techniques
>   Soldering and Brazing Techniques
>   Brass Techniques
>   Woodwind Techniques
>   The Percussion Instruments
>   Mathematics for Band Instrument Repair
>   Human Relations for Band Instrument Repair

Potential Employers:

>   Musical instrument repair shops
>   Manufacturers
>   Colleges and universities

Did You Know?

Musical instrument repairers and tuners earned salaries that ranged from less than $17,050 to $51,940 or more in November 2004. Sporting goods and musical instrument stores are the top employers of professionals in the field. Musical instrument repairers and tuners in these settings earned mean annual salaries of $32,380 in 2004.

Only five postsecondary institutions in the U.S. and Canada offer training in musical instrument repair.

Available At:

Badger State Repair School
204 West Centralia Street, Elkhorn, WI 53121
Degrees available: None (the School offers a 48-week course in brass and woodwind instrument repair)

Keyano College
8115 Franklin Avenue, Fort McMurray, AB T9H 2H7
Canada
800/251-1408, ext. 8979
mir@keyano.ca
http://www.keyano.ca/prospective_students/programs/
certificate_diploma/music_instrument_repair.htm
Degrees available: Diploma

Minnesota State College-SE Technical
308 Pioneer Road, Red Wing, MN 55066
877/853-8324
http://www.southeastmn.edu/Programs
Degrees available: Certificates

Renton Technical College
3000 NE 4th Street, Renton, WA 98056
425/235-2352
http://www.rtc.edu/Programs/TrainingPrograms/BIRT
Degrees available: Certificate, associate degree

Western Iowa Tech Community College
4647 Stone Avenue, Sioux City, IA 51106
800/352-4649
http://www.witcc.com/programs/details.cfm?id=45
Degrees available: Associate degree

For More Information:

Guild of American Luthiers
8222 South Park Avenue, Tacoma, WA 98408-5226
253/472-7853
http://www.luth.org

**National Association of Professional
Band Instrument Repair Technicians**
2026 Eagle Road, PO Box 51, Normal, IL 61761
309/452-4257
napbirt@napbirt.org
http://www.napbirt.org

Piano Technicians Guild
4444 Forest Avenue, Kansas City, KS 66106
913/432-9975
ptg@ptg.org
http://www.ptg.org

Musical Theatre

Musical theatre is an entertaining, fast-paced combination of tuneful songs, choreographed dance routines, and spoken dialogue. Career options in musical theatre include actor, choreographer, dancer, director, playwight, makeup artist, musician, singer, stage chorus actor, stage movement instructor, and stage performer, among others. Due to the competitiveness of the industry, many students who earn an associate degree in musical theatre go on to four-year colleges and earn a bachelor's degree in the field.

Typical Courses:

> Broadway Musical Theatre
> Musical Theatre Practicum
> Musical Comedy
> Acting
> Choreography
> Piano
> Applied Basic Voice
> Applied Intermediate Voice
> Stagecraft
> Stage Makeup
> Introduction to Dance Techniques
> Inprovisation

Potential Employers:

> Theatres
> Performing arts companies
> Opera houses

Did You Know?

Musical theatre originated in the United States. The first musical, *The Black Crook,* was performed in 1866.

Available At:

Community College of Baltimore County-Essex Campus
7201 Rossville Boulevard, Baltimore, MD 21237
410/780-6569
http://www.ccbcmd.edu/liberal_arts/music/musc_thtr_degree.html
Degrees available: Associate degree

San Diego City College
1313 Park Boulevard, San Diego, CA 92101
619/388-3400
http://www.sdcity.edu/academic/vparts/musictheater/default.asp
Degrees available: Associate degree

For More Information:

National Association of Schools of Theatre
11250 Roger Bacon Drive, Suite 21, Reston, VA 20190-5248
703/437-0700
info@arts-accredit.org
http://nast.arts-accredit.org

Theater Communications Group
520 Eighth Avenue, 24th Floor, New York, NY 10018-4156
212/609-5900
tcg@tcg.org
http://www.tcg.org

173

National Technical Institute for the Deaf

Deaf and hard-of-hearing students face many unique challenges as they pursue higher education. To help these students prepare for rewarding careers, Congress established the National Technical Institute for the Deaf (NTID) in 1965. In 1968, the NTID became one of the Rochester Institute of Technology's colleges. Today, 1,100 deaf and hard-of-hearing students attend the Institute. The NTID offers more than 100 campus organizations and activities and dozens of men's and women's varsity, intramural, and club sports.

Available Fields of Study:

Students at the NTID can pursue associate degrees in more than 30 accredited programs and bachelor's and master's degrees in more than 200 programs offered by the Rochester Institute of Technology. In addition, hearing students can pursue associate and bachelor's degrees in American Sign Language-English Interpretations, and deaf and hearing students can pursue master's degrees in Secondary Education of Students who are Deaf or Hard of Hearing. Visit http://www.ntid.rit.edu/prospective/majors.php for more information.

For More Information:

National Technical Institute for the Deaf
Rochester Institute of Technology
52 Lomb Memorial Drive, Rochester, NY 14623
585/475-6700 (Voice/TTY)
http://www.ntid.rit.edu/index_flash.php
Degrees available: Associate degree, bachelor's degree, master's degree

Interview: T. Alan Hurwitz

Dr. T. Alan Hurwitz, Vice President, Rochester Institute of Technology and CEO/Dean, National Technical Institute for the Deaf, was kind enough to talk to the editors of *They Teach That in Community College!?* about the school and its programs.

Q. Please describe the Institute for our readers.

A. The National Technical Institute for the Deaf, part of Rochester Institute of Technology (RIT), provides deaf and hard-of-hearing students with outstanding state-of-the-art technical and professional education programs, complemented by a strong arts and sciences curriculum, that prepares them to live and work in the mainstream of a rapidly changing global community and enhances their lifelong learning. NTID is the recognized world leader in applied research designed to enhance the social, economic, and educational accommodation of deaf and hard-of-hearing people.

Q. What type of services and facilities are available for deaf and hard-of-hearing students at the NTID?

A. Deaf and hard-of-hearing students enjoy a wide array of services including access to interpreters, speech-to-text transcription, note takers, and tutors, as well as other communication strategies. Onsite audiologists provide services related to hearing and hearing aids, assistive devices, and cochlear implants; speech-language pathologists offer a broad range of speech and language services as well.

Dorms and classrooms are fully networked with state-of-the-art computers and multimedia technologies. Students enjoy more than 100 clubs, creative arts programs, student government and religious activities, and sports programs. RIT Campus Safety employs officers who are deaf and also trains hearing officers in various communication strategies.

Q. Does the NTID offer any cooperative educational opportunities or internships?

A. At NTID/RIT, we do offer cooperative educational opportunities and internships. In fact, in most cases, we require it. Employment specialists within the NTID Center on Employment work closely with students throughout their college years to help prepare them for successful, real-world employment. The co-op experience is a critical component of that. The employers—large and small companies throughout the United States—who hire our students for co-op frequently hire the students for permanent jobs. We're proud of our 93 percent employment placement rate at NTID, and we credit that to—in addition to their skills matching to the employers' needs—the fact that we work closely with the student and the employer in the beginning to overcome any challenges that may exist, such as communication. Employers repeatedly tell us how NTID students bring a different kind of preparedness to the job and how they approach challenges with a can-do attitude.

Q. Can you provide a brief overview of your Explore Your Future program for high school juniors?

A. We understand how difficult it is to decide what you want to do the rest of your life, so at our widely popular Explore Your Future week-long summer program, we give high school juniors an opportunity to gain some hands-on experience with a variety of jobs and careers. The students leave with a written summary of experiences and the results of career-interest testing. They meet deaf and hard-of-hearing students from all over the country and participate in sports, dances, multicultural dinners, captioned movies, and more.

Q. What does the future hold for the NTID?

A. We recently announced a new plan that reflects a very bright future for our students! Over the next few years, we will be making exciting changes to our academic programs, access services, and outreach efforts to align even more closely with our students' unique needs. As hearing aid technology continues to improve, and the use of cochlear implants increases, students are using their hearing more than they ever have in the past, which changes their needs for support. In addition, educators and employers around the world have looked to the NTID as a model for technical education programs for deaf and hard-of-hearing students. The knowledge we've acquired from our years of extensive research and experience is unprecedented, and we will be establishing a formal outreach consortium to share information more widely.

Native American Studies

Native American history goes back tens of thousands of years in the Americas. But amidst all of the history, some people may forget that a vibrant contemporary Native American community exists in the United States on Native American reservations and in cities and towns throughout the country. To educate students about the past history and current issues that affect Native Americans, community colleges have created Native American Studies programs. These programs are often offered by community colleges that are sponsored by Indian tribes, as well as those that are near areas, especially the Southwestern and Western United States, where many Indian tribes are located. Students in these programs study Indian history, religion, culture, tribal government, law, and languages. Native American Studies programs offered by tribal community colleges typically focus on educating students about that tribe's culture. For example, students attending the Native American Studies program at Fort Belknap College in Harlem, Montana, focus on the history, culture, and language of the Fort Belknap Gros Ventre and Nakoda (Assiniboine) tribes. Students who choose this major often go on to earn four-year degrees in the social sciences, humanities, and education. Others earn their associate degree or certificate and find work in Native American cultural or social services agencies and in other settings.

Typical Courses:

> Introduction to American Indian Studies
> History of Indians of North America
> Oral Traditions
> Introduction to Tribal Government
> Native American Religion/Philosophy
> Traditional Foods/Plants
> Federal Indian Law
> Native American Education
> Native American Literature
> Native American Cinema
> Intercultural Perspectives
> Native American Language (varies by college)

Potential Employers:

> Social services agencies
> American Indian cultural agencies
> American Indian tribal agencies

Available At:

Fort Belknap College
PO Box 159, Harlem, MT 59526
406/353-2607
http://www.fbcc.edu/html/ais.html
Degrees available: Associate degree

Pima County Community College
4905 East Broadway Boulevard, Tucson, AZ 85709-1010
800/860-PIMA
infocenter@pima.edu
http://www.pima.edu/program/american-indian-studies/index.shtml
Degrees available: Associate degree

Salish Kootenai College
52000 Highway 93, PO Box 70, Pablo, MT 59855
406/275-4800
http://www.skc.edu
Degrees available: Certificate, associate degree

Sisseton Wahpeton College
Agency Village Box 689, Sisseton, SD 57262
605/698-3966
http://www.swc.tc/Academic%20Programs%20Docs/dakst.pdf
Degrees available: Associate degree

For More Information:

Association for the Study of American Indian Literatures
c/o Siobhan Senier
University of New Hampshire
Department of English
Hamilton Smith Hall, 95 Main Street, Durham, NH 03824
http://oncampus.richmond.edu/faculty/ASAIL

Occupational Therapy Assistant

Like their job title implies, *occupational therapy assistants* assist occupational therapists, helping them provide rehabilitative services to people. Occupational therapy assistants (OTAs) may work with people born with mental or developmental disabilities, or people coping with or recovering from illness or injuries. They help their clients to learn how to perform the skills they need for everyday life, such as eating, dressing, grooming, and working. They may do this by showing their clients how to use adaptive equipment or perform exercises designed to increase their ability to function independently. OTAs help the occupational therapist carry out the client's therapy, document the client's progress, and assist with paperwork and billing issues. They work in a variety of settings, such as hospitals, nursing homes, schools, and clinics. The demand for occupational therapy assistants is expected to grow much faster than average, according to the U.S. Department of Labor, providing a perfect opportunity for students interested in a career that allows them to make a difference in people's lives.

Typical Courses:

> Hospitals
> Nursing homes
> Intermediate care facilities
> Public schools
> Mental health centers
> Rehabilitation hospitals
> Home health agencies
> Group homes
> Outpatient clinics

Potential Employers:

> Evaluation and Treatment Principles
> Therapeutic Media
> Activities of Daily Living
> Occupational Therapy Interventions
> Occupational Therapy Group Process
> Psychosocial Dysfunction

> Anatomy & Physiology
> Documentation
> Management Perspectives
> Fieldwork

Available At:

The following list of colleges that offer associate degrees in occupational therapy assisting (OTA) is not exhaustive. Visit the American Occupational Therapy Association's website, http://www.aota.org, for a list of approximately 130 OTA programs that are accredited by the Association.

Bristol Community College
Department of Health Sciences
777 Elsbree Street, Fall River, MA 02720
508/678-2811
http://www.bristolcommunitycollege.edu/catalog/ca6/degree/ca6_occ.html
Degrees available: Associate degree

College of DuPage
Health, Social, and Behavioral Sciences Division
425 Fawell Boulevard, Glen Ellyn, IL 60137
630/942-2495
http://www.cod.edu/academic/acadprog/occ_voc/OccTherA.htm
Degrees available: Associate degree

Community College of Allegheny County-Boyce Campus
595 Beatty Road, Monroeville, PA 15146-1396
724/325-6614
http://www.ccac.edu/default.aspx?id=138733
Degrees available: Associate degree

Community College of Baltimore County-Catonsville Campus
800 South Rolling Road, Baltimore, MD 21228
410/455-4984
http://www.ccbcmd.edu/allied_health/octa_program.html
Degrees available: Associate degree

Community College of Rhode Island-Newport Satellite Campus
Newport Hospital
275 Broadway, Newport, RI 02840
401/847-9800
http://www.ccri.edu/rehabhealth/OTA_faqs.shtml
Degrees available: Associate degree

Did You Know?

According to the American Occupational Therapy Association, occupational therapy can be used to assist those with work-related injuries, arthritis, multiple sclerosis, birth injuries, learning problems, developmental disabilities, mental health issues, spinal cord injuries, burns, amputations, broken bones, difficulties after heart attack or stroke, sports injuries, and vision or cognitive difficulties.

Cuyahoga Community College-Metropolitan Campus
2900 Community College Avenue, Cleveland, OH 44115
216/987-4498
http://www.tri-c.edu/otat/default.htm
Degrees available: Associate degree

Delaware Technical and Community College (multiple campuses)
333 Shipley Street, Wilmington, DE 19801
302/571-5355
http://www.dtcc.edu/wilmington/ah/ota.html
Degrees available: Associate degree

Erie Community College-North Campus
Allied Health Division
6205 Main Street, Williamsville, NY 14221
716/634-0800
http://www.ecc.edu/academics/occupational.asp
Degrees available: Associate degree

Housatonic Community College
900 Lafayette Boulevard, Bridgeport, CT 06604
203/332-5200
http://www.hcc.commnet.edu/academics/programs/dynamic/
progDetail.asp?keyCode=EA77
Degrees available: Associate degree

Kapiolani Community College-University of Hawaii
4303 Diamond Head Road, Honolulu, HI 96816
808/734-9229
hlthhelp@hawaii.edu
http://programs.kcc.hawaii.edu/health/ota/index.htm
Degrees available: Associate degree

Kirkwood Community College
Health Sciences Department
6301 Kirkwood Boulevard, SW, Cedar Rapids, IA 52404
800/363-2220
http://www.kirkwood.edu/site/index.php?t=2&d=2&p=62
Degrees available: Associate degree

Nashville State Community College
120 White Bridge Road, Nashville, TN 37209
615/353-3708
http://www.nscc.edu/depart/ot/index.html
Degrees available: Associate degree

New Hampshire Community Technical College-Claremont
1 College Drive, Claremont, NH 03743
800/837-0658
http://www.claremont.nhctc.edu/ProgramsFrame.html
Degrees available: Associate degree

Salt Lake Community College-Jordan Campus
3491 West 9000 South, West Jordan, UT 84088
801/957-4894
http://www.slcc.edu/pages/1019.asp
Degrees available: Associate degree

Santa Ana College
1530 West 17th Street, Santa Ana, CA 92706
714/564-6833
http://www.sac.edu/faculty_staff/academic_progs/math/therapy/index.htm
Degrees available: Associate degree

For More Information:

American Occupational Therapy Association
4720 Montgomery Lane, PO Box 31220, Bethesda, MD 20824
301/652-2682
educate@aota.org
http://www.aota.org

Orthotics and Prosthetics Assistant and Technician

Orthotics assistants and technicians design, fit, and construct orthopedic braces for people with disabilities. *Prosthetic assistants and technicians* design, fit, and construct artificial limbs for people who have lost limbs due to disease or injury. They fabricate these devices using plastic, metal, wood, plaster, and leather. These allied health professionals work under the supervision of certified orthotists and prosthetists. Prosthetist/orthotist assistants and technicians may be involved with evaluating the individual in need of an orthosis or prosthesis, and the original design, building, and fitting of the device for that individual. They often have the opportunity to work in varied environments, spending time with individuals in need of assistive devices as well as working in the lab to create new orthoses and prostheses. Assistants and technician positions require an associate degree. Only one orthotic and prosthetic assistant training program and four orthotic and prosthetic technician programs are accredited by the National Commission on Orthotic and Prosthetic Education and the Commission on Accreditation of Allied Health Education Programs.

Typical Courses:

>   Introduction to Orthotics and Prosthetics
>   Prosthetic Tools and Materials
>   Orthopedic Equipment and Materials
>   Foot and Ankle Skeletal Structure
>   Clinical Orthotics
>   Below and Above Knee Prosthetics
>   Below and Above Knee Orthotics
>   Below Elbow Prosthetics
>   Above Elbow Prosthetics
>   Upper Limb Prosthetics
>   Spinal Orthotics

Potential Employers:

> Hospitals
> Clinics
> Rehabilitation centers
> U.S. military
> Central fabrication laboratories

Available At:

Orthotic and Prosthetic Assistant Programs
Oklahoma State University-Okmulgee
1801 East 4th Street, Okmulgee, OK 74447
http://www.osu-okmulgee.edu/academics
Degrees available: Associate degree

Orthotic and Prosthetic Technician Programs
Baker College of Flint
1050 West Bristol Road, Flint, MI 48507
https://carina.baker.edu
Degrees available: Associate degree

Century College
3300 Century Avenue North, White Bear Lake, MN 55110
http://www.century.edu/orthoticprosthetic/opsaoverview.aspx
Degrees available: Associate degree

Francis Tuttle-Rockwell Campus
12777 North Rockwell Avenue, Oklahoma City, OK 73142-2789
http://www.francistuttle.com/programs/details.asp?PRGID=13
Degrees available: Associate degree

Spokane Falls Community College
3410 West Fort George Wright Drive, Mail Stop 3060
Spokane, WA 99204-5288
http://tech.spokanefalls.edu/OandP/default.asp?page=Home&OP=1
Degrees available: Certificate, associate degree

For More Information:

American Academy of Orthotists and Prosthetists
526 King Street, Suite 201, Alexandria, VA 22314
http://www.oandp.org

American Orthotic and Prosthetic Association
330 John Carlyle Street, Suite 200, Alexandria, VA 22314
http://www.aopanet.org

National Commission on Orthotic and Prosthetic Education
330 John Carlyle Street, Suite 200, Alexandria, VA 22314
http://www.ncope.org

Interview: Clayton Wright

Clayton Wright is the director of the Orthotics and Prosthetics Technician Program at Spokane Falls Community College in Spokane, Washington. He is also a board certified prosthetist with 13 years of clinical experience. He discussed the school's technician program and the education of students in this field with the editors of *They Teach That in Community College!?*

Q. Please tell us about your program.

A. Our's is a two-year program; one year in the orthotics (orthopedic brace) discipline, one year in the prosthetics (artificial limb) discipline. Successful completion of the two-year program results in an associate of applied science degree. This is a technical arts (vocational) non-transfer degree. Students may choose to take only one discipline instead of both, resulting in a certificate of completion. Our program is accredited by the National Commission on Orthotic Prosthetic Education. A degree or a certificate from our program grants the student eligibility to participate in the American Board for Certification technician registration exam(s).

Q. What high school subjects/activities should students focus on to be successful in this major?

A. A high school diploma or GED is required. Successful technician students need to have good hand skills and fine motor skills. Strong math skills are not required, but a modest background in chemistry and physics are a plus. Good communication skills are very important. Some artistic aptitude is necessary. A student who excels in wood/metal shop and is comfortable in an art class would be an excellent candidate.

Q. How will the field change in the future?

A. The field will continue to expand as baby boomers age and the issues of obesity and diabetes increase. The field will adopt more computer-aided fabrication methods.

Paper Science and Engineering

Papermaking is one of the oldest industries known to man—wood-based papermaking can be traced to ancient China. Today, it is considered a science and involves more than the manufacture of raw paper. Paper scientists and engineers are responsible for finding new uses for paper products, and better and more affordable ways to produce paper, tissue, and other natural fiber products. As *process technicians,* they may help to perfect the recycling of paper and water and other materials used in the papermaking process. As *research technicians,* they may help research engineers extract and work with the various components found in wood or generated by the papermaking process that can be used to create medicines, detergents, and many other goods. Or perhaps they can create new paper products that are compatible with today's high-speed, four-color printers. Graduates of paper science and paper engineering programs may also work in the paper industry in sales, management, and marketing.

Typical Classes:

> Pulp and Paper Manufacturing
> Paper Physics Fundamentals
> Converting and Coating
> Water Quality and Regulations
> Recycling
> Wastewater Engineering
> Surface and Wet End Science
> Solid Waste Treatment
> Process Engineering and Design
> Vector and Multivariate Calculus
> Carbohydrate and Lignin Chemistry

Potential Employers:

> Paper companies
> Chemical suppliers
> Consultants
> Equipment suppliers
> Governmental agencies

Available At:

The following list of schools offering programs in paper science and paper engineering is not exhaustive. For more programs, visit http://www.paperonweb.com.

Alabama Southern Community College-Thomasville Campus
Alabama Center for Excellence in Forestry, Paper and Chemical Technology
PO Box 2000, Thomasville, AL 36784
251/575-3156, ext. 663
http://www.ascc.edu
Degrees available: Associate degree

Tacoma Community College
6501 South 19th Street, Tacoma, WA 98466
253/566-5000
http://www.tacomacc.edu/inst_dept/science/programs.asp
Degrees available: Associate degree

For More Information:

American Forest and Paper Association
1111 19th Street, NW, Suite 800, Washington, DC 20036
800/878-8878
info@afandpa.org
http://www.afandpa.org

Society of Wood Science and Technology
One Gifford Pinchot Drive, Madison, WI 53726-2398
608/231-9347
http://www.swst.org

Paralegal

Paralegals help lawyers perform legal duties. This can include helping a lawyer prepare for trial, draft legal documents, track down necessary legal data, or organize files and information. Paralegals work wherever lawyers work: in law firms, for the government, or in the legal departments of businesses, for example. Like lawyers, paralegals can specialize in particular areas of the law—such as real estate law, labor law, bankruptcy law, or family law—although many paralegals are generalists and perform tasks related to a variety of legal areas. Because paralegals are able to perform many of the tasks a lawyer would need to perform, but do not command a lawyer's salary, it makes economical sense for employers to hire paralegals to share in the legal workload, and many law firms, companies, and government agencies are moving in this direction. The demand for paralegals is expected to grow much faster than average through 2014, according to the U.S. Department of Labor.

Typical Courses:

> Introduction to Paralegal Studies
> Government and the Law
> The American Legal System
> Business Law
> Legal Terminology
> Transcription
> Legal Research and Writing
> Evidence
> Civil Litigation and Procedures
> Family Law
> Real Estate Transactions

Potential Employers:

> Law firms
> Federal government agencies such as the Federal Trade Commission, Treasury Department, Internal Revenue Service, Justice Department, and Department of the Interior
> State and local agencies
> Corporate legal departments

Available At:

The following list of colleges that offer certificates and degrees in paralegal education is not exhaustive. Visit the American Bar Association's website, http://www.abanet.org/legalservices/paralegals/directory/home.html, for a list of programs that are approved by the Association. (Note: Certificates in paralegal studies generally require a previous degree, either at the associate level or the baccalaureate level. A student without a degree of any kind cannot enter a certificate program to become a licensed paralegal.)

Albuquerque TVI Community College
Paralegal Studies Program
717 University, SE, Smith Brasher Hall, Albuquerque, NM 87106
http://oldwww.tvi.edu/bod
Degrees available: Associate degree

University of Arkansas Community College-Fort Smith
5210 Grand Avenue, Fort Smith, AR 72903
479/788-7000
http://www.uacch.edu
Degrees available: Associate degree

Central Texas College
PO Box 1800, Killeen, TX 76540
800/792-3348, ext. 1394
ctc.socad@ctcd.edu
http://www.ctcd.edu/armyedinfo/degree_maps_goarmyed.htm
Degrees available: Associate degree

Columbus State Community College
PO Box 1609, Columbus, OH 43216-1609
800/621-6407
http://www.cscc.edu/DOCS/PARALEGALCURR.HTM
Degrees available: Associate degree, post-degree certificate

Community College of Aurora
16000 East Centre Tech Parkway, Aurora, CO 80011-9036
303/340-7502
http://www.ccaurora.edu
Degrees available: Associate degree, post-degree certificate

Community College of Baltimore County-Dundalk Campus
7200 Sollers Point Road, Baltimore, MD 21222
410/285-9729
http://www.ccbcmd.edu/justice/paralegal/index.html
Degrees available: Associate degree

A paralegal performs research via the telephone.

Community College of Philadelphia
1700 Spring Garden Street, Philadelphia, PA 19130
215/751-8010
http://www.ccp.edu/site/academic/degrees/paralegal.php
Degrees available: Associate degree

Cuyahoga Community College-Western Campus
11000 Pleasant Valley Road, Parma, OH 44130
216/987-5112
http://www.tri-c.edu/paralegal/default.htm
Degrees available: Associate degree, post-degree certificate

Elgin Community College
Paralegal Program
1700 Spartan Drive, Elgin, IL 60123
847/697-1000
http://www.elgin.edu/aca2index.asp?id=471&program=Paralegal
Degrees available: Associate degree, post-degree certificate

Florida Community College-Jacksonville
501 West State Street, Jacksonville, FL 32202
904/381-3589
http://www.fccj.org/prospective/programs/data05_06/2299.html
Degrees available: Associate degree

Did You Know?

Approximately 224,000 paralegals are employed in the United States, according to the U.S. Department of Labor. Seventy percent work for private law firms.

J. Sargeant Reynolds Community College
PO Box 85622, Richmond, VA 23285-5622
804/371-3000
http://www.jsr.vccs.edu/curriculum/programs/
Legal%20AssistingAAS.htm
Degrees available: Associate degree

Kapi'olani Community College-Honolulu
Legal Education Department
4303 Diamond Head Road, Honolulu, HI 96816-4412
http://legal.kcc.hawaii.edu/paralegal/index.htm
Degrees available: Associate degree

Lansing Community College
419 North Capitol Avenue, MC 2100, Lansing, MI 48901
517/483-1528
http://www.lcc.edu/business/legal_asst
Degrees available: Associate degree, post-degree certificate

Laramie County Community College
Legal Assistant Program
1400 East College Drive, Cheyenne, WY 82007
Degrees available: Associate degree
http://www.lccc.wy.edu

Macomb Community College
14500 East 12 Mile Road, Warren, MI 48088
586/445-7153
http://www.macomb.edu/academics/departments/lega/default.asp
Degrees available: Associate degree

Metropolitan Community College
Legal Assistant Program
2909 Ed Babe Gomez Drive, Omaha, NE 68107
http://www.mccneb.edu/legalassistant
Degrees available: Associate degree, post-degree certificate

191

New Hampshire Technical Institute
31 College Drive, Concord, NH 03301-7412
603/271-7104
info@nhti.edu
http://www.nhti.edu/academics/academicprograms/degparaleg.html
and
http://www.nhti.edu/academics/academicprograms/
certparalegal.html
Degrees available: Associate degree, post-degree certificate

Did You Know?

Paralegals earned salaries that ranged from $25,890 to $64,010 or more in November 2004, according to the U.S. Department of Labor. Paralegals employed in the legal services industry (the largest employer of paralegals) earned mean annual salaries of $41,600.

192

Northern Virginia Community College
4001 Wakefield Chapel Road, Annandale, VA 22003-3796
703/323-3000
http://www.nvcc.vccs.edu/curcatalog/programs/legas.htm
Degrees available: Associate degree, post-degree certificate

Oakland Community College
27055 Orchard Lake Road, Farmington Hills, MI 48334
248/522-3627
http://www.oaklandcc.edu/lgl
Degrees available: Associate degree, post-degree certificate

Pikes Peak Community College
5675 South Academy Boulevard, Colorado Springs, CO 80906
800/456-6847
http://www.ppcc.cccoes.edu/CatalogSchedule/Programs/
Programs.cfm?Program=PLAp
Degrees available: Associate degree, post-degree certificate

Pima County Community College-Downtown Campus
1255 North Stone Avenue, Tucson, AZ 85707
520/206-7134
http://www.pima.edu/program/paralegal/index.shtml
Degrees available: Associate degree, post-degree certificate

San Jacinto College-Central Campus
8060 Spencer Highway, Pasadena, TX 77505
281/476-1813
http://www.sjcd.edu/program/paralegal.html
Degrees available: Associate degree

Seminole Community College
100 Weldon Boulevard, Sanford, FL 32773-6199
407/708-2269
http://www.scc-fl.edu/legalassist
Degrees available: Associate degree

Sinclair Community College
Paralegal Program
444 West Third Street, Dayton, OH 45434
http://www.sinclair.edu/academics/bus/departments/par/index.cfm
Degrees available: Associate degree

Tallahassee Community College
444 Appleyard Drive, Tallahassee, FL 32304
850/201-8352
http://www.tcc.cc.fl.us/dept/tpp/programs/as_degrees/
as_paralegal_legal.htm
Degrees available: Associate degree

Tidewater Community College
PO Box 9000, Norfolk, VA 23509-9000
800/371-0898
http://www.tcc.edu/academics/programs/curr/aas/index.htm
Degrees available: Associate degrees

Western Dakota Technical Institute
800 Mickelson Drive, Rapid City, SD 57703
800/544-8765
http://wdti.tec.sd.us/sonisweb/reports/
wdti_programs_detail.cfm?program=696
Degrees available: Associate degree

William Rainey Harper College
Paralegal Studies
1200 West Algonquin Road, Palatine, IL 60067
847/925-6407
http://www.harpercollege.edu/catalog/career/para/index.htm
Degrees available: Associate degree, post-degree certificate

For More Information:

American Association for Paralegal Education
407 Wekiva Springs Road, Suite 241, Longwood, FL 32779
407/834-6688
http://www.aafpe.org

American Bar Association
321 North Clark Street, Chicago, IL 60610
312/988-5522
http://www.abanet.org

Association of Legal Administrators
75 Tri-State International, Suite 222, Lincolnshire, IL 60069-4435
847/267-1252
http://www.alanet.org

National Association of Legal Assistants
1516 South Boston Avenue, Suite 200, Tulsa, OK 74119
918/587-6828
http://www.nala.org

National Federation of Paralegal Associations
2517 Eastlake Avenue East, Suite 200, Seattle, WA 98102
206/652-4120
http://www.paralegals.org

National Paralegal Association
PO Box 406, Solebury, PA 18963
215/297-8333
http://www.nationalparalegal.org

Plastics Science and Engineering

Look around and you will see plastics in almost every aspect of your life. Plastics are used in health care (e.g., surgical gloves, open MRI machines, prosthetic devices), waste treatment, electronics, construction, agriculture, and everyday life (e.g., bottles, food storage, product packaging, and countless other uses). Someday, according to Plastics-car.org, plastics may make up a large percentage of the interior and exterior of cars and other vehicles. In short, the sky's the limit for students interested in careers in plastics. *Plastics engineers,* who design and develop plastic products, typically have associate or bachelor's degrees in plastic or polymer engineering, materials engineering, chemical engineering, industrial engineering, manufacturing engineering, or a related field. *Plastics technicians,* who assist plastics engineers, typically have some postsecondary training or an associate degree.

Typical Courses:

> Overview of the Plastics Industry
> Polymer Processing Survey
> Mathematics
> Chemistry
> 3D CAD and Modeling
> Manufacturing Processes
> Injection Molding
> Mold Design/Maintenance
> Industrial Blow Molding
> Extrusion
> Polymer Testing

Potential Employers:

> Aerospace industry
> Building and construction industry
> Electronics industry
> Packaging industry
> Transportation industry
> Virtually any industry that uses plastics in its products

Available At:

The following list of schools offering programs in plastics science and engineering and related fields is not exhaustive. For more programs, visit http://www.plasticsindustry.org/outreach/institutions.

College of DuPage
Plastics Technology Program
425 Fawell Boulevard, IC 3028, Glen Ellyn, IL 60137-6599
630/942-4343
http://www.cod.edu/academic/acadprog/occ_voc/PlasAcad.htm
Degrees available: Certificate, associate degree

Mount Wachusett Community College
444 Green Street, Gardner, MA 01440
978/632-6600
http://www.mwcc.mass.edu/PDFs/PTProgramSheet.pdf
Degrees available: Associate degree

196

Did You Know?

Plastics are used in countless industries including food packaging and storage, medicine (x-rays on plastic film, artificial hearts, tubing, packaging, artificial tissue, etc.), manufacturing, public safety, and many other fields.

Pennsylvania College of Technology
Plastics and Polymer Technology Department
Breuder Advanced Technology and Health Sciences Center
One College Avenue, Room E134, Williamsport, PA 17701
plastics@pct.edu
http://www.pct.edu/catalog/majors/ps.shtml
Degrees available: Associate degree, bachelor's degree

Quinebaug Valley Community College
729 Main Street, Willimantic, CT 06226
http://www.qvctc.commnet.edu/catalog/c_plastics.asp
and
http://www.qvctc.commnet.edu/catalog/p_plastic.asp
Degrees available: Certificate, associate degree

West Georgia Technical College
303 Fort Drive, LaGrange, GA 30240
706/845-4323
http://www.westgatech.edu/academics/Plastics/Plastics.htm
Degrees available: Certificates, associate degree

For More Information:

American Plastics Council
1300 Wilson Boulevard, Arlington, VA 22209
800/243-5790
http://www.plastics.org

Plastics Institute of America, Inc.
University of Massachusetts-Lowell
333 Aiken Street, Lowell, MA 01854-3686
978/934-3130
info@plasticsinstitute.org
http://www.plasticsinstitute.org

Society of Plastics Engineers
14 Fairfield Drive, PO Box 403, Brookfield, CT 06804-0403
203/775-0471
info@4spe.org
http://www.4spe.org

197

Society of the Plastics Industry
1667 K Street, NW, Suite 1000, Washington, DC 20006
202/974-5200
http://www.socplas.org

Railroad Operations

If you ever dreamed of becoming a railroad conductor, this is the program for you! Designed to provide students with general knowledge and skills for entry-level employment in the railroad industry, this major introduces students to the history of railroading and the various railroad crafts—conducting, mechanics, electronics, and welding. Railroad operations, safety, environment, and quality are additional areas of focus. Business and technical electives provide additional opportunity for students to specialize or prepare for further study. Most programs require students to specialize in one or more areas such as conducting, mechanics, electronics, or welding. Programs typically award certificates and associate degrees. Over the next decade, America's railroads will face an urgent shortage of qualified, well-trained men and women to operate and manage today's modern railroads. Industry experts predict that an additional 60,000 to 210,000 workers will be needed.

Typical Courses:

> History of Railroading
> Railroad Safety, Quality, and Environment
> Physics
> Mechanical Operations
> Construction Management
> Electromechanical Systems
> Industrial Safety
> Metallurgy
> Business Management

Potential Employers:

> Railroads

Available At:

Fewer than 20 community colleges offer programs in railroad operations. Check with academic institutions near you to determine if majors, minors, certificates, or concentrations are available in railroad operations.

There are more than 173,000 miles of railroad track in North America.

199

Dakota County Technical College
1300 145th Street East (County Road 42)
Rosemount, MN 55068-2999
877/937-3282
http://www.dctc.mnscu.edu/programs/rail.htm
Degrees available: Certificate

Johnson County Community College
12345 College Boulevard, Campus Mailbox 63
Overland Park, KS 66210
913/469-3857
http://www.jccc.edu/home/depts/4614
Degrees available: Certificate, associate degrees

Modoc Railroad Academy
PO Box 432, Madison, CA 95653
916/965-5515
mra@modocrailroadacademy.com
http://www.modocrailroadacademy.com/index.asp
Degrees available: Certificate

Sacramento City College
Department of Advanced Transportation Technology
Division of Advanced Technology
3835 Freeport Boulevard, Sacramento, CA 95822
916/558-2491
http://www.scc.losrios.edu/programs/railroad.html
Degrees available: Certificate

Did You Know?

✔ The U.S. rail freight industry is the busiest in the world.
✔ More than 600 freight railroads operate in the U.S., Canada, and Mexico.
✔ The North American railroad industry earns more than $42 billion in annual revenue.

Source: Association of American Railroads

St. Philip's College-Southwest Campus
800 Quintana Road, San Antonio, TX 78211
210/921-4603
http://www.accd.edu/spc/spcmain/swc/railroad.htm
Degrees available: Certificates

Tarrant County College-Northwest Campus
Railroad Dispatcher Training Program
4801 Marine Creek Parkway, Fort Worth, TX 76179
817/515-7271
http://www.tccd.edu/neutral/
DivisionDepartmentPage.asp?pagekey=162&menu=2
Degrees available: Certificate

For More Information:

Association of American Railroads
50 F Street, NW, Washington, DC 20001-1564
202/639-2100
information@aar.org
http://www.aar.org

Recreation Leadership/ Outdoor Education

Calling all nature lovers! Imagine this normal workday: guiding a white water trip through a Class V river run, teaching backpacking safety to a group of first-time campers, or marking a new path for back-country skiing. A major in outdoor education will prepare you for these tasks and much more—and a career in one of the fastest-growing segments of the recreation industry. Programs are based on a theoretical foundation, as well as practical experience ranging from kayaking to avalanche awareness. Most programs focus on the adventure or the environmental aspects interdependently, but students should look into each program in depth to discover programs that focus on one more than another, according to their interests. Programs emphasize outdoor program administration, team building, problem solving, adventure leadership, and natural resource management.

Typical Courses:

> Organization and Management of Adventure Programs
> Environmental Health and Safety
> Mountaineering
> Ecotourism and Natural Resource Management
> Scuba Diving
> Wilderness Survival and First Aid
> Marine Survival
> Fly Fishing
> Backpacking
> Cross Country Skiing
> Sociology of Sport

Potential Employers:

> National Park Service
> National Forest Service
> State and local parks and recreation agencies
> Outward Bound
> College/university outdoor programs
> Adventure-based residential treatment programs for at-risk youth

Available At:

The following list of recreation leadership/outdoor education programs is not exhaustive. Check with academic institutions near you to determine if majors, minors, certificates, or concentrations are available in recreation leadership/outdoor education.

Erie Community College-South Campus
4041 Southwestern Boulevard, Orchard Park, NY 14127
716/648-5400
http://www.ecc.edu/academics/recreation.asp
Degrees available: Associate degree

Recreation leadership majors must be in top physical shape in order to be able to successfully lead clients during outings.

Feather River College
Outdoor Recreation Leadership Program
570 Golden Eagle Avenue, Quincy, CA 95971
530/283-0202, ext. 275, 800/442-9799, ext. 275
http://www.frc.edu/ORL/index.html
Degrees available: Associate degree

National Park Community College
101 College Drive, Hot Springs National Park, AR 71913
501/760-4294
http://www.npcc.edu/Academics/health_sciences_rec.htm
Degrees available: Associate degree

Did You Know?

Approximately 159 million Americans age 16 and over participated in an outdoor activity in 2004, according to the Outdoor Industry Association.

New Hampshire Community Technical College-Claremont
1 College Drive, Claremont, NH 03743
800/837-0658
claremont@nhctc.edu
http://www.claremont.nhctc.edu/ProgramsFrame.html
Degrees available: Associate degree

Suffolk County Community College-Ammerman Campus
533 College Road, Selden, NY 11784-2899
631/451-4000
http://www3.sunysuffolk.edu/Curricula/311.asp
Degrees available: Associate degree

Tallahassee Community College
444 Appleyard Drive, Tallahassee, FL 32304
850/201-8352
http://www.tcc.fl.edu/dept/tpp/programs/as_degrees/as_recreation_technology.htm
Degrees available: Associate degree

Washington County Community College-Eastport Campus
16 Deep Cove Road, Eastport, ME 04631
207/454-1031
http://www.wccc.me.edu/advrec
Degrees available: Associate degree

For More Information:

Outdoor Industry Association
4909 Pearl East Circle, Suite 200, Boulder, CO 80301
303/444-3353
info@outdoorindustry.org
http://www.outdoorindustry.org

Recreation Therapy

People don't often stop to consider the link between recreation and health. Studies have proven that both children and older adults enjoy stronger mental and physical capacity and better social interaction if they recreate. Certified *recreation therapists* use ingenuity and imagination to enhance people's physical, cognitive, and emotional well-being through leisure activities. Recreation therapy (sometimes referred to as therapeutic recreation) interventions include adapted aquatics, adapted fitness activity, adventure programming, animal-assisted therapy, aquatics therapy, creative arts, exercise programs, horticulture, journaling, leisure education, medical play, music, social skills training, stress management, T'ai Chi Chuan, therapeutic horseback riding, wheelchair sports, and Yoga. While all of the listed educational programs focus on using recreation as a therapeutic medium, some programs offer recreation therapy in the department of education as an option in secondary education, while other programs focus primarily on a health sciences curriculum and/or a parks and recreation curriculum.

Typical Courses:

> Introduction to Health Professions
> Contemporary Aspects of Disability
> Professional Seminar
> Research and Evaluation
> Teaching Health Promotion through Leisure Education
> Health Psychology and Human Behavior
> Sport and Recreation for Individuals with Disabilities
> Foundations of Professional Therapeutic Recreation Practice
> TR Assessment and Documentation
> Clinical Procedures in Therapeutic Recreation
> Modalities in Therapeutic Recreation Practice
> Therapeutic Recreation Administration

Potential Employers:

> Hospitals
> Nursing homes
> Adult day programs

> Outpatient centers
> Retirement communities
> Developmental disability centers
> Substance recovery programs
> Schools
> Mental health agencies
> Home health care agencies
> Correctional facilities
> Municipal recreation centers

Available At:

The following list of schools offering programs in recreation therapy is not exhaustive. For more programs, visit http://www.atra-tr.org/curriculumguide.htm or http://www.recreationtherapy.com/trcollg.htm.

Kingsborough Community College-City University of New York
Department of Health, Physical Education and Recreation
2001 Oriental Boulevard, Brooklyn, NY 11235
718/368-5831
http://www.kbcc.cuny.edu/academicDepartments/hper/hphome.htm
Degrees available: Associate degree

Moraine Valley Community College
9000 West College Parkway, Palos Hills, IL 60465-0937
708/974-5227
http://www.morainevalley.edu/programs/program_list.htm
Degrees available: Associate degree

For More Information:

American Therapeutic Recreation Association
1414 Prince Street, Suite 204, Alexandria, VA 22314
703/683-9420
atra@atra-tr.org
http://www.atra-tr.org

Therapeutic Recreation Directory
http://www.recreationtherapy.com

Renewable Energy

Energy use in the United States increased by 17 percent between 1991 and 2000, according to the National Energy Policy Development Group. However, our energy production increased by only 2.3 percent. Public concerns about pollution from fossil fuels, increasing costs for conventional energy sources, and our overdependence on foreign energy supplies have created strong interest in renewable energy resources such as wind energy, solar energy, hydropower energy, geothermal energy, and bioenergy. The National Renewable Energy Laboratory estimates that renewable-energy industries will provide at least 300,000 new jobs for American workers over the next two decades. Courses in renewable-energy-related topics can be found at community colleges throughout the United States, but only a few institutions offer certificates and degrees in the field.

Typical Courses:

> Physics
> Mathematics
> Introduction to Renewable Energy
> Introduction to Energy Management
> Renewable Energy Applications
> Photovoltaic Theory and System Design
> Photovoltaic Installation
> Electrical Systems
> Introduction to Wind Energy
> Introduction to Solar Energy
> Introduction to Hydropower
> Introduction to Geothermal Energy
> Introduction to Bioenergy

Potential Employers:

> Manufacturing companies
> Research and development companies
> Utility companies
> Government agencies (such as the National Renewable Energy Laboratory and the Energy Efficiency and Renewable Energy Clearinghouse)
> Nonprofit groups and agencies

> Colleges and universities
> Trade associations
> Engineering firms
> Architecture firms

Available At:

The following list of colleges that offer courses and majors in renewable energy and related fields is not exhaustive. Visit http://eereweb.ee.doe.gov/education/higher_education_programs.html or http://www.irecusa.org for more programs.

Bismarck State College
Process Plant Technology Program
1500 Edwards Avenue, PO Box 5587, Bismarck, ND 58506
800/852-5685
http://www.bismarckstate.edu/energy/students/prop
Degrees available: Certificate, diploma, associate degree

Lane Community College
Science Department
Renewable Energy Technician Program Option
4000 East 30th Avenue, Building 16, Room 253, Eugene, OR 97405
541/463-3977
http://lanecc.edu/instadv/catalog/science/programs/energy.htm
Degrees available: Associate degrees

Minnesota West Community and Technical College-Granite Falls Campus
Renewable Energy Technology Program
1593 11th Avenue, Granite Falls, MN 56241
800/657-3247
http://www.mnwest.edu/academics/programs/manu/rnewaas.htm
Degrees available: Associate degree

San Juan College
Renewable Energy Program
4601 College Boulevard, Farmington, NM 87402
505/326-3311
http://www.sanjuancollege.edu/reng
Degrees available: Certificate, associate degree

For More Information:

American Solar Energy Society
2400 Central Avenue, Suite A, Boulder, CO 80301
303/443-3130
ases@ases.org
http://www.ases.org

Wind energy is one of the fastest-growing renewable energy technologies.

American Wind Energy Association
1101 14th Street, NW, 12th Floor, Washington, DC 20005
202/383-2500
windmail@awea.org
http://www.awea.org

Association of Energy Engineers
4025 Pleasantdale Road, Suite 420, Atlanta, GA 30340
770/447-5083
http://www.aeecenter.org

Geothermal Education Office
664 Hilary Drive, Tiburon, CA 94920
415/435-4574
geo@marin.org
http://www.geothermal.marin.org

Geothermal Energy Association
209 Pennsylvania Avenue, SE, Washington, DC 20003
202/454-5261
research@geo-energy.org
http://www.geo-energy.org

Interstate Renewable Energy Council
PO Box 1156, Latham, NY 12110-1156
518/458-6059
info@irecusa.org
http://www.irecusa.org

Midwest Renewable Energy Association
7558 Deer Road, Custer, WI 54423
715/592-6595
info@the-mrea.org
http://www.the-mrea.org

National Hydropower Association
1 Massachusetts Avenue, NW, Suite 850, Washington, DC 20001
202/682-1700
help@hydro.org
http://www.hydro.org

National Renewable Energy Laboratory
1617 Cole Boulevard, Golden, CO 80401-3393
303/275-3000
http://www.nrel.gov

Renewable Fuels Association
1 Massachusetts Avenue, NW, Suite 820, Washington, DC 20001
202/289-3835
info@ethanolrfa.org
http://www.ethanolrfa.org

Solar Energy Industries Association
805 15th Street, NW, Suite 510, Washington, DC 20005
202/682-0556
info@seia.org
http://www.seia.org

U.S. Department of Energy
Energy Efficiency and Renewable Energy
100 Independence Avenue, SW, Washington, DC 20585
800/342-5363
http://www.eere.energy.gov and http://eereweb.ee.doe.gov/
education/careers_renewable_energy.html

Interview: Tom Munson and Carl Bickford

San Juan College in Farmington, New Mexico, was the first
community college in the United States to offer an associate
degree in renewable energy. The editors of *They Teach That in
Community College!?* discussed renewable energy and the education of renewable energy students with Tom Munson,
Coordinator of the College's Renewable Energy program, and
Carl Bickford, Associate Professor of Engineering and one of the
founders of the program.

Q. Tell us about the renewable energy program at San Juan College.

A. The renewable energy program at San Juan College gives the student a solid foundation in the science and in the design/installation techniques required to work with renewable energy technologies. We offer Photovoltaic System Design and Installation either as an Associate of Applied Science (AAS) degree or as a One-Year Certificate. The certificate is designed for students who already have a college degree or who currently work in a related industry. Students gain the knowledge and skills necessary to design and safely install electrical energy systems based on current photovoltaic and power conditioning equipment. The curriculum includes hands-on electrical training both in a computer-based laboratory and outdoors doing projects and installations. Training in and compliance with the National Electrical Code is emphasized both in the classroom and during installation practice. For additional information, please visit our website at http://www.sanjuancollege.edu/reng.

Q. What types of students enter your program? What are their career goals and interests?

A. The students who enter the program are looking for a career change and want to make a positive difference in the world. They often want to translate academic knowledge into real-world physical projects.

Q. What type of career path does the average student take upon graduating from your program?

A. Most students end up working in the PV (photovoltaic) industry in varying capacities. Some get jobs working as designers and installers for solar companies that do installation and repair services. Others get jobs working for distributors both in technical support capacities and in sales positions. A few have started their own businesses.

Q. What personal qualities do students need to be successful in your program and in their post-college careers?

A. A concern about the environment, wanting to make a difference, and a desire to make this world a better place to live in are qualities that will help students to be successful in the program.

Basic science and math skills and basic tool skills will be helpful in completing the program. Although it isn't required, skill in working with one's hands and prior electrical knowledge and wiring experience are also beneficial.

Q. What is the future for your program and renewable energy?

A. Our program will grow along with the renewable energy industry, which continues to grow in both this country and the world at large. This is an industry that will be on the leading edge as the consciousness of the society increases.

211

Screenwriting

If you've ever dreamed of winning an Academy Award, and you have a talent for writing, a major in screenwriting might help you develop your skills and give you the background and contacts in the film industry to get your career started. Or maybe your interests lie in writing for television. In television screenwriting programs, you can learn to develop scripts for dramatic forms ranging from action-adventure, to social drama, to situational comedy. No matter your interests, you will learn about the elements of character, dialogue, scene, setting, texture, style, and tone via intensive workshop classes. Writing scenes, short scripts, treatments, and finally full-length feature screenplays—ready to be pitched to agents—is what a student majoring in screenwriting can expect. A combination of creative talent, storytelling ability, and college study will give you a leg up over others in this highly competitive industry. Only a few community colleges offer certificates and associate degrees in screenwriting.

Typical Courses:

> Dramatic Structure
> Editing
> Visual Storytelling
> Film and Television Aesthetics
> Introduction to Screenwriting
> History of Film and Television
> Acting for Non-Actors
> Seminar in Television and Film Writing
> Narrative Theory and Practice for Screenwriters
> Writing Screenplay Adaptations
> Film and Television Genres

Potential Employers:

> Movie studios
> Self-employment (freelance writer)
> Production companies
> Talent agencies
> Advertising agencies

Available At:

Minneapolis Community & Technical College
1501 Hennepin Avenue, Minneapolis, MN 55403
800/247-0911
http://www.minneapolis.edu/screenwriting
Degrees available: Associate degree

Santa Ana College
1530 West 17th Street, Santa Ana, CA 92706
714/564-6000
http://sactv.sac.edu/academic/degrees/index.htm
Degrees available: Certificate

For More Information:

American Screenwriters Association
269 South Beverly Drive, Suite 2600, Beverly Hills, CA 90212-3807
866/265-9091
asa@goasa.com
http://www.asascreenwriters.com

Sundance Institute
8530 Wilshire Boulevard, 3rd Floor, Beverly Hills, CA 90211-3114
310/360-1981
la@sundance.org
http://www.sundance.org

Writers Guild of America-East Chapter
555 West 57th Street, Suite 1230, New York, NY 10019
212/767-7800
http://www.wgaeast.org

Writers Guild of America-West Chapter
7000 West Third Street, Los Angeles, CA 90048
800/548-4532
http://www.wga.org

Screenwriter's Utopia
http://www.screenwritersutopia.com

Interview: Alan Miller

Alan Miller teaches in the film program at Minneapolis
Community & Technical College in Minneapolis, Minnesota.
Students who complete the program earn an associate degree in
screenwriting or film and video. Mr. Miller has been teaching

for 30 years. He discussed the education of students in this field with the editors of *They Teach That in Community College!?*

Q. What high school classes should students focus on to be successful in this major?

A. High school students should place a big emphasis on English, history, and the social sciences.

Q. What are the most important personal and professional qualities for screenwriting students?

A. Students must have dedication and be able to handle arduous tasks on deadline. They obviously need to be creative and imaginative, but at the same time be able to work within specific rules and guidelines.

214

Q. Where do your screenwriting graduates find employment?

A. Throughout the film industry and other allied creative fields, from advertising firms and agencies to whomever deals in film, production, or the like.

Q. What is the employment outlook for graduates of your program?

A. Film is a burgeoning field, particularly with the advent of many production companies, the Internet, and cable television. It is the medium students are probably most familiar with and offers a great opportunity for those willing to work hard, to be prompt with their responsibilities, and to overcome rejection, which is built into the industry, and competition from many others striving for the same goals.

Ski Resort Management

Combine your passion for snow sports with a top-notch college education! Employment opportunities exist at mountain operations and resorts throughout the United States in positions such as resort director, ski instructor, and equipment and operations manager. In postsecondary ski management programs, technical and academic instruction is provided, coupled with practical experience in the form of an internship or fieldwork.

Typical Courses:

> Resort Budgeting and Organization
> Resort Master Planning
> Resort Merchandising
> Resort Mountain Operations
> Snow Science
> Ski Business Management
> Methods for the Professional Ski Teacher
> Ski Lift Construction and Design
> Ski Equipment Mechanics
> Internship in Ski Business and Resort Management

Potential Employers:

> Ski resorts

Available At:

Gogebic Community College
E-4946 Jackson Road, Ironwood, MI 49938
906/932-4231, ext. 269
http://www.gogebic.cc.mi.us/departments/sam_div
Degrees available: Associate degree

For More Information:

National Ski Areas Association
133 South Van Gordon Street, Suite 300, Lakewood, CO 80228
http://www.nsaa.org

Professional Ski Instructors of America
133 South Van Gordon Street, Suite 101, Lakewood, CO 80228
303/987-9390
http://www.psia.org

Southwest Studies

The American Southwest is a lively medley of cultures, ethnic groups, traditions, and history. Southwest studies examines the greater Southwest (Arizona, Colorado, New Mexico, and Utah—some schools also include portions of California and Texas in this group) from anthropological, archeological, artistic, cultural, ethnographic, historical, linguistic, political, and other perspectives. In addition to interdisciplinary study, one of the most exciting aspects of Southwest studies classes are the extensive field trips that most classes take, exploring ancient, but still occupied, Pueblo villages along the Rio Grande River in New Mexico; Anasazi ruins in Arizona, New Mexico, Utah, and Colorado; and multicultural meccas such as Santa Fe, New Mexico.

Typical Courses:

> Southwestern Arts and Culture
> History of the Southwest
> Topics in Anthropology
> Native Peoples of the Southwest
> Contemporary Hispanic Writers of the Southwest
> Sustainable Development
> Social and Cultural Dynamics of the Southwest
> Chicano Studies
> Archaeology of the Borderlands
> Environmental Justice

Potential Employers:

> Colleges and universities
> Secondary schools
> Government agencies
> Research-oriented organizations
> Museums and cultural centers

Available At:

The following list of Southwest studies programs is not exhaustive. Other programs—especially at colleges and universities in the American Southwest—may be available.

University of New Mexico-Los Alamos
4000 University Drive, Los Alamos, NM 87554
505/662-0332, 800/894-5919
stuserv@la.unm.edu
http://www.la.unm.edu/admissions/degrees_certificates.html
Degrees available: Certificate, associate degree

Northern New Mexico Community College-Espanola Campus
921 Paseo de Onate, Espanola, NM 87532
505/747-2213
http://www.nnmcc.edu/academics/catalog/areas/chss/
southweststudies.shtml
Degrees available: Associate degree

Santa Fe Community College
6401 Richards Avenue, Santa Fe, NM 87508-4887
505/428-1370
info@sfccnm.edu
http://www.sfccnm.edu/sfcc/pages/1044.html
Degrees available: Associate degree

For More Information:

American Association of Museums
1575 Eye Street, NW, Suite 400, Washington, DC 20005
http://www.aam-us.org

Spanish-Colonial Furniture Making

The Spanish played a key role in the making of the United States, especially in the Southwestern states of Arizona, California, Texas, and New Mexico. Although Spain long gave up its territories in these states, it has left a lasting imprint on the social and cultural life of the area. One of its most memorable legacies is the art of making Spanish-colonial furniture, a style that combines utility with charming decorative touches including painting, inlaying, gilding, detailed carving, metalwork, and leatherwork. Northern New Mexico Community College offers a certificate and associate degree in the field. Its program teaches the basic concepts of woodworking: selection and preparation of stock, adhesives, abrasives, layout of stock, tools and machines (portable and stationary), basic joinery techniques, and hand carving techniques common to making Spanish-Colonial furniture. According to the school, students spend most of their time working on projects that are facilitated by an instructor. Graduates of the program can go on to work for furniture design companies or open their own design studios.

Typical Courses:

> Introduction to Spanish-Colonial Furniture
> Introduction to Spanish-Colonial Furniture Lab
> Spanish-Colonial Furniture Making Lab
> Advanced Spanish-Colonial Furniture Making Lab
> Traditional Woodcarving
> Introduction to Drafting
> Computer-Aided Drafting
> Introduction to Furniture-Making Tools and Materials

Potential Employers:

> Furniture manufacturers
> Industrial design firms
> Self-employed

Available At:

Northern New Mexico Community College-El Rito Campus
PO Box 160, El Rito, NM 87530
505/581-4115
http://www.nnmcc.edu/academics/catalog/areas/voc
and
http://nnmcc.edu/elrito/culturalprograms/scfm.shtml
Degrees available: Certificate, associate degree

For More Information:

The Furniture Society
111 Grovewood Road, Asheville, NC 28804
828/255-1949
mail@furnituresociety.org
http://www.furnituresociety.org

Spanish Colonial Arts Society
PO Box 5378, Santa Fe, NM 87502-5378
505/982-2226
http://www.spanishcolonial.org

219

Speech Language Pathology Assistant

If you are a patient and caring individual with good people skills, you might consider a career as a *speech language pathology assistant*. Speech language pathology assistants work under the supervision of a certified speech language pathologist to perform speech language screenings and to carry out documented tasks related to a patient's speech and language development. The assistant does not diagnose patients, but follows the supervising pathologist's orders in administering therapies. These professionals have the opportunity to work in school settings with children or in health care settings with individuals of all ages, with an emphasis on the aging population. The speech language pathologist assistant also documents each patient's progress, submits reports to the speech language pathologist, and performs a variety of administrative tasks.

Typical Courses:

> Basic Anatomy & Physiology
> Speech & Language Development
> Human Growth & Development
> Anatomy & Physiology of Speech and Hearing Mechanism
> Language Disorders
> Phonetics
> Disorders of Articulation
> Adult and Geriatric Communication Disorders
> Clinical Procedures in Speech-Language Pathology
> Clinical Fieldwork

Potential Employers:

> Schools
> Day care centers
> Nursing homes
> Medical clinics
> Health maintenance organizations
> Hospitals
> Public health departments
> Research agencies

> Colleges and universities
> Private practice
> Long-term care facilities
> Rehabilitation centers
> Government agencies
> Industrial audiology
> Corporate speech-language pathology programs

Available At:

The following list of speech language pathology assisting programs is not exhaustive. Check with academic institutions near you to determine if majors, minors, certificates, or concentrations are available in speech language pathology assisting.

New Hampshire Community Technical College-Nashua
505 Amherst Street, Nashua, NH 03063
603/882-6923
nashua@nhctc.edu
http://www.nashua.nhctc.edu/Academic%20Programs/
SpeechLangPathAsst.htm
Degrees available: Associate degree

Santa Ana College
1530 West 17th Street, Santa Ana, CA 92706
http://www.sac.edu/degrees/sac/
Speech-Language_Pathology_Assistant.htm
Degrees available: Certificate, associate degree

Williston State College
1410 University Avenue, PO Box 1326, Williston, ND 58802
888/863-9455
http://www.wsc.nodak.edu/academics/career_tech%20programs/
speech_pathology/speech_path_asssistant.htm
Degrees available: Associate degree

221

For More Information:

American Speech-Language-Hearing Association
10801 Rockville Pike, Rockville, MD 20852
800/498-2071, 301/897-5700 (TTY)
http://www.asha.org

National Student Speech Language Hearing Association
10801 Rockville Pike, Rockville, MD 20852
800/498-2071
http://www.nsslha.org

Sports Management

Maybe you dreamed of being a major league baseball player, a grand slam tennis tournament winner, or a professional golfer but your talents never quite reached that of the professional athlete. You can still pursue a passion for sports with a degree in sports management! Health and fitness conscious individuals will gain a business and fitness background that will prepare them for careers as fitness club managers, sales and marketing professionals for professional sports teams, and health educators or program directors for their local parks and recreation department. Individuals of all ages engage in sporting activity as a means for social interaction and a step towards healthy living. If you possess good communication skills and a desire to help individuals reach their fitness goals—while having fun playing sports—a degree in sports management is an excellent means to jump-starting your career. Most programs have options that allow you to concentrate on an area that is most important to you—business management, health and science, or recreation leadership.

Typical Courses:

> Sports Marketing
> Public Relations and Advertising for the Sports Industry
> Accounting
> Fitness Facility Management
> Philosophy, Principles, and Organization of Athletics in Education
> Program Planning and Leadership for Recreation and Physical Education
> Sports and Society
> Current Issues in Sports
> Sports Law
> Health and Fitness Electives

Potential Employers:

> Fitness and health clubs
> Community recreation departments
> Professional sports teams
> Colleges and universities

Available At:

The following list of sports management programs is not exhaustive. Check with academic institutions near you to determine if majors, minors, certificates, or concentrations are available in sports management.

Central Arizona College
8470 North Overfield Road, Coolidge, AZ 85228
http://www.centralaz.edu/portal/
page?_pageid=195,209915&_dad=portal&_schema=PORTAL
Degrees available: Associate degree

New Hampshire Community Technical College-Concord
31 College Drive, Concord, NH 03301-7412
http://nhti.edu/academics/academicprograms/degsprtmgmt.html
and
http://nhti.edu/academics/academicprograms/certsportsmgmt.html
Degrees available: Certificate, associate degree

Mercyhurst College North East
16 West Division Street, North East, PA 16428
800/825-1926
http://northeast.mercyhurst.edu/programs_of_study/
associate_degrees.htm#business_administration_sport
Degrees available: Associate degree

Basketball is one of the five most popular sports in the United States.

New Hampshire Technical Institute
31 College Drive, Concord, NH 03301-7412
603/271-7734
http://www.nhti.edu/academics/academicprograms/
degsprtmgmt.html
and
http://www.nhti.edu/academics/academicprograms/
certsportsmgmt.html
Degrees available: Certificate, associate degree

North Country Community College
23 Santanoni Avenue, PO Box 89, Saranac Lake, NY 12983-0089
518/891-2915, ext.311
http://www.nccc.edu/sports_events_management.html
Degrees available: Associate degree

North Iowa Area Community College
500 College Drive, Mason City, IA 50401
641/422-4281
http://www.niacc.edu/business/sportmanage.html
Degrees available: Associate degree

224

For More Information:

National Association for Sport and Physical Education
1900 Association Drive, Reston, VA 20191-1598
800/213-7193
naspe@aahperd.org
http://www.aahperd.org/naspe/template.cfm

North American Society for Sport Management
http://www.nassm.com

Supply Chain Management

Supply chain management professionals are key players in manufacturing and service industries. According to the Institute for Supply Management, they use their knowledge of purchasing/procurement, transportation/logistics, contract development, negotiation, inventory control, distribution and warehousing, product development, economic forecasting, risk management, and global business to help their companies stay competitive in a global economy. A growing number of colleges and universities are offering degrees in supply chain management (sometimes called logistics and transportation management, global logistics management, operations and supply chain management, transportation and logistics management, and acquisitions management) at the certificate through graduate levels. Other schools offer study in the field via supply chain management concentrations that are part of degrees in business, business administration, business information systems, management, marketing, or other fields.

Typical Classes:

> Introduction to Supply Chain Management
> Economics
> Transportation Management
> Strategic Warehouse Management
> Sales
> Negotiations: Theory and Practice
> Information Technology Tools
> Forecasting in the Supply Chain
> Quality Process Management
> Supply Chain Research and Analysis Techniques
> Inventory Strategies
> E-Commerce and the Supply Chain
> Customer Relationships

Potential Employers:

> Technology companies
> Manufacturing companies
> Service organizations
> Consulting firms
> Any organization that offers products or services

Available At:

The following list of schools offering programs in supply chain management is not exhaustive. For more programs, visit the following website: http://www.ism.ws/ISMMembership/SchoolsOfferingCourses.cfm.

University of Alaska-Anchorage
College of Business and Public Policy
3211 Providence Drive, Anchorage, AK 99508
907/786-4100
http://www.scob.alaska.edu/logistics.asp
Degrees available: Certificate, associate degree, bachelor's degree, master's degree

Cecil Community College
One Seahawk Drive, North East, MD 21901
410/287-1000
http://www.cecilcc.edu/programs/programs-05-07/
transportation-logistics/transportation-management.asp
Degrees available: Certificate, associate degree

Columbus State Community College
PO Box 1609, Columbus, OH 43216-1609
800/621-6407
http://www.cscc.edu/DOCS/logcurr.htm
Degrees available: Certificates, associate degree

Cuyahoga Community College (multiple campuses)
Administrative Offices
700 Carnegie Avenue, Cleveland, OH 44115
216/987-4000
http://www.tri-.edu/CATALOG/0507/sequences/programs/
purchasing.htm
Degrees available: Associate degree

Greenville Technical College-Barton Campus
PO Box 5616, Greenville, SC 29607
864/250-8111
http://greenvilletech.com/academic_programs/
materials_management.html
and
http://greenvilletech.com/academic_programs/
supply_chain_management_certificate.html
Degrees available: Certificate, associate degree

Harper College
1200 West Algonquin Road, Palatine, IL 60067
847/925-6707
http://goforward.harpercollege.edu
Degrees available: Certificate, associate degree

Illinois Central College
Business and Information Systems Department
1 College Drive, Technology Center, Room 205
East Peoria, IL 61635-0001
http://www.icc.edu/bis/cat_display.asp?id=97
Degrees available: Certificate

Did You Know?

U.S. News & World Report recently selected supply chain management as a hot track career field.

Ivy Tech Community College of Indiana-Indianapolis Campus
50 West Fall Creek Parkway North Drive, Indianapolis, IN 46208
888/489-5463
http://www.ivytech.edu/programs/log
Degrees available: Associate degree

227

Johnson County Community College
12345 College Boulevard, Overland Park, KS 66210-1299
913/469-8500
http://www.jccc.net/home/catalog/default/toccareerprograms/
careerprograms/AAS-BUSLOGIS
Degrees available: Associate degree

Lakeshore Technical College
1290 North Avenue, Cleveland, WI 53015-1414
888/468-6582
http://www.gotoltc.com/programs
Degrees available: Certificate, associate degree

Lenoir Community College
PO Box 188, Kinston, NC 28502-0188
252/527-6223, ext. 613
http://www.lenoir.cc.nc.us/nsite/academicprogs/globalogA25170.htm
Degrees available: Associate degree

Northeast Wisconsin Technical College
PO Box 19042, Green Bay, WI 54307-9042
920/498-5444
http://www.nwtc.edu/Programs
Degrees available: Certificate, associate degree

Northern Virginia Community College-Alexandria Campus
3001 North Beauregard Street, Room AA 362, Alexandria, VA 22311
703/845-6313
http://www.nvcc.edu/alexandria/business/ACQProgram.asp
Degrees available: Certificate, associate degree

Northwood University
1900 West Big Beaver, Suite 200, Troy, MI 48084
248/649-5111
http://www.northwood.edu/uc/locations/michigan/troy/
default.asp?section=asm
Degrees available: Associate degree

Oakton Community College
1600 East Golf Road, Des Plaines, IL 60016
847/635-1600
http://www.oakton.edu/acad/career/mgt_p3.htm#pmcert
Degrees available: Certificate

Palo Alto College
1400 West Villaret, San Antonio, TX 78224
210/921-5151
http://www.accd.edu/pac/mgt/Degrees.htm
Degrees available: Certificate, associate degree

Riverside Community College-Norco Campus
2001 Third Street, Norco, CA 92860-2600
951/372-7000
http://www.academic.rcc.edu/logisticsmanagement
Degrees available: Certificates, associate degrees

Shoreline Community College
6101 Greenwood Avenue North, Shoreline, WA 98133-5696
206/297-9290
http://success.shoreline.edu/jbaker
Degrees available: Certificates, associate degree

Sinclair Community College
444 West Third Street, Dayton, OH 45402-1460
800/315-3000
http://www.sinclair.edu/stservices/cppc/EmployerServices/
DegreeandCertificatePrograms/index.cfm
Degrees available: Certificate, associate degree

Tulsa Community College-Northeast Campus
Business and Information Technology Division
3727 East Apache, Tulsa, OK 74115
918/595-7439
http://www.tulsacc.edu
Degrees available: Certificates, associate degree

For More Information:

American Society of Transportation and Logistics
1700 North Moore Street, Suite 1900, Arlington, VA 22209
703/524-5011
astl@nitl.org
http://www.astl.org

Council of Supply Chain Management Professionals
2805 Butterfield Road, Suite 200, Oak Brook, IL 60523-1170
630/574-0985
cscmpadmin@cscmp.org
http://www.cscmp.org

Institute for Supply Management
PO Box 22160, Tempe, AZ 85285-2160
800/888-6276
http://www.ism.ws

Interview: Rex Beck

Rex Beck is an assistant professor in the Logistics Management Program at Riverside Community College-Norco Campus in Norco, California. He has more than 20 years of experience in logistics management, including materials management, logistics analysis and administrative support, logistics customer field and call center support, warehouse management system implementation, reverse logistics, warehouse management, and quality system implementation and management. Mr. Beck discussed Riverside's logistic management program and the education of students in this field with the editors of *They Teach That in Community College!?*

Q. What educational options are available to students in your program?

A. We offer two certificates (in Logistics Management, and Business Administration with a Logistics Management Concentration) and two AS degrees (also in Logistics Management, and Business Administration with a Logistics Management Concentration).

Q. What high school subjects/activities should students focus on to be successful in this major?

A. Although vocational-level coursework related to the logistics industry would be helpful, such coursework is usually not available at the high school level. Coursework, both available and necessary, would include classes that develop the strong written, verbal, mathematical, and computer skills demanded by both industry and our academic program.

As an educator of future managers, we would find high school activities providing the opportunity to develop leadership skills an excellent starting point. During the high school years, students may also find opportunities for entry-level work within the industry. Such hands-on experience is always a positive.

Q. What are the most important personal and professional qualities for logistics management students?

A. The most important thing to us is that our graduates have the skills necessary to thrive as managers in the demanding environment of our logistics industry. One of the exciting things about this industry is the opportunity to utilize a broad base of knowledge and skills. A wide variety of technical and managerial skills are necessary to be a competent contributor. To go beyond this and join the ranks of the best managers requires much more than technical skills and the application of management skills such as planning, organizing, and controlling. These things are table stakes. True excellence requires great commitment and a highly motivational leadership style.

Q. What educational level is typically required for logistics management graduates to land good jobs in the industry?

A. The history of our industry tells us individuals with excellent potential as managers can rise from entry-level positions to responsible management positions with nothing beyond a high school diploma. These days are behind us for all but a few employers. It is now common for employers to require a general bachelor's degree before promoting an individual into a management position. Because our program is unique in educating students specifically as logistics managers, we are finding our associate degree graduates to be very competitive.

Q. Where do logistics management graduates find employment?

A. Logistics management graduates find employment in positions involving warehousing, purchasing, contract management, transportation and traffic, inventory management, and numerous other activities related to the movement and delivery of goods from the point of origin to the final consumer. Logistics management has become so critical to commerce that many logistics practitioners are making the jump to general executive management.

Q. How will the field of logistics management change in the future?

A. Logistics management often involves finding the right trade-off between technology, labor, and facilities. Since technology is becoming increasing economical over time, while labor and facilities only rise in cost with the passage of time, we will continue to see technology used more extensively. This will likewise create a future in which the logistics manager will work in an environment which is increasingly driven by technology. Pressures for these future managers to be formally educated will logically continue to increase as well.

Surgical Technology

You've probably seen enough operating-room scenes on television and in the movies to know that there are many health care professionals present during a surgery—far more than just surgeons and nurses. *Surgical technologists* are part of this group. Preparing the operating room, creating and maintaining the sterile field, and gathering and organizing necessary equipment and supplies are just some of the vital pre-operative responsibilities of this professional. During surgery, the surgical technologist passes instruments to the surgeon and must be skilled enough to anticipate the needs of the surgeon. He or she also handles and prepares medications and specimens. When the surgery has concluded, the surgical technologist is responsible for maintaining the sterile field until the patient is transported and removing any instruments or equipment. The operating room can be a stressful environment, and the surgical technologist must be able to work well under pressure. The surgical technologist's role is indeed vital to a successful surgery—he or she plays a role in saving lives. According to the U.S. Department of Labor, the demand for surgical technologists is expected to increase at a rate of 21 to 35 percent through 2012. An aging population along with advances in medical technology create the need for trained individuals who are able to meet the needs of this growing profession.

Typical Courses:

> Surgical Instrumentation, Equipment and Supplies
> Principles of Asepsis and Sterile Technique
> Surgical Procedures
> Medical Terminology
> Anatomy and Physiology
> Microbiology
> Surgical Pharmacology and Anesthesia Techniques
> Safety Standards in the Operating Room
> General Patient Care and Safety
> Legal, Moral, and Ethical Issues
> Postoperative Considerations

Potential Employers:

> Hospital surgical units

> Obstetric departments
> Specialized surgical units (cardiac, pediatric, etc.)
> Outpatient care centers
> Physician's offices
> Medical corporations
> Military
> Labor and delivery departments
> Medical sales

Available At:

The following list of colleges that offer degrees in surgical technology is not exhaustive. The Commission on Accreditation of Allied Health Education Programs accredits surgical technology programs. Visit its website, http://www.caahep.org, for a complete list of programs.

Bunker Hill Community College
250 New Rutherford Avenue, Boston, MA 02129-2925
http://www.bhcc.mass.edu/AR/ProgramsOfStudy/
Programs2005.php?programID=47
Degrees available: Certificate

College of DuPage
425 Fawell Boulevard, Glen Ellyn, IL 60137
630/562-2804
http://www.cod.edu/academic/OccVocEd/surgical/tech.htm
Degrees available: Associate degree

College of Southern Idaho
315 Falls Avenue, PO Box 1238, Aspen Building, Room 153
Twin Falls, ID 83303-1238
800/680-0274, ext. 6706
http://www.csi.edu/l4.asp?SurgicalTech
Degrees available: Certificate

Columbus State Community College
PO Box 1609, Columbus, OH 43216-1609
800/621-6407
http://www.cscc.edu/DOCS/surgcurr.htm
Degrees available: Certificate, associate degree

Community College of Allegheny County-Boyce Campus
595 Beatty Road, Monroeville, PA 15146-1396
http://www.ccac.edu/default.aspx?id=144958
and
http://www.ccac.edu/default.aspx?id=138749
Degrees available: Certificate, associate degree

Eastern Idaho Technical College
1600 South 25th East, Idaho Falls, ID 83404
800/662-0261
http://www.eitc.edu/pdf/catalog/Surgical%20Technology.pdf
Degrees available: Associate degree

Flathead Valley Community College-Kalispell Campus
777 Grandview Drive, Kalispell, MT 59901
406/756-3846
http://www.fvcc.edu/academics/catalog/2005/SurgicalTechnology.shtml
Degrees available: Associate degree

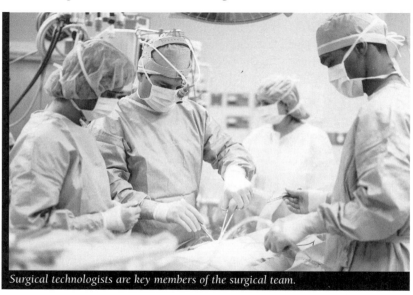

Surgical technologists are key members of the surgical team.

Florida Community College at Jacksonville
501 West State Street, Jacksonville, FL 32202
904/766-6585
info@fccj.edu
http://www.fccj.org/prospective/programs/data05_06/5667.html
Degrees available: Associate degree

Ivy Tech Community College of Indiana (multiple campuses)
50 West Fall Creek Parkway North Drive, Indianapolis, IN 46208
888-489-5463
http://www.ivytech.edu/programs/sur
Degrees available: Associate degree

Kirkwood Community College
6301 Kirkwood Boulevard, SW, Cedar Rapids, IA 52404
800/363-2220, ext 5566
info@kirkwood.edu.cc.ia.us
http://www.kirkwood.edu/site/index.php?t=2&d=2&p=65
Degrees available: Diploma

Lansing Community College
PO Box 40010, Lansing, MI 48901-7210
800/644-4522
selectiveadmissions@lcc.edu
http://www.lcc.edu/health/surgical_tech
Degrees available: Associate degree

Macomb Community College
14500 East 12 Mile Road, Warren, MI 48088
586/286-2192
answer@macomb.edu
http://www.macomb.edu/ProgramDescriptions/
SurgicalTechnology.asp
Degrees available: Certificates, associate degree

Madison Area Technical College
Health Occupations Department
3550 Anderson Street, Madison, WI 53704
608/246-6280
http://matcmadison.edu/matc/ASP/showprogram.asp?ID=3086
Degrees available: Diploma

Montgomery College-Takoma Park/Silver Spring Campus
Department of Surgical Technology
7600 Takoma Avenue, Health Science Center, Room 359
Takoma Park, MD 20912
301/562-5541
http://www.mc.cc.md.us/surgtech
Degrees available: Certificate, associate degree

Nashville State Community College
120 White Bridge Road, Nashville, TN 37209
615/353-3340
http://www.nscc.edu/depart/surg/index.html
Degrees available: Certificate

Nassau Community College
One Education Drive, Garden City, NY 11530
516/572-7345
http://www.ncc.edu/dptpages/ahs/ST/Frame1.html
Degrees available: Associate degree

Oakland Community College
2480 Opdyke Road, Bloomfield Hills, MI 48304
248/341-2000
http://www.oaklandcc.edu/FutureStudents/DegreePrograms.asp
Degrees available: Associate degree

Salt Lake Community College
4600 South Redwood Road, Salt Lake City, UT 84123
801/957-4161
http://www.slcc.edu/pages/1043.asp
Degrees available: Certificate, associate degree

San Jacinto College-Central Campus
8060 Spencer Highway, Pasadena, TX 77505
281/476-1816
http://www.sjcd.edu/program/surgical_tech.html
Degrees available: Certificate, associate degree

Santa Fe Community College-Northwest Campus
3000 Northwest 83rd Street, Gainesville, FL 32606
352/395-5000
http://inst.sfcc.edu/~health/surgtech
Degrees available: Associate degree

Southeast Community College-Lincoln Campus
8800 O Street, Lincoln, NE 68520-1299
800/642-4075, ext. 2785
http://www.southeast.edu/SURT/surt_welcome.html
Degrees available: Associate degree

Western Dakota Technical Institute
800 Mickelson Drive, Rapid City, SD 57703
800/544-8765
http://wdti.tec.sd.us/sonisweb/reports/
wdti_programs_detail.cfm?program=580
Degrees available: Diploma

For More Information:

Association of Surgical Technologists
7108-C South Alton Way, Centennial, CO 80112
303/694-9130
http://www.ast.org

Interview: Kathleen Uribe

Kathleen Uribe is the program chair of the Surgical Technology Program at Southeast Community College in Lincoln, Nebraska. Students who complete the program receive an associate of applied science degree. The program is also noteworthy in that it is the only CAAHEP-accredited program to offer its entire program online. Kathleen discussed the school's program and the education of students in this field with the editors of *They Teach That in Community College!?*

Q. Tell us about the career of surgical technologist.

A. Surgical technologists are highly skilled and uniquely pre-pared to their role as a valuable and integral part of the surgi-cal team. Surgical technologists perform a wide variety of tasks in the operating room. They anticipate the needs of the surgical team, handle instruments, and assist the surgeon by holding retractors, cutting suture, suctioning the wound, adjusting lights and applying dressings, to name a few. Additional responsibilities are to operate the sterilizer; set up the room in preparation for the procedure; care and handling of instruments before, during, and after the procedure; and to prepare for the next day's schedule. The primary focus is keeping patient care number one. The motto of the surgical technologist is, "Aeger Primo-The Patient Comes First."

Q. Tell us about the online aspects of your program.

A. In this day and age, the average student is so busy with their lives and work that they really like the opportunity for web-based learning. The online program allows distance educa-tion students the convenience to work at home online for the didactic portion of the program; the labs and clinicals are conducted at a hospital in the student's area that is willing to take them on as a student under our guidance. Distance edu-cation also gives students-especially those in rural areas-the opportunity to learn surgical technology even if it is not available at a school near them. It also helps to provide quali-fied surgical technologists in rural areas.

Q. What high school subjects/activities should students focus on to be successful in this major?

A. High school students should focus on the sciences, such as anatomy and physiology, biology, and microbiology.

Q. What are the most important personal and professional qualities for surgical technology students and professionals in the field?

A. A successful student and surgical technologist is highly motivated, a self-starter, honest, and has integrity. They should be able to handle difficult and stressful situations. They also should be physically capable to stand for long periods of time and lift heavy objects.

Q. Where do surgical technology graduates find employment?

A. Job opportunities include hospitals, medical centers, surgery outpatient centers, doctor's offices, labor and delivery departments, the sterile processing and distribution department of a hospital, education departments, and medical sales, to name a few. Surgical technology is also a great stepping stone as preparation to become a physician's assistant. There is also the opportunity to advance to the position of first assistant. The certified first assistant's main impetus is to assist the surgeon during surgery above and beyond the tasks and skills of the certified surgical technologist. Additional schooling and certification is required to function as a certified first assistant.

Q. How will the change in the future?

A. At this time only a few states require the surgical technologist to maintain his or her professional certification. As the profession grows and becomes stronger, we hope that at some point it will become mandatory that a surgical technologist will need to be licensed in each state. At this time there is a shortage of qualified certified surgical technologists, and this need will continue as the baby boomers age. The national professional organization, the Association of Surgical Technologists, is in support of all surgical technology programs granting the associate degree of applied science.

Television, Film, and Radio Production

Every time you turn on your television and watch your favorite sitcom, nightly newscast, pay-per-view movie, or television commercial, an entire team of behind-the-scenes production personnel was involved in the creation of what you see on the screen. Lighting and sound technicians, camera operators, and video editors are just a few positions on this team of professionals who work together to make what we see and hear a visual and auditory success. Students in television, film, and radio production technology programs can expect to get significant hands-on experience, as much of the mastery of these types of skills comes from practice. This is a competitive field, so students should be strong-willed, hardworking, and willing to do a lot of grunt work in the beginning. You may find yourself on-location at a video shoot for a commercial, in the studio mixing sound or editing film, or on assignment shooting a live news report. Graduates will find work inside and outside the studio, and individuals who seek flexibility in their work environment will find a career in television, film, and radio production a perfect match.

Typical Courses:

> Directing for Television and Film
> Remote Production/Video Editing
> Television Studio Production for Business
> Audio for Motion Pictures and Television
> Physics of Sound
> Cinematography
> Pre-Production for Motion Pictures and Film
> Film/Video Production Aesthetics and History
> Radio Production
> Post-Production Techniques
> Lighting for Television and Video
> Practicum/Fieldwork

Potential Employers:

> Television and radio stations
> Motion picture studios

> Video production companies
> Large corporations with in-house advertising departments

Available At:

The following list of television, film, and radio production programs is not exhaustive. Check with academic institutions near you to determine if majors, minors, certificates, or concentrations are available in television, film, and radio production.

**Borough of Manhattan Community College-
City University of New York**
Speech, Communications, and Theatre Arts Department
199 Chambers Street, New York, NY 10007
212/220-8090
http://www.bmcc.cuny.edu/speech/VAT/VAT.html
Degrees available: Associate degree

College of DuPage
Liberal Arts Division
425 Fawell Boulevard, Glen Ellyn, IL 60137
630/942-2047
http://www.cod.edu/academic/acadprog/occ_voc/ComArtSc.htm
Degrees available: Certificate, associate degrees

Lansing Community College
PO Box 40010, Lansing, MI 48901-7210
800/644-4522
welcome@lcc.edu
http://www.lcc.edu/mait/motion_picture/index.htm
and
http://www.lcc.edu/mait/media/index.htm
Degrees available: Certificates, associate degrees

Montgomery College-Rockville Campus
51 Mannakee Street, Rockville, MD 20850
301/279-5000
http://www.montgomerycollege.edu/curricula/descriptions/
cdcommunications.htm#tv
and
http://www.montgomerycollege.edu/curricula/descriptions/
cdcommunications.htm#tvcert
Degrees available: Certificates, associate degrees

Palm Beach Community College
4200 Congress Avenue, Lake Worth, FL 33461
561/207-5421
http://www.pbcc.edu/programs/programsheet.asp?id=72
Degrees available: Associate degree

Piedmont Community College
Department of Film and Video Production Technology
PO Box 1150, Yanceyville, NC 27379
336/694-5707
http://www.pccfilm.com
Degrees available: Associate degree

Southern Maine Community College
2 Fort Road, South Portland, ME 04106
207/741-5500
http://www.smccme.edu
Degrees available: Associate degree

Suffolk County Community College-Ammerman Campus
533 College Road, Selden, NY 11784-2899
631/451-4000
http://www3.sunysuffolk.edu/Curricula/306.asp
Degrees available: Associate degree

For More Information:

International Alliance of Theatrical Stage Employees, Moving Picture Technicians, Artists and Allied Crafts
1430 Broadway, 20th Floor, New York, NY 10018
212/730-1770
http://www.iatse-intl.org

National Association of Broadcast Employees and Technicians
nabet@nabetcwa.org
http://nabetcwa.org

Society of Broadcast Engineers
9102 North Meridian Street, Suite 150, Indianapolis, IN 46260
317/846-9000
mclappe@sbe.org
http://www.sbe.org

Society of Motion Picture and Television Engineers
3 Barker Avenue, White Plains, NY 10601
http://www.smpte.org

Travel Industry Management

Do you love traveling to exotic places? Do you enjoy planning every minute detail of a family vacation? Are you fascinated with the behind-the-scenes world of the travel industry? If so, here is the job for you! Career opportunities abound in travel management—one of the nation's largest industries. As a travel management professional, you'll be responsible for helping consumers get the most for their vacation dollars. You'll advise, coordinate, and give alternatives for destinations, modes of travel, and accommodations. Programs, varying from certificate to a master's degree, stress business skills to prepare students for management positions throughout the travel industry. Practical work is also required, with onsite experience gained in a variety of travel and tourism settings.

Typical Courses:

> Hotel and Restaurant Management
> Food and Beverage Management
> Travel Industry Marketing
> Destination Development and Marketing
> Managerial Economics
> Accounting
> Business Law
> Human Resource Management
> Travel Industry Financial Analysis and Controls
> Passenger Transportation Management

Potential Employers:

> Hotels
> Restaurants
> Airlines
> Cultural institutions
> Museums
> Convention bureaus
> Travel agencies
> Tour operators
> Consulting agencies
> Government agencies

Available At:

The following list of travel industry management programs is not exhaustive. Check with academic institutions near you to determine if majors, minors, certificates, or concentrations are available in travel industry management.

Broward Community College
111 East Las Olas Boulevard, Fort Lauderdale, FL 33301
954/201-7400
http://www.broward.edu
Degrees available: Associate degree

College of DuPage
Travel and Tourism Program
425 Fawell Boulevard, IC 1031B, Glen Ellyn, IL 60137-6599
http://www.cod.edu/academic/acadprog/occ_voc/Travel
Degrees available: Certificates, associate degrees

Did You Know?

In 2004, there were 760 million international tourist arrivals—an all-time record according to the World Tourism Organization. The 10 most popular tourism destinations in the world (in descending order) in 2003 were France, Spain, the United States, Italy, China, United Kingdom, Austria, Mexico, Germany, and Canada.

Community College of Allegheny County-North Campus
8701 Perry Highway, Pittsburgh, PA 15237-5372
412/369-3600
http://www.ccac.edu/default.aspx?id=147243
Degrees available: Associate degree

Houston Community College-Central College
1300 Holman, PO Box 7849, Houston, TX 77270-7849
713/718-6072
http://ccollege.hccs.edu/workforc/hotel/travel/travel.htm
Degrees available: Certificate, associate degree

Miami Dade College (multiple campuses)
305/237-8888
mdccinfo@mdc.edu
https://sisvsr.mdc.edu/ps/sheet.aspx
Degrees available: Associate degree

Moraine Valley Community College
9000 West College Parkway, Palos Hills, IL 60465-0937
708/974-4300
http://www.morainevalley.edu
Degrees available: Certificate, associate degree

Northern Virginia Community College (multiple campuses)
Administrative Offices
4001 Wakefield Chapel Road, Annandale, VA 22003-3796
703/323-3000
http://www.nv.cc.va.us/curcatalog/programs/tratou.htm
Degrees available: Associate degree

Palm Beach Community College
4200 Congress Avenue, Lake Worth, FL 33461
561/868-3353
http://www.pbcc.edu/programs/department.asp?dept_id=35
Degrees available: Associate degree

For More Information:

National Tour Association
546 East Main Street, Lexington, KY 40508
859/226-4444, 800/682-8886
questions@ntastaff.com
http://www.ntaonline.com

Outdoor Industry Association
4909 Pearl East Circle, Suite 200, Boulder, CO 80301
303/444-3353
info@outdoorindustry.org
http://www.outdoorindustry.org

Travel Industry Association of America
1100 New York Avenue, NW, Suite 450, Washington, DC 20005
202/408-8422
http://www.tia.org

Turfgrass Management

Do you love the look, smell, and feel of a healthy lawn? Ever wonder who was responsible for maintaining the pristine look of your local golf course? Turfgrass managers are currently in demand by golf course facilities, nurseries, and athletic field owners to manage and keep grass green and healthy. Your coursework will include training in different types of turf—from the hardy grass found at golf courses and playing fields, to the plants and sod raised by nurseries and greenhouses. Not only will you be an expert at the different types of grass, but also the ways in which to keep them healthy using irrigation and pest control techniques. Many programs offered by community colleges offer non-traditional methods of degree completion such as video or Web-based classes. Some schools, such as Virginia's Tidewater Community College offer work/study programs at local facilities. Students put their classroom knowledge to the test while at the same time earning valuable work experience.

Typical Courses:

> Introduction to Golf and Turf Management
> Soil and Water Management
> Principles of Plant Growth
> Putting Green Management
> Applied Ecology
> Landscape Plans
> Turf and Athletic Field Maintenance
> Greenhouse Production and Garden Center Management
> Soils and Plant Nutrition
> Horticulture Management

Potential Employers:

> Golf courses
> Greenhouses and nurseries
> Athletic fields
> Landscape design companies

Available At:

The following list of turfgrass management programs is not exhaustive. Check with academic institutions near you to determine if majors, minors, certificates, or concentrations are available in turf-grass management.

Cincinnati State Technical and Community College
3520 Central Parkway, Cincinnati, OH 45223
513/861-7700
http://www.cinstate.cc.oh.us/FutureStudent/Academics/
AcademicDivisions/BusinessTechnologies/tur.htm
and
http://www.cincinnatistate.edu/CurrentStudent/Academics/
AcademicDivisions/BusinessTechnologies/turc.htm
Degrees available: Certificate, associate degree

Delaware Technical and Community College (multiple campuses)
400 Stanton-Christiana Road, Newark, DE 19713
302/588-5288
http://www.dtcc.edu/stanton-wilmington/programs/
tech_sheets_web/TurfManagement.pdf
Degrees available: Certificate, diploma, associate degree

For More Information:

Golf Course Superintendents Association of America
1421 Research Park Drive, Lawrence, KS 66049-3859
800/472-7878
infobox@gcsaa.org
http://www.gcsaa.org

Professional Grounds Management Society
720 Light Street, Baltimore, MD 21230-3816
800/609-7467
pgms@assnhqtrs.com
http://www.pgms.org

Professional Landcare Network
950 Herndon Parkway, Suite 450, Herndon, VA 20170
800/395-2522
http://www.landcarenetwork.org/cms/home.html

Sports Turf Managers Association
805 New Hampshire, Suite E, Lawrence, KS 66044
800/323-38755
http://www.sportsturfmanager.org

Web Design/Development

Every website you visit, whether it's a company or personal site, was designed by someone. Some are trained professionals and others are not. If you've been to a website that contained hard-to-find information, out-of-date links, and visually chaotic graphics, you understand the importance of good design in attracting people to a site. The advent of the Internet for the mainstream population created an instant demand for individuals to create aesthetically pleasing, user-friendly websites for businesses of all sizes. *Website developers and designers* create and maintain highly professional and complex websites for corporations, associations, schools, and more. The website designer plays an integral role in an organization's ability to communicate a message, attract and maintain customers, and disseminate pertinent information. He or she must have an eye for design and an aptitude for computer technology. The U.S. Department of Labor notes that among design occupations, there will be an increase in graphic design jobs through 2014, particularly for graphic designers with website design experience. However, competition in this field is significant, and individuals entering the field must be prepared for a competitive marketplace upon graduation.

Typical Courses:

> Design Process and Technology
> Drawing for Graphic Designers
> Multimedia Technology
> HTML
> Photoshop
> InDesign
> Dreamweaver
> Internet Graphics
> Fireworks
> Flash
> 3-D Modeling & Animation

Potential Employers:

> Advertising agencies
> Corporations with in-house designers
> Graphic design firms

> Internet service providers
> Consulting agencies
> Freelance opportunities (self-employment)

Available At:

The following list of Web design/development programs is not exhaustive. Check with academic institutions near you to determine if majors, minors, certificates, or concentrations are available in Web design/development.

Bergen Community College
400 Paramus Road, Paramus, NJ 07652
201/447-7195
http://www.bergen.edu/ecatalog/
programview.asp?program.cbn=22&semester.rm=1
Degrees available: Associate degree

Cecil Community College
One Seahawk Drive, North East, MD 21901
410/287-1000
information@cecilcc.edu
http://www.cecilcc.edu/programs/programs-05-07/
art-science/arts-web-design.asp
Degrees available: Certificate, associate degree

Cincinnati State Technical and Community College
3520 Central Parkway, Cincinnati, OH 45223
513/861-7700
http://www.cinstate.cc.oh.us/FutureStudent/Academics/
AcademicDivisions/InformationTechnologies/MWEB.htm
Degrees available: Associate degree

Community College of Vermont (multiple campuses)
inquire@ccv.edu
http://www.ccv.edu/degree/AAS/web_design
Degrees available: Associate degree

Dawson Community College
300 College Drive, PO Box 421, Glendive, MT 59330
800/821-8320
http://www.dawson.edu/academics/Catalog/
DCCAASDegreePlansofStudy.asp#WebDevelopment
Degrees available: Associate degree

Delaware County Community College-Marple Campus
Information Technology Department
901 South Media Line Road, Media, PA 19063-1094
610/359-5050
http://www.dccc.edu/catalog/
career_programs.html#web_development
Degrees available: Associate degree

Eastern Idaho Technical College
1600 South 25th East, Idaho Falls, ID 83404
800/662-0261
http://www.eitc.edu/pdf/catalog/
Web%20Development%20Specialist.pdf
Degrees available: Associate degree

Hudson Valley Community College
80 Vandenburgh Avenue, Troy, NY 12180
518/629-7225
business@hvcc.edu
https://www.hvcc.edu/bus/cwd/index.html
Degrees available: Associate degree

Mohawk Valley Community College
1101 Sherman Drive, Utica, NY 13501
315/792-5348
http://www.mvcc.edu/acdmcs/dprtmnts/bit/wbdsgnmngmt.cfm
Degrees available: Certificate, associate degree

Portland Community College (multiple campuses)
PO Box 19000, Portland, OR 97280-0990
866/922-1010
http://www.pcc.edu/pcc/pro/progs/wsd
Degrees available: Certificate

Santa Fe Community College
6401 Richards Avenue, Santa Fe, NM 87508-4887
505/428-1693
info@sfccnm.edu
http://www.sfccnm.edu/sfcc/pages/1093.html
Degrees available: Associate degree (web design)

Spokane Falls Community College
3410 West Fort George Wright Drive, MS 3011
Spokane, WA 99224-5288
888/509-7944
http://tech.spokanefalls.edu/AppliedVisualArts/
default.asp?menu=2&page=AASWebDesign
Degrees available: Associate degree

249

Williston State College
1410 University Avenue, PO Box 1326, Williston, ND 58802
888/863-9455
http://www.wsc.nodak.edu
Degrees available: Certificate, associate degree (web design)

For More Information:

International Webmasters Association
119 East Union Street, Suite F, Pasadena, CA 91103
626/449-3709
http://www.iwanet.org

World Organization of Webmasters
9580 Oak Avenue Parkway, Suite 7-177, Folsom, CA 95630
916/608-1597
info@joinwow.org
http://www.joinwow.org

Wood Science and Technology

When most people think of forest products, they think of paper or the wood that is used to build furniture or construct houses. But there is a lot more to forest products than just paper and wood. Did you know that forest products, according to the Society of Wood Science and Technology, are used to create an anti-cancer drug, rayon clothing, molded panels in automobiles, vanilla flavoring in ice cream, and other products? *Wood science technology workers* study the physical, chemical, and biological properties of wood and the methods of growing and processing it for use in everyday life. Students who complete two-year wood science programs can enter the field as wood science technicians. Other students go on to earn a bachelor's or master's degree in the field—allowing them improved job opportunities.

Typical Classes:

> Introduction to Forest Biology
> Introduction to Forest Resources
> Introduction to Wood Science and Technology
> Wood Anatomy and Structure
> Physical and Mechanical Properties of Wood
> Wood Chemistry
> Adhesion and Adhesives Technology
> Harvesting Forest Products
> Wood Composites
> Wood Deterioration and Preservation
> Forest Products Business Management
> Forest Resource Economics

Potential Employers:

> Mills
> Manufacturers of wood products
> Wood suppliers
> Forest products associations
> Pulp and paper companies
> Government agencies
> Colleges and universities

Did You Know?

Approximately 1.4 million people are employed in the U.S. forest products industry, according to the Society of Wood Science and Technology.

Available At:

Morrisville State College
PO Box 901, Morrisville, NY 13408
315/684-6032
http://www.morrisville.edu/Academics/Sci_Tech/
Wood_Products_Tech/index.htm
Degrees available: Associate degree

For More Information:

Society of Wood Science and Technology
One Gifford Pinchot Drive, Madison, WI 53726-2398
608/231-9347
vicki@swst.org
http://www.swst.org

Appendix A: Community Colleges in the United States by State

The following appendix lists all of the two-year colleges in the United States. While all do not offer unique programs, this section will help you learn more about educational options in your state.

Alabama

Alabama Southern Community College
http://www.ascc.edu

Bevill State Community College
http://www.bscc.edu

Bishop State Community College
http://www.bscc.cc.al.us

Calhoun Community College
http://www.calhoun.cc.al.us

Central Alabama Community College
http://www.cacc.cc.al.us

Chattahoochee Valley Community College
http://www.cv.edu

Enterprise State Junior College
http://www.esjc.cc.al.us

Gadsden State Community College
http://www.gadsdenst.cc.al.us

J. F. Drake State Technical College
http://www.dstc.cc.al.us

J. F. Ingram State Technical College
http://www.ingram.cc.al.us

James H. Faulkner State Community College
http://www.faulkner.cc.al.us

Jefferson Davis Community College
http://www.jeffdavis.cc.al.us/mainindex.php

Jefferson State Community College
http://www.jscc.cc.al.us

Lawson State Community College
http://www.ls.cc.al.us

Lurleen B. Wallace Community College
http://www.lbwcc.edu

Marion Military Institute
http://www.marionmilitary.edu

Northeast Alabama Community College
http://www.nacc.cc.al.us

Northwest-Shoals Community College
http://www.nwscc.cc.al.us

Prince Institute of Professional Studies
http://www.princeinstitute.edu

Reid State Technical College
http://www.rstc.cc.al.us

Shelton State Community College
http://www.sheltonstate.edu/sscc

Snead State Community College
http://www.snead.cc.al.us

Southern Union State Community College
http://www.suscc.cc.al.us

Trenholm State Technical College
http://www.trenholmtech.cc.al.us

Virginia College
http://www.vc.edu/index.html

Wallace Community College-Dothan
http://www.wallace.edu

Wallace Community College-Selma
http://www.wccs.edu

Alaska

Ilisagvik
http://www.ilisagvik.cc

Kodiak College University of Alaska Anchorage
http://www.koc.alaska.edu

Prince William Sound Community College
http://www.pwscc.edu

Arizona

Apollo College
http://www.apollocollege.com

Arizona Automotive Institute
http://www.azautoinst.com/home.htm

Arizona Western College
http://www.azwestern.edu

The Bryman School
http://www.hightechinstitute.edu/locations/the-bryman-school-of-phoenix

Central Arizona College
http://www.centralaz.edu

Chandler-Gilbert
Community College
http://www.cgc.maricopa.edu

Cochise College
http://www.cochise.cc.az.us

Coconino County
Community College
http://www.coconino.edu

Dine College
http://www.dinecollege.edu

Eastern Arizona College
http://www.eac.edu

Estrella Mountain
Community College
http://www.emc.maricopa.edu

Gateway Community College
http://www.gatewaycc.edu

Glendale Community College
http://www.gc.maricopa.edu

High-Tech Institute
http://www.hightechschools
.com/locations/details.php?l
ocation=PHX

Lamson College
http://www.lamsoncollege.
com

Long Technical College
http://www.longtechnicalcol
lege.com

Mesa Community College
http://www.mc.maricopa.edu

Mohave Community College
http://www.mohave.edu

Northland Pioneer College
http://www.northland.cc.az
us

Paradise Valley Community
College
http://www.pvc.maricopa.edu

Paralegal Institute, Inc.
http://www.theparalegalinsti
tute.edu

Phoenix College
http://www.pc.maricopa.edu

Pima County Community
College
http://www.pima.edu

Pima Medical Institute
http://www.pmi.edu

RainStar University
http://www.rainstaruniversity
.com

The Refrigeration School
http://www.refrigerationsch
ool.com

Rio Salado College
http://www.rio.maricopa.edu

Scottsdale Community
College
http://www.sc.maricopa.edu

Scottsdale Culinary
Institute
http://www.chefs.edu

South Mountain
Community College
http://www.southmountaincc
.edu

Southwest Institute of
Healing Arts
http://www.swiha.org

Universal Technical Institute
http://www.uticorp.com

Yavapai College
http://www2.yc.edu

Arkansas

Arkansas Community
College-Batesville,
University of
http://www.uaccb.edu

Arkansas Community
College-Hope, University of
http://www.uacch.edu

Arkansas Community
College-Morrilton,
University of
http://www.uaccm.edu

Arkansas Northeastern
College
http://www.anc.edu

Arkansas State University-
Beebe
http://www.asub.edu

Arkansas State University-
Mountain Home
http://www.asumh.edu/
indexns.htm

Arkansas State University-
Newport
http://www.asun.edu

Black River Technical
College
http://www.blackrivertech.org

Cossatot Community
College
http://ctc.tec.ar.us

Crowley's Ridge College
http://www.crowleysridgeco
llege.edu

East Arkansas Community
College
http://www.eacc.cc.ar.us

Mid-South Community
College
http://www.midsouthcc.edu

National Park Community
College
http://www.npcc.edu

North Arkansas College
http://pioneer.northark.
cc.ar.us

NorthWest Arkansas
Community College
http://www.nwacc.edu

Ouachita Technical College
http://www.otc.tec.ar.us

Ozarka College
http://www.ozarka.edu

Petit Jean College
http://www.state.ar.us/pjc

Phillips Community
College of the University of
Arkansas
http://www.pccua.edu

Pulaski Technical College
http://www.pulaskitech.edu

Rich Mountain Community
College
http://www.rmcc.cc.ar.us

South Arkansas
Community College
http://www.southark.edu

Southeast Arkansas College
http://www.seark.org

Southern Arkansas
University Tech
http://www.sautech.edu

California

Alameda, College of
http://alameda.peralta.edu
Canyons, College of the
http://www.coc.cc.ca.us

Allan Hancock College
http://www.hancockcollege.
edu

American River College
http://www.arc.losrios.edu

Antelope Valley College
http://www.avc.edu

Bakersfield College
http://www.bc.cc.ca.us

Barstow Community College
http://www.barstow.cc.ca.us

Butte College
http://www.butte.cc.ca.us

Cabrillo College
http://www.cabrillo.edu

Canada College
http://canadacollege.net

Cerritos College
http://www.cerritos.edu

Cerro Coso Community
College
http://www.cerrocoso.edu

Chabot College
http://www.chabotcollege.
edu/Default.asp

Chaffey College
http://www.chaffey.edu

Citrus College
http://www.citruscollege.edu

City College of San Francisco
http://www.ccsf.edu

Coastline Community
College
http://coastline.cccd.edu

Columbia College
http://columbia.yosemite.cc.
ca.us/default.htm

Compton Community
College
http://www.compton.cc.ca.
us/index.html

Contra Costa College
http://www.contracosta.cc.
ca.us

Cosumnes River College
http://www.crc.losrios.edu

Copper Mountain College
http://www.cmccd.edu

Crafton Hills College
http://www.craftonhills.edu

Cuesta College
http://www.cuesta.edu

Cuyamaca College
http://www.cuyamaca.net

Cypress College
http://www.cypresscollege.edu

De Anza College
http://www.deanza.edu

Desert, College of the
http://www.collegeofthedese
rt.edu

Diablo Valley College
http://www.dvc.edu

East Los Angeles College
http://www.elac.cc.ca.us

El Camino College
http://www.elcamino.edu

Evergreen Valley College
http://www.evc.edu

Fashion Institute of Design
and Merchandising
http://www.fidm.com

Feather River College
http://www.frcc.cc.ca.us

Folsom Lake College
http://www.flc.losrios.edu

Foothill College
http://www.foothill.fhda.
edu/index.php

Fresno City College
http://www.fresnocitycollege
.edu

Fullerton College
http://www.fullcoll.edu

Gavilan Joint Community
College District
http://www.gavilan.cc.ca.us

Glendale Community College
http://www.glendale.edu

Golden West College
http://gwc.info

Grossmont College
http://www.grossmont.edu

Hartnell College
http://www.hartnell.cc.ca.us

Imperial Valley College
http://www.imperial.cc.ca.us

Irvine Valley College
http://www.ivc.edu

Lake Tahoe Community
College
http://www.ltcc.cc.ca.us

Laney College
http://laney.peralta.edu

Las Positas Community
College
http://www.laspositascollege
.edu

Lassen Community College
http://www.lassencollege.edu

Long Beach City College
http://www.lbcc.cc.ca.us

Los Angeles City College
http://www.lacitycollege.edu
Los Angeles Harbor College
http://www.lahc.cc.ca.us/

Los Angeles Mission
College
http://www.lamission.edu

Los Angeles Pierce College
http://www.lapc.cc.ca.us

Los Angeles Southwest College
http://lasc.edu

Los Angeles Trade Tech College
http://www.lattc.cc.ca.us

Los Angeles Valley College
http://www.lavc.cc.ca.us

Los Medanos College
http://www.losmedanos.net

Mendocino College
http://www.mendocino.edu

Merced College
http://www.mccd.edu

Merritt College
http://www.merritt.edu

Mira Costa College
http://www.miracosta.cc.ca.us

256

Mission College
http://www.missioncollege.org

Modesto Junior College
http://mjc.yosemite.cc.ca.us

Monterey Peninsula College
http://www.mpc.edu/homex.asp

Moorpark College
http://www.moorpark.cc.ca.us

Mt. San Antonio College
http://www.mtsac.edu

Mt. San Jacinto College
http://www.msjc.edu

Napa Valley College
http://www.napavalley.edu

Ohlone College
http://www.ohlone.cc.ca.us

Orange Coast College
http://www.orangecoastcollege.edu

Oxnard College
http://www.oxnard.cc.ca.us

Palomar College
http://www.palomar.edu

Pasadena City College
http://www.pasadena.edu

Porterville College
http://www.pc.cc.ca.us

Redwoods, College of the
http://www.redwoods.cc.ca.us

Reedley College
http://www.reedleycollege.com

Rio Hondo College
http://www.riohondo.edu

Riverside Community College
http://www.rcc.edu

Sacramento City College
http://www.scc.losrios.edu

Saddleback College
http://www.saddleback.cc.ca.us

San Bernadino Valley College
http://www.valleycollege.edu

San Diego City College
http://www.city.sdccd.cc.ca.us

San Diego Mesa College
http://www.sandiegomesacollege.net

San Diego Miramar College
http://www.miramar.sdccd.net

San Joaquin Delta College
http://www.deltacollege.edu

San Jose City College
http://www.sjcc.edu

San Mateo, College of
http://gocsm.net

Santa Ana College
http://www.sac.edu/homex.asp

Santa Barbara City College
http://www.sbcc.cc.ca.us

Santa Monica College
http://www.smc.edu

Santa Rosa Junior College
http://www.santarosa.edu

Santiago Canyon College
http://www.sccollege.edu/homex.asp

Sequoias, College of the
http://www.cos.edu

Shasta College
http://www.shastacollege.edu

Sierra College
http://www.sierracollege.edu

Siskiyous, College of the
http://www.siskiyous.edu

Skyline College
http://skylinecollege.net

Solano Community College
http://www.solano.edu

Southwestern College
http://www.swc.cc.ca.us

Taft College
http://www.taft.cc.ca.us

Ventura College
http://www.venturacollege.edu

Victor Valley College
http://www.vvc.edu

West Hills Community College
http://www.westhillscollege.com

West Los Angeles College
http://www.wlac.cc.ca.us

West Valley College
http://www.westvalley.edu

Yuba College
http://www.yccd.edu/yuba

Colorado

Aims Community College
http://www.aims.edu

Arapahoe Community College
http://www.arapahoe.edu

Aurora, Community College of
http://www.ccaurora.edu

Bel-Rea Institute of Animal Technology
http://www.bel-rea.com

Blair College
http://www.blair-college.com
Boulder College of Massage Therapy
http://www.bcmt.org

Cambridge College
http://www.hightechschools.com

College America Denver
http://www.collegeamerica.edu

Colorado Mountain College
http://www.coloradomtn.edu

Colorado Northwestern Community College
http://www.cncc.edu

Colorado School of Trades
http://www.schooloftrades.com

Denver, Community College of
http://www.ccd.rightchoice.org

Denver Academy of Court Reporting
http://www.dacr.org

Denver Automotive and Diesel College
http://www.dadc.com

Durango Air Service
http://www.durangoair.com

Front Range Community College
http://www.frcc.cc.co.us

Heritage College
http://www.heritage-education.com

IntelliTec College
http://www.intelliteccollege.com

Johnson and Wales University
http://www.jwu.edu/denver/index.htm

Lamar Community College
http://www.lamarcc.edu

Morgan Community College
http://www.morgancc.edu

Northeastern Junior College
http://www.njc.edu

Otero Junior College
http://www.ojc.edu

Parks College
http://www.parks-college.com

Pikes Peak Community College
http://www.ppcc.edu

Pueblo Community College
http://www.pueblocc.edu

Red Rocks Community College
http://www.rrcc.edu

Trinidad State Junior College
http://www.trinidadstate.edu

Westwood College
http://www.westwoodcollege.com

Connecticut

Asnuntuck Community-Technical College
http://www.acc.commnet.edu

Briarwood College
http://www.briarwood.edu

Capital Community College
http://www.ccc.commnet.edu

Gateway Community College
http://www.gwctc.commnet.edu

Housatonic Community College
http://www.hcc.commnet.edu

Manchester Community College
http://www.mcc.commnet.edu

Middlesex Community-Technical College
http://www.mxctc.commnet.edu

Mitchell College
http://www.mitchell.edu

Naugatuck Valley Community College
http://www.nvcc.commnet.edu

Northwestern Connecticut Community College
http://www.nwctc.commnet.edu

Norwalk Community College
http://www.nctc.commnet.edu/default.asp

Quinebaug Valley Community College
http://www.qvcc.commnet.edu

St. Vincent's College
http://www.stvincentscollege.edu

Three Rivers Community-Technical College
http://www.trcc.commnet.edu

Tunxis Community College
http://www.tunxis.commnet.edu

Delaware

Delaware Technical and Community College
http://www.dtcc.edu

Florida

ATI Career Training Center
http://ati.edu-search.com

Brevard Community College
http://www.brevard.cc.fl.us

Broward Community College
http://www.broward.edu

Central Florida College
http://www.trade-schools.net/central-florida-college

Central Florida Community College
http://www.cfcc.cc.fl.us

Central Florida Institute
http://www.cfinstitute.com

Chipola Junior College
http://www.chipola.edu

Daytona Beach Community
College
http://www.dbcc.cc.fl.us

Edison Community College
http://www.edison.edu

Florida Career College
http://www.careercollege.
edu

Florida College of Natural
Health
http://www.fcnh.com

Florida Community College
-Jacksonville
http://www.fccj.org

Florida Keys Community
College
http://www.fkcc.edu

Florida National College
http://www.fnc.edu
Florida Technical College
http://www.flatech.edu

Gulf Coast Community
College
http://www.gc.cc.fl.us

High Tech Institute
http://www.hightechinstitute
.com

Hillsborough Community
College
http://www.hccfl.edu

Key College
http://www.keycollege.edu

Lake City Community
College
http://www.lakecity.cc.fl.us

Lake-Sumter Community
College
http://www.lscc.cc.fl.us

Manatee Community
College
http://www.mccfl.edu

Miami Dade College
http://www.mdc.edu/home

National School of
Technology
http://nst.career-edu.net

North Florida Community
College
http://www.nfcc.edu

Okaloosa-Walton
Community College
http://www.owcc.cc.fl.us

Palm Beach Community
College
http://www.pbcc.cc.fl.us

Pasco-Hernando
Community College
http://www.pasco-
hernandocc.com

Polk Community College
http://www.polk.edu

Santa Fe Community
College
http://www.santafe.cc.fl.us

Seminole Community College
http://www.scc-fl.edu

South Florida Community
College
http://www.sfcc.cc.fl.us

Southwest Florida College
http://www.collegesurfing.
com/ce/swfc

St. Johns River Community
College
http://www.sjrcc.cc.fl.us

Tallahassee Community
College
http://www.tcc.fl.edu

Valencia Community
College
http://www.valencia.cc.fl.us

Webster College
http://www.webstercollege.
edu

Georgia

Abraham Baldwin
Agricultural College
http://www.abac.peachnet.
edu

Albany Technical College
http://www.albanytech.org

Altamaha Technical College
http://www.altamahatech.org

Andrew College
http://www.andrewcollege.edu

Appalachian Technical
College
http://www.apptec.org

Ashworth College
http://www.ashworthcollege
.com

Athens Technical College
http://www.athenstech.edu

Atlanta Metropolitan
College
http://www.atlm.edu/
amc_site

Atlanta Technical College
http://www.atlantatech.org

Augusta Technical College
http://www.augusta.tec.ga.us

Bainbridge College
http://www.bainbridge.edu

Bauder College
http://www.bainbridge.edu

Central Georgia Technical
College
http://www.cgtcollege.org

Chattahoochee Technical
College
http://www.chattcollege.com

Coastal Georgia
Community College
http://www.cgcc.edu

Columbus Technical College
http://www.columbustech.org

Coosa Valley Technical
College
http://www.cvtcollege.org

Dalton State College
http://www.daltonstate.edu

Darton College
http://www.darton.edu

DeKalb Technical College
http://www.dekalbtech.edu

East Central Technical
College
http://www.ectcollege.org

East Georgia College
http://www.ega.edu

Flint River Technical College
http://www.flint.tec.ga.us

Gainesville College
http://www.gc.peachnet.edu

Georgia Aviation and
Technical College
http://www.gavtc.org

Georgia Military College
http://www.gmc.cc.ga.us

Georgia Perimeter College
http://www.gpc.edu

Gordon College
http://www.gdn.peachnet.edu

Griffin Technical College
http://www.griftec.org

Gupton Jones College of
Funeral Service
http://www.gupton-jones.edu

Gwinnett Technical College
http://www.gwinnetttechnicalcollege.com

Heart of Georgia Technical
College
http://www.hgtc.org

Herzing College
http://www.herzing.edu

Interactive College of
Technology
http://www.ict-ils.edu

Lanier Technical College
http://www.lanier.tec.ga.us

Macon State College
http://www.maconstate.edu

Middle Georgia College
http://www.mgc.edu

Middle Georgia Technical
College
http://www.middlegatech.edu

Moultrie Technical College
http://www.moultrietech.edu

North Georgia Technical
College
http://www.clarkes.tec.ga.us

North Metro Technical
College
http://www.northmetrotech.edu

Northwestern Technical
College
http://www.nwtcollege.org

Ogeechee Technical
Institute
http://www.ogeechee.tec.ga.us

Okefenokee Technical
College
http://www.okefenokeetech.org

Sandersville Technical
College
http://www.sandersvilletech.org

Savannah Technical College
http://www.savannahtech.edu

South University
http://www.southuniversity.edu

South Georgia College
http://www.sgc.peachnet.edu

South Georgia Technical
College
http://www.sgtcollege.org

Southeastern Technical
College
http://www.southeasterntech.org

Southwest Georgia
Technical College
http://www.swgtc.net

Swainsboro Technical College
http://www.swainsborotech.edu

Truett McConnell College
http://www.truett.edu

Valdosta Technical College
http://www.valdostatech.org

Waycross College
http://www.waycross.edu

West Central Technical
College
http://www.westcentral.org

West Georgia Technical
Institute
http://www.westga.tec.ga.us

Young Harris College
http://www.yhc.edu

Hawaii

Hawaii Business College
http://www.hbc.edu

Hawaii Community
College, University of
Hawaii
http://www.hawcc.hawaii.edu

Hawaii Tokai International
College
http://www.tokai.edu

Heald College
http://www.heald.edu

Honolulu Community
College, University of
Hawaii
http://honolulu.hawaii.edu

Kapiolani Community
College, University of
Hawaii
http://www.kcc.hawaii.edu/page/Home

Kauai Community College,
University of Hawaii
http://www.kauaicc.hawaii.edu

Leeward Community
College, University of
Hawaii
http://www.lcc.hawaii.edu

Maui Community College,
University of Hawaii
http://www.maui.hawaii.edu

Windward Community
College, University of
Hawaii
http://www.wcc.hawaii.edu

TransPacific Hawaii College
http://www.transpacific.org

Idaho

American Institute of
Health Technology
http://www.aiht.com

259

Brigham Young University-Idaho
http://www.byui.edu

Eastern Idaho Technical College
http://www.eitc.edu

Larry G. Selland College of Applied Technology
http://selland.boisestate.edu

North Idaho College
http://www.nic.edu

Southern Idaho, College of
http://www.csi.edu

Illinois

Black Hawk College
http://www.bhc.edu

Career Colleges of Chicago
http://www.careerchi.com

Carl Sandburg College
http://www.sandburg.edu

Cooking and Hospitality Institute of Chicago, Inc.
http://www.chic.edu

Danville Area Community College
http://www.dacc.cc.il.us

DeVry, Inc.
http://www.devry.edu

DuPage, College of
http://www.cod.edu

Elgin Community College
http://www.elgin.edu

Fox College
http://www.foxcollege.edu

Frontier Community College
http://www.iecc.cc.il.us/fcc

Harold Washington College
http://hwashington.ccc.edu

Heartland Community College
http://www.hcc.cc.il.us

Highland Community College
http://www.highland.edu

Illinois Central College
http://www.icc.edu

Illinois Valley Community College
http://www.ivcc.edu

ITT Technical Institute
http://www.itt-tech.edu

John A. Logan College
http://www.jal.cc.il.us

John Wood Community College
http://www.jwcc.edu

Joliet Junior College
http://www.jjc.cc.il.us

Kankakee Community College
http://www.kcc.cc.il.us

Kaskaskia College
http://www.kc.cc.il.us

Kennedy-King College
http://kennedyking.ccc.edu

Kishwaukee College
http://kish.cc.il.us

Lake County, College of
http://www.clcillinois.edu

Lake Land College
http://www.lakeland.cc.il.us

Lewis and Clark Community College
http://www.lc.edu

Lincoln College
http://www.lincolncollege.edu

Lincoln Land Community College
http://www.llcc.cc.il.us

Lincoln Trail College
http://www.iecc.cc.il.us/ltc

MacCormac College
http://www.maccormac.edu

Malcolm X College
http://malcolmx.ccc.edu

McHenry County College
http://www.mchenry.edu

Midstate College
http://www.midstate.edu

Moraine Valley Community College
http://www.morainevalley.edu

Morrison Institute of Technology
http://www.morrison.tec.il.us/About.htm

Morton College
http://www.morton.edu

Northwestern Business College
http://www.northwesternbc.edu

Oakton Community College
http://www.oakton.edu

Office Technology, College of
http://www.cotedu.com

Olive Harvey College
http://oliveharvey.ccc.edu

Olney Central College
http://www.iecc.cc.il.us/occ

Parkland College
http://www.parkland.edu

Prairie State College
http://www.prairie.cc.il.us

Rend Lake College
http://www.rlc.cc.il.us

Richard J. Daley College
http://daley.ccc.edu

Richland Community College
http://www.richland.edu

Rock Valley College
http://www.rockvalleycollege.edu

Rockford Business College
http://www.rbcsuccess.com

St. Augustine College
http://www.st-aug.edu/

Sauk Valley Community College
http://www.svcc.edu

Shawnee Community College
http://www.shawneecc.edu

South Suburban College
http://www.ssc.cc.il.us

Southeastern Illinois College
http://www.sic.cc.il.us

Southwestern Illinois
College
http://www.southwestern.cc
.il.us

Spoon River College
http://www.spoonrivercollege
.net

Springfield College in
Illinois
http://www.sci.edu

Triton College
http://www.triton.edu

Truman College
http://www.trumancollege.c
c/index.php

Wabash Valley College
http://www.iecc.edu/wvc

Waubonsee Community
College
http://www.wcc.cc.il.us

Wilbur Wright College
http://wright.ccc.edu

William Rainey Harper
College
http://goforward.harpercollege
.edu

Worsham College of
Mortuary Science
http://www.worshamcollege
.com

Indiana

Ancilla College
http://www.ancilla.edu

Brown Mackie College
http://www.cbcaec.com

Court Reporting, College of
http://www.ccredu.com

Indiana Business College
http://www.ibcschools.edu

International Business
College
http://www.ibcindianapolis.
edu

Ivy Tech State College
http://www.ivytech.edu

Lincoln Technical Institute
http://www.lincolntech.com

Michiana College
http://www.universities.com
/On-Campus/
Michiana_College.html

Mid-America College of
Funeral Service
http://www.mid-
america.edu

Professional Careers
Institute
http://www.pcicareers.com

Sawyer College, Inc.
http://www.sawyercollege.edu

Vincennes University
http://www.vinu.edu

Iowa

AIB College of Business
http://www.aib.edu

Clinton Community
College
http://www.eicc.edu/general
/clinton

Des Moines Area
Community College
http://www.dmacc.cc.ia.us

Eastern Iowa Community
College District
http://www.eicc.edu

Ellsworth Community
College
http://www.iavalley.cc.ia.us/
ecc

Hamilton College
http://www.hamiltonia.edu

Hawkeye Community
College
http://www.hawkeye.cc.ia.us

Indian Hills Community
College
http://www.ihcc.cc.ia.us

Iowa Central Community
College
http://www.iccc.cc.ia.us

Iowa Lakes Community
College
http://www.ilcc.cc.ia.us

Iowa Wesleyan College
http://www.iwc.edu

Iowa Western Community
College
http://www.iwcc.cc.ia.us

Kirkwood Community
College
http://www.kirkwood.cc.ia.us

Marshalltown Community
College
http://www.iavalley.cc.ia.us/
mcc

Muscatine Community
College
http://www.eicc.edu/general
/muscatine

North Iowa Area
Community College
http://www.niacc.cc.ia.us

Northeast Iowa Community
College
http://www.nicc.edu

Northwest Iowa
Community College
http://www.nwicc.com

Scott Community College
http://www.eicc.edu

Southeastern Community
College
http://www.secc.cc.ia.us

Southwestern Community
College
http://www.swcc.cc.ia.us

Western Iowa Tech
Community College
http://www.witcc.com

Kansas

Allen County Community
College
http://www.allencc.edu

Barton County Community
College
http://www.bartonccc.edu

261

Butler County Community
College
http://www.butlercc.edu

Cloud County Community
College
http://www.cloud.edu

Coffeyville Community
College
http://www.ccc.cc.ks.us

Colby Community College
http://www.colbycc.edu

Cowley County
Community College
http://www.cowley.cc.ks.us

Dodge City Community
College
http://www.dccc.cc.ks.us

Donnelly College
http://www.donnelly.edu

Fort Scott Community
College
http://www.fortscott.edu

Garden City Community
College
http://www.gccks.edu

Highland Community
College
http://www.highlandcc.edu

Independence Community
College
http://www.indy.cc.ks.us
Johnson County
Community College
http://www.johnco.cc.ks.us

Kansas City Kansas
Community College
http://www.kckcc.cc.ks.us

Labette Community
College
http://www.labette.cc.ks.us

Neosho County
Community College
http://www.neosho.edu

Pratt Community College
http://www.pcc.cc.ks.us

Seward County Community
College
http://www.sccc.edu

Kentucky

Ashland Community
College
http://www.kctcs.net

Ashland Technical College
http://www.kctcs.net

Beckfield College
http://www.beckfield.edu

Big Sandy Community and
Technical College
http://www.kctcs.net/bigsandy

Daymar College
http://www.daymarcollege.edu

Draughons Junior College
http://www.draughons.edu

Elizabethtown Community
College
http://www.elizabethtowncc
.com

Gateway Community &
Technical College
http://www.gateway.kctcs.edu

Hazard Community College
http://www.hazard.kctcs.
edu

Henderson Community
College
http://www.hencc.kctcs.net

Hopkinsville Community
College
http://www.hopcc.kctcs.net

Jefferson Community College
http://www.jcc.kctcs.edu

Jefferson Technical College
http://www.jefferson.kctcs.
edu

Lexington Community
College
http://www.bluegrass.kctcs.
edu/LCC

Louisville Technical Institute
http://www.louisvilletech.com

Madisonville Community
College
http://www.madcc.kctcs.net

Maysville Community
College
http://www.maycc.kctcs.net

Midway College
http://www.midway.edu

National College of
Business & Technology
http://www.ncbt.edu

Owensboro Community
College
http://www.octc.kctcs.edu

St. Catherine College
http://www.sccky.edu

Somerset Community
College
http://www.somcc.kctcs.net/

Southeast Community
College
http://www.secc.kctcs.net/

Brown Mackie College-
Northern Kentucky
http://www.retsaec.com/
locations.asp?locid=7

Southwestern College of
Business
http://www.swcollege.net/
c_florence_ky.php

Spencerian College
http://www.spencerian.edu

West Kentucky Community
and Technical College
http://www.westkentucky.
kctcs.edu

Louisiana

Baton Rouge Community
College
http://www.brcc.cc.la.us

Bossier Parish Community
College
http://www.bpcc.cc.la.us

Delgado Community College
http://www.dcc.edu

Herzing College
http://www.herzing.edu

Louisiana State University-
Alexandria
http://www.lsua.edu

262

Louisiana State University-Eunice
http://www.lsua.edu

Nunez Community College
http://www.nunez.edu

South Louisiana Community College
http://www.slcc.cc.la.us

Southern University at Shreveport/Bossier City
http://www.susla.edu

Maine

Andover College
http://www.andovercollege.com

Beal College
http://www.andovercollege.com

Central Main Medical Center School of Nursing
http://www.cmmcson.org

Central Maine Community College
http://www.cmtc.com

Eastern Maine Community College
http://www.emcc.edu

Husson College
http://www.husson.edu

Kennebec Valley Community College
http://www.kvcc.me.edu

Mid-State College
http://www.midstate.edu
Northern Maine Community College
http://www.nmcc.edu

Southern Maine Community College
http://www.smccme.edu

Washington County Community College
http://www.wccc.me.edu

York County Community College
http://www.yccc.edu

Maryland

Allegany College of Maryland
http://www.ac.cc.md.us

Anne Arundel Community College
http://www.aacc.cc.md.us

Baltimore City Community College
http://www.bccc.edu/baltimoreccc/site/default.asp

Baltimore County, Community College of
http://www.ccbcmd.edu

Carroll Community College
http://www.carrollcc.edu

Cecil Community College
http://www.cecilcc.edu

Chesapeake College
http://www.chesapeake.edu

Frederick Community College
http://www.frederick.edu

Garrett Community College
http://www.garrettcollege.edu

Hagerstown Business College
http://www.hagerstownbusinesscol.org

Hagerstown Community College
http://www.hcc.cc.md.us

Harford Community College
http://www.harford.edu

Howard Community College
http://www.howardcc.edu

Maryland College of Art and Design
http://www.mcadmd.org

Montgomery College
http://www.mc.cc.md.us

Prince George's Community College
http://pgweb.pg.cc.md.us

Southern Maryland, College of
http://www.csmd.edu

TESST College of Technology
http://www.tesst.com

Wor-Wic Community College
http://www.worwic.cc.md.us

Massachusetts

Bay State College
http://www.baystate.edu

Berkshire Community College
http://cc.berkshire.org/flash.html

Bristol Community College
http://srvweb.bristol.mass.edu/index.cfm

Bunker Hill Community College
http://www.bhcc.mass.edu

Cape Cod Community College
http://www.capecod.mass.edu

Dean College
http://www.dean.edu

Fisher College
http://www.fisher.edu

Greenfield Community College
http://www.gcc.mass.edu

Holyoke Community College
http://www.hcc.edu

Massachusetts Bay Community College
http://www.massbay.edu

Massasoit Community College
http://www.massasoit.mass.edu

Middlesex Community College
http://www.middlesex.mass.edu

Mount Wachusett
Community College
http://www.mwcc.mass.edu

North Shore Community
College
http://www.northshore.edu

Northern Essex
Community College
http://www.necc.mass.edu

Quincy College
http://www.quincycollege.edu

Quinsigamond Community
College
http://www.qcc.edu

Springfield Technical
Community College
http://www.stcc.edu

Michigan

Alpena Community College
http://www.alpena.cc.mi.us

Bay de Noc Community
College
http://www.baydenoc.cc.mi.
us

Bay Mills Community
College
http://www.bmcc.edu

Charles S. Mott
Community College
http://www.mcc.edu/
indexmain.shtml

Delta College
http://www.delta.edu

Glen Oaks Community
College
http://www.glenoaks.cc.mi.
us

Gogebic Community College
http://www.gogebic.cc.mi.us

Grand Rapids Community
College
http://www.grcc.cc.mi.us

Henry Ford Community
College
http://www.hfcc.edu

ITT Technical Institute
http://www.itt-tech.edu

Jackson Community College
http://www.jackson.cc.mi.us

Kalamazoo Valley
Community College
http://www.kvcc.edu

Kellogg Community College
http://www.kellogg.cc.mi.us

Kirtland Community College
http://www.kirtland.edu

Lake Michigan College
http://www.lakemichigancol
lege.edu

Lansing Community College
http://www.lansing.cc.mi.us

Lewis College of Business
http://www.lewiscollege.edu

Macomb Community College
http://www.macomb.edu

Mid Michigan Community
College
http://www.midmich.cc.mi.
us

Monroe County
Community College
http://www.monroeccc.edu

Montcalm Community
College
http://www.montcalm.cc.mi
.us

Muskegon Community
College
http://www.muskegon.cc.mi
.us

North Central Michigan
College
http://www.ncmc.cc.mi.us

Northwestern Michigan
College
http://www.nmc.edu

Oakland Community
College
http://www.oaklandcc.edu

Saginaw Chippewa Tribal
College
http://www.sagchip.org/
tribalcollege

St. Clair County
Community College
http://www.stclair.cc.mi.us

Schoolcraft College
http://www.schoolcraft.cc.
mi.us

Southwestern Michigan
College
http://www.smc.cc.mi.us

Washtenaw Community
College
http://www.wccnet.edu

Wayne County Community
College
http://www.wcccd.edu

West Shore Community
College
http://www.westshore.edu

Minnesota

Alexandria Technical College
http://web.alextech.edu

Anoka-Hennepin Technical
College
http://www.ank.tec.mn.us

Anoka-Ramsey Community
College
http://www.an.cc.mn.us

Central Lakes College
http://www.clc.mnscu.edu

Century College
http://www.century.cc.mn.us

Dakota County Technical
College
http://www.dctc.mnscu.edu

Fergus Falls Community
College
http://www.minnesota.edu/c
ampuses/fergus_falls/

Fon du Lac Tribal and
Community College
http://www.fdl.cc.mn.us

Hibbing Community
College
http://www.hcc.mnscu.edu

Inver Hills Community
College
http://www.inverhills.edu

Lake Superior College
http://www.lsc.edu

Leech Lake Tribal College
http://www.leechlaketribalc
ollege.org

Minneapolis Community
and Technical College
http://www.mctc.mnscu.edu

Minnesota State College-
Southeast Technical
http://www.southeasttech.
mnscu.edu

Minnesota West
Community &
Technical College
http://www.mnwest.mnscu.
edu

Normandale Community
College
http://www.nr.cc.mn.us

North Hennepin
Community College
http://www.nhcc.edu

Northland Community and
Technical College
http://www.northlandcollege
.edu

Northwest Technical
College
http://www.ntcmn.edu

Pine Technical College
http://134.29.165.192

Rainy River Community
College
http://www.rrcc.mnscu.edu

Ridgewater College
http://www.ridgewater.
mnscu.edu

Riverland Community
College
http://www.riverland.edu

Rochester Community and
Technical College
http://www.rctc.edu

Saint Cloud Technical
College
http://www.sctc.edu

Saint Paul Technical
College
http://www.saintpaul.edu

South Central Technical
College
http://southcentral.edu

White Earth Tribal and
Community College
http://www.wetcc.org

Mississippi

Antonelli College
http://www.antonellic.com

Coahoma Community
College
http://www.ccc.cc.ms.us

Copiah-Lincoln
Community College
http://www.colin.edu

East Central Community
College
http://www.eccc.cc.ms.us

East Mississippi
Community College
http://www.emcc.cc.ms.us

Hinds Community College
http://www.hindscc.edu

Holmes Community
College
http://www.holmes.cc.ms.us

Itawamba Community
College
http://www.icc.cc.ms.us

Jones County Junior College
http://www.jcjc.cc.ms.us

Meridian Community College
http://www.mcc.cc.ms.us

Mississippi Delta
Community College
http://www.mgccc.edu

Northeast Mississippi
Community College
http://www.necc.cc.ms.us

Northwest Mississippi
Community College
http://www.northwestms.edu

Pearl River Community
College
http://www.prcc.edu

Southwest Mississippi
Community College
http://www.smcc.cc.ms.us

Virginia College
http://www.vc.edu/gulfcoast

Missouri

Blue River Community
College
http://kcmetro.edu
home.asp?C=1&QLinks=
Blue+River

Cottey College
http://www.cottey.edu

Crowder College
http://www.crowder.edu

East Central College
http://www.eastcentral.edu

Jefferson College
http://www.jeffco.edu

Linn State Technical
College
http://www.linnstate.edu

Longview Community
College
http://kcmetro.edu
home.asp?C=2&QLinks=Lo
ngview

Maple Woods Community
College
http://kcmetro.edu
home.asp?C=3&QLinks=
Maple+Woods

Mineral Area College
http://www.mineralarea.edu

Missouri College
http://www.missouricollege.
com

Moberly Area Community
College
http://www.macc.cc.mo.us

North Central Missouri
College
http://www.ncmc.cc.mo.us

265

Ozarks Technical
Community College
http://www.otc.cc.mo.us

Penn Valley Community
College
http://kcmetro.edu/
home.asp?C=4&QLinks=Pe
nn+Valley

Ranken Technical College
http://www.ranken.edu

Sanford-Brown College
http://www.sanford-
brown.edu

Saint Louis Community
College
http://www.stlcc.cc.mo.us

Missouri State University-
West Plaines
http://www.wp.missouristate
.edu

St. Charles Community
College
http://www.stchas.edu

State Fair Community
College
http://www.sfcc.cc.mo.us

Three Rivers Community
College
http://www.trcc.commnet.
edu

Montana

Blackfeet Community
College
http://www.bfcc.org

Chief Dull Knife College
http://cdkc.edu

College of Technology,
University of Montana
http://www.cte.umt.edu

Dawson Community
College
http://www.dawson.cc.mt.us

Flathead Valley Community
College
http://www.fvcc.edu

Fort Belknap College
http://www.fbcc.edu

Fort Peck Community
College
http://www.fpcc.edu

Little Big Horn College
http://www.lbhc.cc.mt.us

Miles Community College
http://www.milescc.edu

Montana Tech-University of
Montana
http://www.mtech.edu

Stone Child College
http://www.montana.edu/
wwwscc

Nebraska

Central Community
College
http://www.cccneb.edu

The Creative Center
http://www.thecreativecenter
.com

Hamilton College-Lincoln
http://www.hamiltonlincoln
.edu

Hamilton College-Omaha
http://www.hamiltonomaha.
edu

ITT Technical Institute
http://www.itt-tech.edu/
campus/school.cfm?lloc_
num=66

Little Priest Tribal College
http://www.lptc.bia.edu

Metropolitan Community
College
http://www.mccneb.edu

Mid-Plains Community
College
http://www.mpcc.edu

Nebraska Indian
Community College
http://www.thenicc.edu

Northeast Community
College
http://www.northeastcollege
.com

Southeast Community
College
http://www.southeast.edu

Vatterott College
http://www.vatterott-
college.com

Western Nebraska
Community College Area
http://hannibal.wncc.cc.ne.
us

Nevada

Art Institute of Las Vegas
http://www.ailv.artinstitutes.
edu

Career College of Northern
Nevada
http://www.ccnn4u.com

Great Basin College
http://www.gbcnv.edu

Heritage College
www.heritagecollege.com

ITT Technical Institute
http://www.itt-tech.edu

Las Vegas College
http://www.lasvegas-
college.com

Southern Nevada,
Community College of
http://www.ccsn.nevada.edu

Truckee Meadows
Community College
http://www.tmcc.edu

Western Nevada
Community College
http://www.wncc.nevada.edu

New Hampshire

New Hampshire
Community Technical
College-Berlin
http://www.berlin.nhctc.edu

New Hampshire
Community Technical
College-Claremont
http://www.claremont.nhctc
.edu

New Hampshire
Community Technical
College-Laconia
http://www.laconia.nhctc.edu

New Hampshire Community Technical College-Manchester/Stratham
http://www.ms.nhctc.edu

New Hampshire Community Technical College-Nashua
http://www.nashua.nhctc.edu

New Hampshire Technical Institute
http://www.nhti.net

New Jersey

Atlantic Cape Community College
http://www.atlantic.edu

Bergen Community College
http://www.atlantic.edu

Berkeley College
http://www.berkeleycollege.edu

Brookdale Community College
http://www.brookdalecc.edu

Burlington County College
http://www.bcc.edu

Camden County College
http://www.camdencc.edu

County College of Morris
http://www.ccm.edu

Cumberland County College
http://www.cccnj.edu

Essex County College
http://www.essex.edu

Gloucester County College
http://www.gccnj.edu

Hudson County Community College
http://www.hudson.cc.nj.us

Mercer County Community College
http://www.mccc.edu

Middlesex County College
http://www.middlesex.cc.nj.us

Ocean County College
http://www.ocean.edu

Passaic County Community College
http://www.pccc.cc.nj.us

Raritan Valley Community College
http://www.raritanval.edu

Sussex County Community College
http://www.sussex.edu

Union County College
http://www.ucc.edu/default.htm

Warren County Community College
http://www.warren.cc.nj.us

New Mexico

Albuquerque Technical Vocational Institute
http://www.tvi.cc.nm.us

Clovis Community College
http://www.clovis.edu

Eastern New Mexico University-Roswell
http://www.roswell.enmu.edu

Institute of American Indian Arts
http://www.iaiancad.org

Luna Community College
http://www.luna.cc.nm.us

New Mexico-Gallup, University of
http://www.gallup.unm.edu

New Mexico-Los Alamos, University of
http://www.la.unm.edu

New Mexico-Taos, University of
http://www4.unm.edu/taos

New Mexico-Valencia, University of
http://www.unm.edu/~unmvc

New Mexico Junior College
http://www.nmjc.edu

New Mexico Military Institute
http://www.nmmi.cc.nm.us

New Mexico State University-Alamogordo
http://alamo.nmsu.edu

New Mexico State University-Carlsbad
http://artemis.nmsu.edu

New Mexico State University-Dona Ana Branch Community College
http://dabcc.nmsu.edu

New Mexico State University-Grants
http://grants2.nmsu.edu

Northern New Mexico Community College
http://nnmcc.edu

San Juan College
http://www.sjc.cc.nm.us

Santa Fe Community College
http://www.santafe.cc.fl.us

Southwestern Indian Polytechnic Institute
http://www.sipi.bia.edu

New York

Adirondack Community College
http://www.sunyacc.edu

Bramson O R T College
http://www.bramsonort.org

Briarcliffe College
http://www.bcl.org

Bronx Community College
http://www.bcc.cuny.edu

Broome Community College
http://www.sunybroome.edu

Cayuga County Community College
http://www.cayuga-cc.edu

Clinton Community College
http://www.clintoncc.suny.edu

Columbia-Greene Community College
http://www.sunycgcc.edu

Corning Community College
http://www.corning-cc.edu

267

Dutchess Community College
http://www.sunydutchess.edu

Erie Community College
http://www.ecc.edu

Fashion Institute of Technology
http://www.collegeprofiles.com/fit.html

Finger Lakes Community College
http://www.flcc.edu

Fulton-Montgomery Community College
http://www.fmcc.suny.edu

Genesee Community College
http://www.genesee.suny.edu

Herkimer County Community College
http://www.hccc.suny.edu

Hostos Community College-City University of New York
http://www.hostos.cuny.edu

Hudson Valley Community College
http://www.hvcc.edu

Jamestown Community College
http://www.sunyjcc.edu

Jefferson Community College
http://www.sunyjefferson.edu

Kingsborough Community College-City University of New York
http://www.kbcc.cuny.edu

LaGuardia Community College-City University of New York
http://www.lagcc.cuny.edu

Manhattan Community College, Borough of
http://www.bmcc.cuny.edu

Mohawk Valley Community College
http://www.mvcc.edu

Monroe Community College
http://www.monroecc.edu

Nassau Community College
http://www.ncc.edu

National Technical Institute for the Deaf
http://www.ntid.rit.edu

Niagara County Community College
http://www.sunyniagara.cc.ny.us

North Country Community College
http://www.nccc.edu

Onondaga Community College
http://www.sunyocc.edu

Orange County Community College
http://www.orange.cc.ny.us

Queensborough Community College-City University of New York
http://www.qcc.cuny.edu

Rockland Community College
http://www.sunyrockland.edu

Sage Junior College of Albany
http://www.sage.edu

Schenectady County Community College
http://www.sunysccc.edu

SUNY College-Morrisville
http://www.morrisville.edu

Suffolk County Community College
http://www3.sunysuffolk.edu/index.asp

Sullivan County Community College
http://www.sullivan.suny.edu

Tompkins-Cortland Community College
http://www.sunytccc.edu

Ulster County Community College
http://www.sunyulster.edu

Westchester Community College
http://www.sunywcc.edu

North Carolina

Alamance Community College
http://www.alamance.cc.nc.us/newsite

Albemarle,College of the
http://www.albemarle.cc.nc.us

Asheville-Buncombe Technical Community College
http://www.abtech.edu

Beaufort County Community College
http://www.beaufort.cc.nc.us

Bladen Community College
http://www.bladen.cc.nc.us

Blue Ridge Community College
http://www.by.cc.va.us

Brunswick Community College
http://www.brunswick.cc.nc.us

Caldwell Community College and Technical Institute
http://www.caldwell.cc.nc.us

Cape Fear Community College
http://cfcc.edu/index.php

Carolinas College of Health Sciences
http://www.carolinascollege.org

Carteret Community College
http://www.carteret.edu

Catawba Valley Community College
http://www.cvcc.edu

Central Carolina Community College
http://www.cccc.edu

Central Piedmont Community College
http://www1.cpcc.edu

Cleveland Community College
http://www.cleveland.cc.nc.us

Coastal Carolina Community College
http://www.coastalcarolina.edu

Craven Community College
http://www.craven.cc.nc.us

Davidson County Community College
http://www.davidson.cc.nc.us

Durham Technical Community College
http://www.durhamtech.org

ECPI Technical College
http://www.ecpi.net

Edgecombe Community College
http://www.edgecombe.cc.nc.us

Fayetteville Technical Community College
http://www.faytechcc.edu

Forsyth Technical Community College
http://www.forsyth.tec.nc.us

Gaston College
http://www.gaston.cc.nc.us

Guilford Technical Community College
http://technet.gtcc.cc.nc.us

Halifax Community College
http://www.hcc.cc.nc.us

Haywood Community College
http://www.haywood.edu

Isothermal Community College
http://www.isothermal.edu

James Sprunt Community College
http://www.sprunt.com

Johnston Community College
http://www.johnstoncc.edu

King's College
http://www.kingscollegecharlotte.edu

Lenoir Community College
http://www.lenoir.cc.nc.us

Louisburg College
http://www.louisburg.edu

Martin Community College
http://www.martin.cc.nc.us

Mayland Community College
http://www.mayland.cc.nc.us

McDowell Technical Community College
http://www.mcdowelltech.cc.nc.us

Miller-Motte Technical College
http://www.miller-motte.com

Mitchell Community College
http://www.mitchellcc.edu

Montgomery Community College
http://www.montgomery.cc.nc.us

Nash Community College
http://www.nash.cc.nc.us

Pamlico Community College
http://www.pamlico.cc.nc.us/default.htm

Piedmont Community College
http://www.piedmont.cc.nc.us

Pitt Community College
http://www.pitt.cc.nc.us

Randolph Community College
http://www.randolph.cc.nc.us

Richmond Community College
http://www.richmond.cc.nc.us

Roanoke-Chowan Community College
http://www.roanoke.cc.nc.us

Robeson Community College
http://www.robeson.cc.nc.us

Rockingham Community College
http://www.rcc.cc.nc.us

Rowan-Cabarrus Community College
http://www.rccc.cc.nc.us

Sampson Community College
http://www.sampson.cc.nc.us

Sandhills Community College
http://www.sandhills.cc.nc.us

South Piedmont Community College
http://www.spcc.edu/

Southeastern Community College
http://www.sccnc.edu

Southwestern Community College
http://www.southwest.cc.nc.us

Stanly Community College
http://www.stanly.cc.nc.us

Surry Community College
http://www.surry.cc.nc.us

Tri-County Community College
http://www.tccc.cc.nc.us

Vance-Granville Community College
http://www.vgcc.cc.nc.us

Wake Technical Community College
http://www.wake.tec.nc.us

Wayne Community College
http://www.waynecc.edu

Western Piedmont Community College
http://www.wp.cc.nc.us

Wilkes Community College
http://www.wilkes.cc.nc.us

Wilson Technical
Community College
http://www.wilsontech.cc.nc
.us

North Dakota

Aakers Business College
http://www.aakers.edu

Bismarck State College
http://www.bismarckstate.edu

Cankdeska Cikana
Community College
http://www.littlehoop.edu/
cccc/home.html

Fort Berthold Community
College
http://www.fbcc.bia.edu

Lake Region State College
http://www.lrsc.nodak.edu

Minot State University-
Bottineau
http://www.misu-b.
nodak.edu

North Dakota State College
of Science
http://www.ndscs.nodak.edu

Sitting Bull College
http://www.sittingbull.edu

Turtle Mountain
Community College
http://www.turtle-
mountain.cc.nd.us

United Tribes Technical
College
http://www.uttc.edu

Williston State College
http://www.wsc.nodak.edu

Ohio

Advertising Art, School of
http://www.saacollege.com

AEC Southern Ohio
College
http://www.socaec.com

Antonelli College
http://www.antonellic.com

Art Institute of Cincinnati
http://www.theartinstituteof
cincinnati.com

ATS Institute of Technology
http://www.atsinstitute.com

Belmont Technical College
http://www.btc.edu

Bohecker's Business College
http://www.boheckercollege
.edu

Bowling Green State
University Firelands
College
http://www.firelands.bgsu.
edu

Bradford School
http://www.collegeforsuccess
.com/bsc

Bryant & Stratton College
http://www.bryantstratton.edu

Central Ohio Technical
College
http://www.cotc.edu

Chatfield College
http://www.chatfield.edu

Cincinnati State Technical
and Community College
http://www.cinstate.cc.oh.us

Clark State Community
College
http://www.clark.cc.oh.us

Clermont College
http://www.clc.uc.edu

Cleveland Institute of
Electronics
http://www.cie-wc.edu/
Distance-Learning.asp

Columbus State
Community College
http://www.cscc.edu

Cuyahoga Community
College
http://www.tri-c.cc.oh.us

Davis College
http://www.daviscollege.edu

Edison State Community
College
http://www.edison.cc.oh.us

Gallipolis Career College
http://www.gallipoliscareerc
ollege.com

Hocking Technical College
http://www.hocking.edu

Hondros College
http://hondroscollege.com

International College of
Broadcasting
http://www.icbcollege.com

ITT Technical Institute
http://www2.itt-tech.edu

James A. Rhodes State
College
http://www.rhodesstate.edu

Jefferson Community
College
http://ns3.jeffersonccc.org/
jcc/default.htm

Kent State University-
Ashtabula
http://www.ashtabula.kent.
edu

Kent State University-East
Liverpool
http://www.kenteliv.kent.edu

Kent State University-
Trumbull
http://www.trumbull.kent.edu

Lakeland Community
College
http://www.lakeland.cc.oh.us

Lorain County Community
College
http://www.lorainccc.edu/L
CCC/LorainCountyCommu
nityCollege.lccc

Mercy College of Northwest
Ohio
http://www.mercycollege.edu
/elizabeth.html

Miami-Jacobs College
http://www.miamijacobs.
edu

Miami University-
Middletown
http://www.mid.muohio.edu

North Central State College
http://www.ncstatecollege.edu

Northwest State
Community College
http://www.nscc.cc.oh.us

270

Ohio Business College
http://ohiobusinesscollege.
com

Ohio College of
Massotherapy
http://www.ocm.edu

Ohio Institute of
Photography and
Technology
http://www.oipt.com

Ohio State University
Agricultural Technical
Institute
http://www.ati.osu.edu

Ohio Technical College
http://www.ohiotechnicalcol
lege.com

Ohio University-Chillicothe
http://oucweb.chillicothe.
ohiou.edu/index.html

Ohio University-South
http://www.southern.ohiou.
edu

Owens Community College
https://www.owens.edu

Professional Skills Institute
http://www.proskills.com

Raymond Walters College
http://www.rwc.uc.edu

Remington College-
Cleveland
http://www.remingtoncollege
.edu/cleveland

Rio Grande Community
College
http://www.rio.edu

Sinclair Community
College
http://www.sinclair.edu

Southeastern Business
College
http://www.careersohio.com

Southern State Community
College
http://www.sscc.edu

Southwestern College of
Business
http://www.swcollege.net

Stark State College of
Technology
http://www.starkstate.edu

Stautzenberger College
http://www.stautzen.com

Summit College
http://sc.uakron.edu

Terra State Community
College
http://www.terra.edu

Trumbull Business College
http://www.tbc-
trumbullbusiness.com

Vatterott College-Cleveland
http://www.vatterott-
college.com/About/
campuses/?ShowCampus=01

Washington State
Community College
http://www.wscc.edu

Wayne College, University
of Akron
http://www.wayne.uakron.
edu

Wright State University-
Lake Campus
http://www.wright.edu/lake

Oklahoma

Carl Albert State College
http://www.casc.cc.ok.us

Connors State College
http://www.connors.cc.ok.us

Eastern Oklahoma State
College
http://www.eosc.cc.ok.us

Metropolitan College
http://www.metropolitancoll
ege.edu

Murray State College
http://www.msc.cc.ok.us

Northeastern Oklahoma
A&M College
http://www.neoam.cc.ok.us

Northern Oklahoma College
http://www.north-ok.edu

Oklahoma City Community
College
http://www.okccc.edu

Oklahoma State University-
Oklahoma City
http://www.osuokc.edu

Redlands Community
College
http://www.redlandscc.net

Rose State College
http://www.rose.edu

Seminole State College
http://www.ssc.cc.ok.us

Tulsa Community College
http://www.tulsacc.edu

Vaterott College
http://www.vatterott-
college.com/home

Western Oklahoma State
College
http://www.western.cc.ok.us

Oregon

Blue Mountain Community
College
http://www.bmcc.cc.or.us

Central Oregon
Community College
http://www.cocc.edu

Chemeketa Community
College
http://www.chemek.cc.or.us

Clackamas Community
College
http://www.clackamas.cc.or.
us

Clatsop Community
College
http://www.clatsopcc.edu

Columbia Gorge
Community College
http://www.cgcc.cc.or.us

Everest College
http://western-college.com

Klamath Community
College
http://www.kcc.cc.or.us

271

Lane Community College
http://www.lanecc.edu

Linn-Benton Community
College
http://www.lbcc.cc.or.us

Mt. Hood Community
College
http://www.mhcc.cc.or.us/
pages/1.asp

Oregon Coast Community
College
http://www.occc.cc.or.us

Pioneer Pacific College
http://www.pioneerpacificco
llege.com

Portland Community
College
http://www.pcc.edu

Rogue Community College
http://www.roguecc.edu

Southwestern Oregon
Community College
http://www.southwestern.cc
.or.us

Tillamook Bay Community
College
http://www.tbcc.cc.or.us

Treasure Valley Community
College
http://www.tvcc.cc

Umpqua Community
College
http://www.umpqua.cc.or.us

Western Culinary Institute
http://www.wci.edu

Pennsylvania

Allegheny County,
Community College of
http://www.ccac.edu

Beaver County, Community
College of
http://www.ccbc.edu

Bucks County Community
College
http://www.bucks.edu

Butler County Community
College
http://bc3.cc.pa.us

Delaware County
Community College
http://www.dccc.edu

Harcum College
http://www.collegeprofiles.
com/harcum.html

Harrisburg Area
Community College
http://www.hacc.edu

Keystone College
http://www.keystone.edu

Lehigh Carbon Community
College
http://www.lccc.edu

Luzerne County
Community College
http://www.luzerne.edu

Manor College
http://www.manor.edu

Montgomery County
Community College
http://www.mc3.edu

Northampton Community
College
http://www.northampton.edu

Pennsylvania College of
Technology
http://www.pct.edu

Philadelphia, Community
College of
http://www.ccp.edu/site

Reading Area Community
College
http://www.racc.edu

Thaddeus Stevens College
of Technology
http://www.stevenstech.org

Valley Forge Military
College
http://www.vfmac.edu

Westmoreland County
Community College
http://www.wccc-pa.edu

Rhode Island

New England Institute of
Technology
http://www.neit.edu

Rhode Island, Community
College of
http://www.ccri.edu

South Carolina

Aiken Technical College
http://www.aik.tec.sc.us

Central Carolina Technical
College
http://www.sum.tec.sc.us

Denmark Technical College
http://www.denmarktech.edu

ECPI Technical College
http://www.ecpi.net

Florence-Darlington
Technical College
http://www.fdtc.edu

Greenville Technical
College
http://www.greenvilletech.
com

Horry-Georgetown
Technical College
http://www.hor.tec.sc.us

Lowcountry, Technical
College of the
http://www.tcl.edu

Midlands Technical College
http://www.midlandstech.
com

Northeastern Technical
College
http://www.netc.edu

Orangeburg-Calhoun
Technical College
http://www.octech.org/
octech/default.asp

Piedmont Technical College
http://www.ptc.edu

Spartanburg Technical
College
http://www.stcsc.edu

Tri-County Technical College
http://www.tctc.edu

Trident Technical College
http://www.tridenttech.org

272

Williamsburg Technical College
http://www.williamsburgtech.com

York Technical College
http://www.yorktech.com/default.asp

South Dakota

Kilian Community College
http://www.kilian.edu

Lake Area Technical Institute
http://www.lati.tec.sd.us

Mitchell Technical Institute
http://www.mti.tec.sd.us

Sisserton-Wahpeton Community College
http://www.swc.tc

Southeast Technical Institute
http://www.southeasttech.com/sti_web

Western Dakota Technical Institute
http://www.westerndakotatech.org

Tennessee

Chattanooga State Technical Community College
http://www.chattanoogastate.edu

Cleveland State Community College
http://www.clscc.cc.tn.us

Columbia State Community College
http://www.coscc.cc.tn.us

Concorde Career College
http://concorde.edu-search.com

Draughons Junior College
http://www.draughons.edu

Dyersburg State Community College
http://www.dscc.edu/homepage.asp

High Tech Institute
http://www.hightechschools.com/index.php

Hiwassee College
http://www.hiwassee.edu

Jackson State Community College
http://www.jscc.edu

John A. Gupton College
http://www.guptoncollege.com

Medvance Institute
http://www.medvance.edu

Miller-Motte Technical College
http://www.miller-motte.com

Motlow State Community College
http://www.mscc.cc.tn.us

Nashville Auto-Diesel College
http://www.nadcedu.com

Nashville State Community College
http://www.nscc.edu

National College of Business & Technology
http://www.ncbt.edu

North Central Institute
http://www.nci.edu

Northeast State Technical Community College
http://www.nstcc.cc.tn.us

Nossi College of Art
http://www.nossi.com

Pellissippi State Technical Community College
http://www.pstcc.edu

Remington College
http://remington.edu-search.com

Roane State Community College
http://www.rscc.cc.tn.us/index.asp

South College
http://south.college-info.org

Southwest Tennessee Community College
http://www.southwest.tn.edu

Volunteer State Community College
http://www.vscc.cc.tn.us

Walters State Community College
http://www.ws.edu

Texas

Alvin Community College
http://www.alvincollege.edu

Amarillo College
http://www.actx.edu

Angelina College
http://www.angelina.cc.tx.us

Art Institute of Dallas
http://www.aid.edu

Art Institute of Houston
http://www.artinstitutes.edu/houston

Austin Community College
http://www.austincc.edu
Blinn College
http://www.blinn.edu

Brazosport College
http://www.brazosport.cc.tx.us

Brookhaven College
http://www.brookhavencollege.edu

Cedar Valley College
http://www.cedarvalleycollege.edu

Central Texas College
http:// www.ctcd.cc.tx.us

Cisco Junior College
http://www.cisco.cc.tx.us

Clarendon College
http://www.clarendoncollege.net
Coastal Bend College
http://vct.coastalbend.edu

Collin County Community Colleges
http://www.ccccd.edu

273

Dallas County Community
Colleges
http://www.dcccd.edu

Del Mar College
http://www.delmar.edu

Eastfield College
http://www.efc.dcccd.edu

El Centro College
http://www.ecc.dcccd.edu

El Paso Community College
http://www.epcc.edu

Frank Phillips College
http://www.fpc.cc.tx.us

Galveston College
http://www.gc.edu/gc

Grayson County College
http://www.grayson.edu

Hill College
http://www.hillcollege.edu

Houston Community
College-Central
http://ccollege.hccs.edu

Houston Community
College-Coleman
http://www.hccs.edu/coleman

Houston Community
College-Northwest
http://nwc.hccs.edu

Houston Community
College-Southeast
http://secollege.hccs.edu

Houston Community
College-Southwest
http://swc2.hccs.edu

Howard College
http://www.howardcollege.
edu

Kilgore College
http://www.kilgore.edu

Kingwood College
http://kcweb.nhmccd.edu

Lamar State College-Orange
http://www.orange.lamar.edu

Lamar State Collgee-Port
Arthur
http://www.pa.lamar.edu

Laredo Community College
http://www.laredo.cc.tx.us

Lee College
http://www.lee.edu

Lon Morris College
http://www.lonmorris.edu

Mainland, College of the
http://www.com.edu

McLennan Community
College
http://www.mclennan.edu

Midland College
http://www.midland.edu

Montgomery College
http://www.montgomery-
college.com

Mountain View College
http://www.mvc.dcccd.edu

Navarro College
http://www.navarrocollege.
edu

North Central Texas College
http://www.nctc.edu

North Harris Montgomery
College
http://www.nhmccd.edu

North Lake College
http://www.northlakecollege
.edu

Northeast Texas
Community College
http://www.ntcc.edu

Northwest Vista College
http://www.accd.edu/nvc

Odessa College
http://www.odessa.edu

Palo Alto College
http://www.accd.edu/pac/htm

Panola College
http://www.panola.edu

Paris Junior College
http://www.parisjc.edu

Ranger College
http://www.ranger.cc.tx.us

Richland College
http://www.rlc.dcccd.edu

St. Philips College
http://www.accd.edu/spc/
spcmain/spc.htm

San Antonio College
http://www.accd.edu/sac/
sacmain/sac.htm

San Jacinto College
http://www.sjcd.cc.tx.us

South Plains College
http://www.southplainscollege
.edu

South Texas Community
College
http://www.southtexascollege
.edu

Southwest Texas Junior
College
http://www.southtexascollege
.edu

Tarrant County College
District
http://www.tccd.edu

Temple College
http://www.templejc.edu

Texakana College
http://www.tc.cc.tx.us

Texas Southmost College
http://www.utb.edu

Texas State Technical
College-Harlingen
http://www.harlingen.tstc.edu

Texas State Technical
College-Marshall
http://www.marshall.tstc.
edu

Texas State Technical
College-Waco
http://www.waco.tstc.edu

Texas State Technical
College-West Texas
http://www.sweetwater.tstc.
edu

Tomball College
http://wwwtc.nhmccd.edu

Trinity Valley Community
College
http://www.tvcc.cc.tx.us

Tyler Junior College
http://www.tyler.cc.tx.us

Vernon College
http://www.vernoncollege.
edu

Victoria College
http://www.vc.cc.tx.us

Wade College
http://www.wadecollege.edu

Weatherford College
http://www.wc.edu

Westen Texas College
http://www.wtc.edu

Wharton County Junior
College
http://www.wcjc.cc.tx.us

Utah

Certified Careers Institute
http://www.cciutah.edu

Dixie State College of Utah
http://www.dixie.edu

Eastern Utah, College of
http://www.ceu.edu

Latter-Day Saints Business
College
http://www.ldsbc.edu

Mountain West College
http://www.mwcollege.com

Provo College
http://www.provocollege.com

Salt Lake Community
College
http://www.slcc.edu

Snow College
http://www.snow.edu

Stevens-Henager College
http://www.stevenshenager.
edu

Utah Career College
http://www.utahcollege.com

Utah Valley State College
http://www.uvsc.edu

Vermont

Landmark College
http://www.landmarkcollege
.org

Sterling College
http://www.sterlingcollege.
edu

Vermont, Community
College of
http://www.ccv.vsc.edu

Woodbury College
http://www.woodbury-
college.edu

Virginia

Blue Ridge Community
College
http://www.by.cc.va.us

Central Virginia
Community College
http://www.cvcc.vccs.edu

Dabney S. Lancaster
Community College
http://www.dl.cc.va.us

Danville Community
College
http://www.dcc.vccs.edu

Eastern Shore Community
College
http://www.es.vccs.edu

ECPI Technical College
http://www.ecpi.net

Germanna Community
College
http://www.gc.cc.va.us

J. Sargeant Reynolds
Community College
http://www.jsr.vccs.edu

John Tyler Community
College
http://www.jt.cc.va.us

Lord Fairfax Community
College
http://www.lf.vccs.edu

Mountain Empire
Community College
http://www.me.cc.va.us

New River Community
College
http://www.nr.vccs.edu

Northern Virginia
Community College
http://www.nvcc.vccs.edu

Patrick Henry Community
College
http://www.ph.vccs.edu

Paul D. Camp Community
College
http://www.pc.vccs.edu

Piedmont Virginia
Community College
http://www.pvcc.cc.va.us

Rappahannock Community
College
http://www.rcc.vccs.edu

Richard Bland College
http://www.rbc.edu

Southside Virginia
Community College
http://www.sv.vccs.edu

Southwest Virginia
Community College
http://www.sw.vccs.edu

Thomas Nelson
Community College
http://www.tncc.vccs.edu

Tidewater Community
College
http://www.tcc.vccs.edu

Virginia Highlands
Community College
http://www.vhcc.edu

Virginia Western
Community College
http://www.vw.vccs.edu

Wytheville Community
College
http://www2.wcc.vccs.edu

Washington

Art Institute of Seattle
http://www.ais.edu

Bates Technical College
http://www.bates.ctc.edu

275

Bellevue Community
College
http://www.bcc.ctc.edu

Bellingham Technical
College
http://www.btc.ctc.edu

Big Bend Community
College
http://www.btc.ctc.edu

Cascadia Community
College
http://www.cascadia.ctc.edu

Centralia College
http://www.centralia.ctc.edu

Clark College
http://www.centralia.ctc.edu

Clover Park Technical
College
http://www.cptc.ctc.edu

276

Columbia Basin College
http://www.columbiabasin.
edu

Edmonds Community
College
http://www.edcc.edu

Everett Community College
http://www.evcc.ctc.edu

Grays Harbor College
http://www.ghc.ctc.edu

Green River Community
College
http://www.greenriver.edu

Highline Community
College
http://www.highline.edu

Lake Washington Technical
College
http://www.lwtc.ctc.edu

Lower Columbia College
http://www.lcc.ctc.edu

North Seattle Community
College
http://www.northseattle.edu

Northwest Indian College
http://www.nwic.edu

Northwest School of
Wooden Boatbuilding
http://www.nwboatschool.
org

Olympic College
http://www.olympic.edu

Peninsula College
http://www.pc.ctc.edu

Pierce College
http://www.pierce.ctc.edu

Renton Technical College
http://www.rtc.edu

Seattle Central Community
College
http://www.seattlecentral.org

Shoreline Community
College
http://www.seattlecentral.org

Skagit Valley College
http://www.skagit.edu

South Puget Sound
Community College
http://www.spscc.ctc.edu

South Seattle Community
College
http://www.southseattle.edu

Spokane, Community
Colleges of
http://www.ccs.spokane.cc.
wa.us

Spokane Community College
http://www.scc.spokane.edu

Spokane Falls Community
College
http://www.sfcc.spokane.cc.
wa.us

Tacoma Community College
http://www.tacomacc.edu

Walla Walla Community
College
http://www.wwcc.edu/home

Wenatchee Valley College
http://www.wvc.edu

Whatcom Community
College
http://www.whatcom.ctc.edu

Yakima Valley Community
College
http://www.yvcc.edu

West Virginia

Bluefield State Community
and Technical College
http://www.bluefield.wvnet.
edu

Corinthian School-National
Institute of Technology
Campus
http://www.cci.edu

Eastern West Virginia
Community and Technical
College
http://www.eastern.wvnet.
edu

Fairmont State College
http://www.fairmontstate.edu

Huntington Junior College
http://www.huntingtonjunio
rcollege.edu

Marshall University
Community and Technical
College
http://www.marshall.edu/ctc

Mountain State College
http://www.mountainstate.
org

Potomac State College-West
Virginia University
http://www.potomacstatecol
lege.edu

Shepherd College
http://www.shepherd.edu

Southern West Virginia
Community and Tehcnical
College
http://www.southern.wvnet.
edu/default.htm

Valley College of Technology
http://www.vct.edu

West Virginia Junior College
http://www.wvjc.com

West Virginia Northern
Community College
http://www.northern.wvnet.
edu

West Virginia State
Community and Technical
College
http://www.wvsctc.edu/

West Virginia University
Institute of Technology
http://www.wvutech.edu

West Virginia University-
Parkersburg
http://www.wvup.edu

Wisconsin

Blackhawk Technical College
http://www.blackhawk.edu

Bryant & Stratton College
http://www.bryantstratton.
edu

Chippewa Valley Technical
College
http://www.cvtc.edu

Fox Valley Technical College
http://www.fvtc.edu

Gateway Technical College
http://www.gtc.edu

Lac Courte Oreilles Ojibwa
Community College
http://www.lco.edu

Lakeshore Technical
College
http://www.gotoltc.com

Madison Area Technical
College
http://matcmadison.edu/matc

Menominee Nation, College
of the
http://www.menominee.edu

Mid-State Technical College
http://www.midstate.tec.wi.
us

Milwaukee Area Technical
College
http://www.milwaukee.tec.
wi.us

Moraine Park Technical
College
http://www.moraine.tec.wi.
us

Nicolet Area Technical
College
http://www.nicolet.tec.wi.us

Northcentral Technical
College
http://www.ntc.edu

Northeast Wisconsin
Technical College
http://www.nwtc.edu

Southwest Wisconsin
Technical College
http://www.swtc.edu

Waukesha County
Technical College
http://www.wctc.edu

Western Wisconsin
Technical College
http://www.western.tec.wi.us

Wisconsin Indianhead
Technical College
http://www.witechcolleges.
com

Wyoming

Casper College
http://www.caspercollege.edu

Central Wyoming College
http://www.cwc.edu

Eastern Wyoming College
http://ewcweb.ewc.whecn.
edu

Laramie County
Community College
http://www.lccc.cc.wy.us

Northwest College
http://www.northwestcollege
.edu

Sheridan College
http://www.sheridan.edu

Western Wyoming
Community College
http://www.wwcc.wy.edu

Wyoming Techncial
Institute
http://www.wyotech.com

277

Appendix B:
Top Community Colleges

The following community colleges awarded the most associate degrees in 2005, according to a *Community College Week* analysis of U.S. Department of Education data. Note: colleges are listed in descending order in terms of number of degrees awarded.

Valencia Community College
http://www.valencia.cc.fl.us

Broward Community College
http://www.broward.edu

Nassau Community College
http://www.ncc.edu

Florida Community College at Jacksonville
http://www.fccj.cc.fl.us

Northern Virginia Community College
http://www.nvcc.vccs.edu

Salt Lake Community College
http://www.slcc.edu

Suffolk County Community College
http://www.sunysuffolk.edu

Monroe Community College
http://www.monroecc.edu

Santa Fe Community College
http://www.santafe.cc.fl.us

Sierra College
http://www.sierracollege.edu

Palm Beach Community College
http://www.pbcc.cc.fl.us

Central Texas College
http://www.ctcd.edu

Tarrant County College
http://www.tccd.edu

City University of New York Borough of Manhattan Community College
http://www.bmcc.cuny.edu/j2ee/index.jsp

Tulsa Community College
http://www.tulsacc.edu

Hillsborough Community College
http://www.hccfl.edu

Brevard Community College
http://www.brevard.cc.fl.us

Riverside Community College
http://www.rcc.edu

Bellevue Community College
http://www.bcc.ctc.edu

Tallahassee Community College
http://www.tcc.fl.edu

Oakland Community College
http://www.oaklandcc.edu

Pasadena City College
http://www.pasadena.edu

College of DuPage
http://www.cod.edu

Kirkwood Community College
http://www.kirkwood.cc.ia.us

Pima County Community College
http://www.pima.edu

Erie Community College
http://www.ecc.edu

Kingsborough Community College-City University of New York
http://www.kbcc.cuny.edu

North Harris Montgomery Community College District (five colleges)
http://www.nhmccd.cc.tx.us

Houston Community College System (six colleges)
http://www.hccs.cc.tx.us

Columbus State Community College
http://www.cscc.edu

Portland Community College
http://www.pcc.edu

Mesa Community College
http://www.mc.maricopa.edu

San Joaquin Delta College
http://www.deltacollege.edu

Hudson Valley Community College
http://www.hvcc.edu

University of Wisconsin Colleges
http://www.uwc.edu

Community College of Allegheny County
http://www.ccac.edu

Cuyahoga Community College
http://www.tri-c.cc.oh.us/home/default.htm

Community College of Philadelphia
http://www.ccp.edu

Brookdale Community College
http://www.brookdalecc.edu

San Jacinto College-Central Campus
http://www.sjcd.cc.tx.us

Montgomery College
http://www.mc.cc.md.us

Community College of Baltimore County
http://www.ccbcmd.edu

Southeast Community College
http://www.southeast.edu

Santa Ana College
http://www.sac.edu/homex.asp

Daytona Beach Community College
http://www.dbcc.cc.fl.us

Seminole Community College
http://www.scc-fl.edu

Mt. San Antonio College
http://www.mtsac.edu

Orange Coast College
http://www.orangecoastcollege.edu

Pensacola Junior College
http://pjc.edu

Georgia Perimeter College
http://www.gpc.edu

Santa Monica College
http://www.smc.edu

Milwaukee Area Technical College
http://www.matc.edu

Fashion Institute of Design and Merchandising-Los Angeles
http://www.fidm.com

Macomb Community College
http://www.macomb.edu/main.asp

LaGuardia Community College/CUNY
http://www.lagcc.cuny.edu

American River College
http://www.arc.losrios.edu

De Anza College
http://www.deanza.edu

Sinclair Community College
http://www.sinclair.edu/index.cfm

El Paso Community College
http://www.epcc.edu

Harrisburg Area Community College
http://www.hacc.edu

Vincennes University
http://www.vinu.edu

Madison Area Technical College
http://matcmadison.edu/matc

Modesto Junior College
http://mjc.yosemite.cc.ca.us

East Los Angeles College
http://www.elac.edu

Grand Rapids Community College
http://www.grcc.cc.mi.us

Palomar College
http://www.palomar.edu

Mississippi Gulf Coast Community College
http://www.mgccc.edu

Santa Barbara City College
http://www.sbcc.edu

El Camino College
http://www.elcamino.edu

Community College of Rhode Island
http://www.ccri.edu

Camden County College
http://www.camdencc.edu

Moorpark College
http://www.moorpark.cc.ca.us

Cerritos College
http://www.cerritos.edu

Indian River Community College
http://www.ircc.edu

Edison Community College
http://www.edison.edu

Seattle Community Colleges-Central Campus
http://seattlecentral.org

San Diego Mesa College
http://www.sdmesa.sdccd.cc.ca.us

Chaffey College
http://www.chaffey.edu/welcome.shtml

City College of San Francisco
http://www.ccsf.cc.ca.us

Grossmont College
http://www.grossmont.edu

Delgado Community College
http://www.dcc.edu

Lansing Community College
http://www.lcc.edu

Moraine Valley Community College
http://www.morainevalley.edu

Santa Rosa Junior College
http://www.santarosa.edu

Spokane Community College
http://www.scc.spokane.edu

Anne Arundel Community College
http://www.aacc.cc.md.us

279

Appendix C: Community College Associations

The following professional organizations provide resources and support to community college students and educators.

American Association of Community Colleges
One Dupont Circle, NW, Suite 410, Washington, DC 20036
202/728-0200
http://www.aacc.nche.edu

Community College Week
Box 1305, Fairfax, VA 22038
703/978-3535
http://www.ccweek.com

Distance Education and Training Council
1601 18th Street, NW, Washington, DC 20009
202/234-5100
http://www.detc.org

League for Innovation in the Community College
4505 East Chandler Boulevard, Suite 250, Phoenix, AZ 85048
480/705-8200
http://www.league.org/index.cfm

School Index

The following is an alphabetical list of the colleges covered in *They Teach That in Community College!?*

Schools By State Index

The following is a list of the schools covered in *They Teach That in Community College!?* by geographic region.

288

West Virginia

Wisconsin

Wyoming

Locations Throughout the United States

Canada

Association/Organization Index

The following is an alphabetical list of the associations and organizations mentioned in *They Teach That in Community College!?*

293

Also from
College & Career Press!
College Spotlight newsletter!

"What college to choose and what programs to examine are topics that are increasingly complex for senior high school students. *College Spotlight* will help them and their counselors in a way that no other publication really does."

—*Essential Resources for Schools and Libraries,* March/April 2002

College Spotlight (ISSN 1525-4313) is a 12-page newsletter published in September, October, November, January, March, and May of each school year to help those concerned with selecting, applying to, evaluating, and entering college, as well as to provide other alternatives for today's high school graduates.

Each issue of *College Spotlight* offers:

✔ Fascinating and informative cover stories such as "Major revisions in store for the SAT" and "The forensic science major: so popular, it's a crime"

✔ Regular features, such as Free & Low-Cost Guidance Materials, Book Reviews, Financial Aid, and Diversity Issues (including stories such as "More minorities and women needed in computer science")

✔ Useful education statistics, surveys, and other interesting research

Read a sample issue and learn how to order by visiting www.collegeandcareerpress.com!

Subscription Rates:
1 year/$30 ($25 if payment accompanies your order)
2 years/$50 ($45 if payment accompanies your order)
3 years/$65 ($60 if payment accompanies your order)